Living in a Law Transformed

Living in a Law Transformed

Encounters with the Works of James Boyd White

Edited by Julen Etxabe & Gary Watt

Maize Books: An Imprint of Michigan Publishing

Copyright © 2014 by Julen Etxabe and Gary Watt

All rights reserved

This book may not be reproduced, in whole or in part, including illustrations, in any form (beyond that copying permitted by Sections 107 and 108 of the U.S. Copyright Law and except by reviewers for the public press), without written permission from the publisher.

Published in the United States of America by

Michigan Publishing

Manufactured in the United States of America

2017   2016   2015   2014   4 3 2 1

DOI: http://dx.doi.org/10.3998/maize.12982987.0001.001

ISBN 978-1-60785-336-7 (paper)

ISBN 978-1-60785-337-4 (e-book)

Contents

	Editors' Introduction **Julen Etxabe and Gary Watt**	1
1.	Law and Literature Redux? Some Remarks on the Importance of the Legal Imagination **Jeanne Gaakeer**	13
2.	Towards a Critique of Narrative Reason **François Ost**	37
3.	Imagining Rhetoric, Approaching Justice **Willem Witteveen**	52
4.	It's Not All About Pretty Human Rights Adjudication in a Life and Death Situation **Julen Etxabe**	68
5.	Slow Reading and Living Speech James Boyd White on What a Constitutional Law Opinion is For **H. Jefferson Powell**	89
6.	The Impossible Prayers of James Boyd White **Jack L. Sammons**	107
7.	Silence and Justice **Richard Dawson**	126
8.	Meaning In the Natural World **Joseph Vining**	144
9.	Reading Materials The Stuff that Legal Dreams are Made On **Gary Watt**	155
10.	Reimagining "The True North Strong and Free" Reflections on Going to the Movies with James Boyd White **Rebecca Johnson**	173

11. Generating Law   190
    Learning How to Take Care of What One Has Started
    Thomas D. Eisele

12. A Gift in Yellow Clothing   204
    Learning and Teaching with *The Legal Imagination*
    Mark Weisberg

    Select Bibliography   221
    Contributors   227

Editors' Introduction

Julen Etxabe and Gary Watt

In March 2013, the Association for the Study of Law, Culture and the Humanities (ASLCH) convened its annual conference in London. It was the first time that the conference had been held outside the United States, and, with a happy correspondence, it fell in an important anniversary year for a U.S. scholar who has profoundly influenced legal thought and practice far beyond his home horizons. 2013 marks the fortieth anniversary of the publication of James Boyd White's *The Legal Imagination*, of which we will shortly say more. 2013 is also, incidentally, the seventy-fifth anniversary of the "publication" of the man himself. The present collection of essays draws together a group of scholars who have gathered in gratitude to the works, wisdom, and personal warmth of Professor James Boyd White. Contributors come from many countries—from The United States, Canada, the Netherlands, Belgium, the United Kingdom, the Basque Country, and New Zealand.

We are delighted that the first contribution to the collection is from Jeanne Gaakeer, who at the 2013 conference joined the roll of distinguished winners of the ASLCH's annual James Boyd White Award. Many of the contributors to this volume had the pleasure of meeting at the London conference, and for some of us, including one of the editors of this collection, that was the first occasion of their meeting face-to-face with the man himself after several years of correspondence. For other contributors it was a welcome chance to meet again the tutor, colleague, and friend whom they know simply as Jim. Indeed, a very good thing about Jim White is that, thanks to his lack of pretension and the clarity of his communication, students and scholars *can* know him "simply." Having said that, it is only through serious attention that we come to appreciate the deep challenges that lie beneath the simple things he has to say about living in the law. It is with that effort of attention, and not only to celebrate amity and anniversaries, that we present this publication of twelve essays.

The main title of our book, *Living in a Law Transformed*, is intended to remove the artificial barrier that we all too often erect between our life and our work. If we see work in purely metric terms of so-called human resources, as being those hours that we do not devote to love and leisure and all the rest of life, what damage do we do to true human resources? The answer is that we make a wasteland of the world of work, and thereby deaden a huge portion of our lives. Even more dangerous than that, we deaden the lives of the students, clients, and colleagues who meet us in the law. What a difference would it make for those of us who work as jurists, if we were to acknowledge that we (and our clients, colleagues, and students) are bound to live in law? What a difference might it make if we were to bring our life to work and bring our work to life? James Boyd White challenges us to ask such questions as these.

One of the threads that weaves its way through this collection is that an integration of life and law has transformed the contributors' experience as scholars, students, and teachers, as well as our vision of law. This collection of essays therefore constitutes an invitation to encounter White's work—and the contributors' collective experience of their own encounters—as an experience of living in a law transformed. For just as Odysseus had to learn to recognize Ithaca at his return, White invites us to look at the law anew and to learn to recognize it as something like our own true home.

James Boyd White's *The Legal Imagination* is widely regarded as the founding document of the modern "law and literature" movement. It is therefore appropriate that this collection should start and move from there. The movement takes us through narrative critique, with special attention to critical readings of law as literature. From there, the collection moves to consider the potential for meaningful experience that is to be found in the spaces and silences that exist within and around text and speech. The next group of chapters engages with extratextual sources; the authors travel with White toward an appreciation of paintings, places, movies, and even a simple stone in a stream. This leads us, finally, to the place of practice, not only in the classroom, the court, or the lawyer's office, but wherever we live and work. Thus the journey of the book leads to hope of real transformation.

One feature stressed by many of the contributors to this volume is

White's personal style of writing and the apparent straightforwardness with which he conveys complex and often controversial thoughts. His voice is dialogical in nature, engaging the reader on a personal level. White is not motivated by any desire to prove other views or writers wrong, but by a desire to make his readers participate in his own sense of wonder. He leaves space for their own—your own—judgments.

So what judgment do we, as editors, reach on the works of White? In one sense the jury must always be "out" when it comes to a judgment of this sort. That is perhaps the one unanimous verdict of the twelve contributors to this volume.

It is not so much that James Boyd White's work is hard to classify, but rather that it has created a world of its own. White has developed a personal vocabulary, where each term is defined in relation to every other term, in ways that challenge, and redefine, conventional understandings of language, rhetoric, authority, community, constitution, translation, ethics, and of course, law. In his writings, all these terms acquire a rich array of meanings that are less conceptual and analytic than performative and compositional. White's way of reading legal texts—a contract, a statute, a judicial opinion, a will, the Declaration of Independence, or the U.S. Constitution—entails an invitation to live in a law radically transformed.

Contrary to the extended notion of law as a system of norms, White has invited us to view law as a culture of argument constantly being made and remade out of the resources of a given language. Consequently, he has rejected the dominant scientific model of law, and instead views law as an art or activity brought to life by the individual people engaged in it. One should not see in this rejection a refusal to speak about questions of theory. (Quite the opposite—there is a sense in which White's work is deeply theoretical.) However, he rejects any suggestion that a theory can do away with the tensions, ambiguities, and perplexities of law. At bottom, his work evinces a profound skepticism for any attempt to reduce the world into a "system," wherein every element can be neatly defined or assigned exactly the same value and meaning regardless of its particular context. A strictly systemic way of proceeding ignores what he calls the "radical literariness of life," conveying the simple idea that life is more complex than any theory could possibly explain it.

One could do much worse than to call James Boyd White a humanist of law. Nowadays humanism is a loaded term, often decried for its undertones of anthropocentrism and the imperialism of the Western white man imposing his own culture under the pretense of universality. Humanism is also evocative of worn-out debates about the "literary canon" and certain sentimental pieties about human nature. Sharing none of these postulates, White's humanism is not the kind that puts "man" at the center of the universe and the world at his feet, but one that emphasizes, against the odds of existence, the human quest and potential for meaning.

Likewise, he is not interested in defining an essence of "man" to raise him above other forms of life, or to distinguish individuals from one another in clans or islands. White speaks certainly from the perspective of a particular time, context, and culture, but his work is infused with a love for cultures different to his own. Performing the task of a translator (a favorite metaphor), he develops a practice of slow reading through which that which was foreign and unknown may become increasingly familiar, even if never fully owned. For White, this process begins by learning the language—be it the Greek of Homer, the Latin of Augustine, or the Italian of Dante—which may grant us access to others' social and political worlds, their terms of value, their ways of speaking about the natural world, their cosmology, and their conceptions of the transcendent.

White's selection of texts has never been shaped by a canon of purported high literature. Rather, he has followed those texts that spoke to him regardless of their provenance, finding illumination equally in African masks, literature written by children, or the paintings of Vermeer. More importantly, when he reads "canonical literature," including Plato, Emily Dickinson, and George Herbert, his readings unsettle and defy our usual understandings of these texts.

White's writings contain a core of optimism about human potential and capacities. However, it would be a mistake to interpret this as naïve or sentimental, which is a vice he has often denounced. White has warned against the ugliness and corruption of certain forms of life and against the violent and dehumanizing practices of what he calls "the empire of force," including appalling practices of torture.

White's humanism can be connected with the importance and the centrality he grants to language. For him language is not an inert system of signs to be codified, but something that exists in interaction between speakers, in real-life encounters and misencounters. His works also focus on the limits of language: what language cannot express, access, and what it distorts or destroys in the form of dead language, empty slogans, and propaganda. Yet, language is arguably all that we have to communicate with each other, in whatever form this is expressed: physical gestures, facial expressions, bodily language, or awkward silences.

In positing language as central to law, the critic may point out the risk of downplaying the political and coercive elements in law. Admittedly,

White has not been interested in the kind of issues often discussed under the heading of "politics." Still, he has time and again stressed that our ways of speaking and talking to and about each other are fundamentally ethical and political—for they are invitations to constitute different kinds of communities. Such forms of community are not based on any purported commonality of interest and purpose, nor are they necessarily cozy and friendly. Rather, these are rhetorical in kind, sometimes as fleeting as the expressions that imagine them; other times long-lasting and solid as institutions.

The present volume also wishes to pay tribute to White's inspiring work as a teacher, through which he has created innovative courses with a healthy atmosphere of collaboration and mutual respect. In the area of legal education, he has written against the colonization of the law by the instrumental rationality of cold-calculus economics—a particular way of translating everything into a utilitarian calculation of costs and benefits—that sets itself up as universal and neutral. His writings also provide inspiration for legal practice, which as one contributor to this collection reminds us, calls for our personal ethical participation.

The chapters in this collection are, accordingly, a call to participate in the contributors' own struggle to read and appreciate and to search for meaning in it all. Each of the contributors will acknowledge that the works of Professor White have placed us at the uncomfortable cutting edge of meaning. White coaxes his readers to appreciate all things in which meaning may be found. There might even be meaning in the fact that, out of the extensive oeuvre of James Boyd White, two of the contributors happened to pick as the starting point for their chapters the same short passage from the same book. What should we read into the shared choice of that one passage out of thousands? There is surely a danger of reading too much into it. There is certainly a danger of reading too little into it, for coincidence itself is sometimes meaningful.

A particular struggle that the editors of this volume have faced is the challenge of ordering the chapters in a meaningful sequence. The editors' choice might be expressed as a choice between structure and freedom, or rather as an appreciation of the need to keep structure and freedom in productive tension. What James Boyd White offers as our guide is to reflect upon "The Silken Tent" of Robert Frost's eponymous poem, which "in guys ... gently sways at ease." He might have helped us to a specific reading of the poem, but our sense is that it is enough to learn (which we had not otherwise guessed) that the poem can be read as an attempt to express the very tension between structure and freedom that we must somehow get a feel for as people living in law and, specifically now, as editors of this book. So we turn to a brief introduction to each of the twelve chapters in the order in which, through some combination of chance and design, we have placed them.

In "Law and Literature Redux? Some Remarks on the Importance of the Legal Imagination," Jeanne Gaakeer traces the development of literary-legal studies over recent decades and discusses the future of humanistic legal education and practice, in light of James Boyd White's seminal contributions to the legal imagination. From at least three perspectives, Gaakeer stresses the *methodological* implications of law and literature for our views on law (e.g., as a positivist "science" or an hermeneutic "art"), the *paideic* potential of law and literature for contemporary legal education, and the *historical* relevance of the *studia humanitatis* and their exemplary contribution toward high-quality interdisciplinary research and the modern practice of law.

François Ost's "Towards a Critique of Narrative Reason" aims to rehabilitate narrative, against the dominant paradigm of thought which disqualifies it. The fact that we have all been nurtured by stories should make this effort an easy one, but the prevailing doctrine tends to discredit narrative, presenting it as subjective and frivolous. In his analysis, Ost focuses on the constitutive character of narrative, both as the collective story, memory, and history of a people, and as the personal novel each one of us tells to himself, in order to create his own identity. Ost suggests that such a conception of the human as *homo fabulans* (or storytelling animal) could lead to an outline of a "Critique of Narrative Reason," out of which theoretical reason and practical reason will emerge.

In his essay "Imagining Rhetoric, Approaching Justice," Willem Witteveen turns to the contemporary relevance of rhetoric as one of the arts essential for democratic citizenship, for arguing a case in court as an effective and responsible lawyer, and for deciding issues of law and justice as a judge. However, the fear that rhetoric functions merely to disguise naked forms of power makes it necessary to return to the classical rhetorical tradition, in order to reimagine for our own time what rhetoric as an art or *technè* can actually mean. Inspired by James Boyd White's reading of *Gorgias* in *When Words Lose their Meaning*, Witteveen argues for small but meaningful steps toward an open-ended ideal of justice beyond procedural fairness; namely, as a set of virtues and ethical relationships manifested in communication, which he illustrates with Giotto's paintings on the walls of the Capella della Scrovegni.

Continuing the theme of justice, Julen Etxabe's "It's Not All About Pretty: Human Rights Adjudication in a Life and Death Situation" unfolds judicial opinions using the methods of White's *Justice as Translation*. Against ways of assessing judicial opinions in terms of the concrete result they reach or the policy they recommend, White proposes a "standard of excellence" that focuses on the democratic quality of the conversations that are opened by every opinion, bringing us close to Bakhtin's multi-voicedness and dialogism. Such a way of reading does not wish to dilute political concerns into a matter of *style*, but rather the opposite, to reveal the profundity, and ethical and political implications, of what is often dismissed as mere style. Etxabe illustrates the possibilities of this analysis with the European Court of Human Rights case of *Pretty v UK*, a decision involving a case of euthanasia, and argues for the continued relevance of this kind of analysis in human-rights adjudication.

Continuing the exploration of judicial opinions, in "Slow Reading and Living Speech: James Boyd White on What a Constitutional Law Opinion is For," Jeff Powell examines White's practice of "slow reading" as an approach that demands openness to the points of tension, fracture, or contradiction that are central to its meaning. On this view, it is a mistake to act too quickly on the impulse to harmonize discordant elements in a serious piece of writing, including legal writing. Powell illustrates his argument through a brief consideration of White's book on George Herbert's "poetry of voices" and then turns to Justice Jackson's famous concurring opinion in *Youngstown* on the limits of executive power, which has become a trite doctrinal formula. A slow reading of Jackson's various voices, however, shows how that usual reading is untenable. In Powell's view, Jackson's accomplishment lies precisely in making it plain to the reader the unavoidable uncertainties that accompany, and should accompany, momentous constitutional decisions. After noting the difficulties of contemporary constitutional law to approach such "living speech," Powell argues that White's approach to reading has far-ranging implications for how we teach and think about the law.

Taking the issue of voice into a different register, Jack Sammons suggests that much of White's lifetime of work can be read as an attempt to address through performances the very personal issue of how to speak in a religious voice. This may present an almost insurmountable challenge, for how can a religious voice be audible in a world where the mode of thought demanded by religion has gone missing? Beyond an obvious problem of translation, Sammons surmises a more radical inability to have experiences we call religious and to make sense of them in any language. "The Impossible Prayers of James Boyd White" addresses this challenge through an inquiry into White's way of reading literary texts, in which the text's "imagined world" can provoke a "cultural dislocation" that transforms both us and our culture. For texts to have such emancipatory effect, however, texts must be read in a particular way, so that meaning is not chosen based on other values, but as experienced as the mystery of being moved by a "nothing" other to us yet real. This leads us away from the imaginative transformations opened by readings to the ontological character of the identities uncovered and, ultimately, to something prior: the creative capacity of meaning—the meaning of our seeking meaning—which is an assumption underlying White's work, offering us an experience phenomenologically undistinguishable from what he call religious.

While the essays of Etxabe, Powell, and Sammons focus on issues of voice—the many-voicedness of judicial opinions, the competing voices of a single judge, and the voices of Jim White the author—Richard Dawson turns his attention to silence, which is not to be understood as the mere counterpart, or absence, of voice. In "Justice and Silence," Dawson argues that a distinctive aspect of White's work *is* a concern with the topic of silence. Rather than focus on the dehumanizing tendencies of some forms of silence(ing)—including economics—Dawson connects silence with a pressure toward the inexpressible, which signals a fracture in the social bonds and structures of meaning, and takes us to the limits of our imaginations. For Dawson, an encounter with such forms of silence may enable us to attune to the conditions of our existence in life and law alike. Drawing on a number of texts (including *Huckleberry Finn*, *Billy Budd*, Shakespeare's *Richard II*, and Herbert's *The Temple*), Dawson points to the intimate connection between silence and justice, sensing in justice-related silence not a defect, but a gift beyond language. This brings us, next, to our capacity to appreciate the speech and silence of stuff other than formal languages and texts.

While James Boyd White has devoted much of his work to the rescue of meaning in language, art, and the human world, Joseph Vining wonders about the extent to which modern law is amenable to such kinds of "close reading." In "Meaning in the Natural World," Vining frames the question as the problem of the *object trouvé* (e.g., a stone smoothed by the waters of a river that Jim White kept at his desk), which cannot be read in the same way that a piece of visual art, or music, or written text can. In essence, the problem posed by the (putative) meaning of inanimate objects might be the same facing legal operators when they attribute meaning to words found in a piece of legislation, or an administrative or judicial opinion. For, whenever law is viewed not as an expression of mind, but as the product of "sociocultural forces," the issue arises as to the meaning that can be attributed to the outcome of such impersonal processes.

In "Reading Materials: The Stuff that Legal Dreams are Made On," Gary Watt enquires into the "materiality" of words and the intrinsic force that material stuff works upon the human mind. Offering multiple examples, Watt fosters a Whitean approach towards a meaningful appreciation of material culture beyond text and speech. In his view, such an approach might open the way to improved environmental respect, to more just and finely attuned judgments, and to an appropriately harmonious, touching, and responsive social constitutions. One of the examples that attracts Watt is, remarkably, the same smoothed stone that attracted Vining that attracted White. Watt finds it intriguingly akin in its properties to the kind of solidity and balance we find admirable in law and certain sculptures. According to Watt, such a form of balance is not based on a strict or equal symmetry, but rather in its asymmetry: a form of dynamic balance that expresses motion and energy created by oppositions, contrast, and disequilibrium. Following James Tully's reading of Bill Reid's *The Spirit of Haida Gwaii*, Watt sees another Canadian First Nations' sculpture *The Dance Screen* (*The Scream Too*) as a material example of a constitutional disposition that stands for more than strict equality, and which calls to be completed by the touch and endless engagement of the public.

The authors did not plan it, but the previous chapter and the next one follow neatly from each other by keeping us with the First Nations people of Canada. In "Reimagining 'The True North Strong and Free': Reflections on Going to the Movies with James Boyd White," Rebecca Johnson describes her personal experiences in designing, and teaching, a seminar in Inuit law and film to a group of primarily non-Inuit law students at the University of Victoria. Despite the veritable revival of Inuit culture and political activism in the last twenty years, and the fact that Indigenous scholars have become increasingly fluent in "Canadian Law," Johnson avows that there has been insufficient engagement with Indigenous legal orders on their own terms. Faced with the challenge of devising such a trans-systemic course, Johnson found invaluable theoretical and practical tools in the works of James Boyd White (including *The Legal Imagination, Justice as Translation,* and *The Edge of Meaning*). Taking as a given White's insight about learning to *live* within a language, a culture, and a legal order, the purpose of the course was to enable non-Inuit students to begin to "inhabit" the Inuit North and make possible, also, the imagination of law as something other than a universal colonial force. In this setting, films by or about Inuit function not as examples of "the truth," but as places where students can work at inhabiting a space of imagination and mutual engagement.

If the encounters with the works of James Boyd White are an invitation to live in a law transformed, it is only fitting that this volume should include an experience that changed the life of a practicing lawyer. In his essay, Thomas Eisele describes an experience of self-discovery after early years of law practice in which he could not find vitality in his work. After receiving a review copy of *The Legal Imagination*, Eisele realized that none of his legal work breathed life and that the instruments, memos, and letters he was drafting were "forgeries" borrowed from form-books and other available models. Although *The Legal Imagination* offered no apparent "method" to become a competent lawyer, the book's invitation to consider the lawyer as a kind of artist and the law as a kind of literature made an impact. With the help of White's instruction, and his self-tutelage working through the materials of *The Legal Imagination*, Eisele came to realize that the forms and formulas he had emulated prescribed no solutions to the legal problems facing him and his client. Rather, the competent legal solution could be made manifest (or failed to be made so) only in so far as one could manage to create it out of those materials. If "generativity" can be defined as the ability to come to some understanding of what one cares about most in life and to take care of that passion, *The Legal Imagination* allowed Eisele to generate legal instruments that could speak to the difficulties and complexities of life in which the lawyer and the client find themselves.

The concluding chapter of this collection is Mark Weisberg's "A Gift in Yellow Clothing: Learning and Teaching with *The Legal Imagination*." When the book arrived on his desk in 1979, the combination of fiction, history, poetry, and law; the refreshing questions and comments of the author; the challenging and provocative writing assignments; and the voice that addressed students as individuals in a jargon-free manner, were all qualities that attracted Weisberg and compelled him to offer a course modeled after it. Working with *The Legal Imagination* ever since, Weisberg not only discovered his own vocation as a teacher, but afforded students the opportunity to experience their work as the product of independent minds; to define their own responsibilities as writers and participants in a community; and to develop the associative and imaginative dimensions of thought and language on top of the cognitive and logical ones.

Anyone familiar with Jim White's teaching style and method will recognize many of the strategies described by Weisberg, including a remarkable form of "silence" that the teacher can productively use to foster shared responsibility in an atmosphere of mutual respect. Those who have not had the privilege of attending any of Jim White's courses and seminars will obtain a rare glimpse into what the theoretical claims of the author look like, and can accomplish, in the real environment of the classroom.

In the four decades since the publication of *The Legal Imagination*, and for even longer than that, James Boyd White has repeated his distinctive call for personal ethical participation in the life of law, and he has repeatedly been the first to respond to that call. To look back on his life's work is to look at the first forty years of the modern law and humanities movement, but the advantage of anniversaries is that they come in perpetuity and prompt us to look to the future. A good deal of our hope for law's future lies in the life that the works of James Boyd White can bring to law. Looking back, James Boyd White was pleased to tell us that the "life of writing has given me friends." Looking forward, we hope that we, a few of his friends, have produced a book that will encourage new readers to experience the life in his writing.

After this book was sent to press, we have been saddened by the terrible news that Willem Witteveen, his wife and daughter were amongst the passengers of flight MH 17 to Kuala Lumpur where they were headed to visit their son and brother. This book wishes to honor our good friend Willem and his family.

[1]

Law and Literature Redux?

Some Remarks on the Importance of the Legal Imagination
Jeanne Gaakeer

"As by some tyrant's stern command,
A wretch forsakes his native land ...
So I from thee, thus doom'd to part,
Gay queen of fancy, and of art,
Reluctant move with doubtful mind ...
Me wrangling courts and cities draw
To smoke, and crowds, and stubborn law ...
Then welcome business, welcome strife
Welcome the cares and thorns of life"
–W BLACKSTONE, "THE LAWYER'S FAREWELL TO HIS MUSE"[1]

"A lawyer without history or literature is a mechanic, a mere working mason; if he possesses some knowledge of these, he may venture to call himself an architect"
–W SCOTT, *GUY MANNERING*[2]

Law and Literature 1.01

"Law and literature" began in 1973. It is an Anglo-American phenomenon. To start an overview of interdisciplinary scholarship in the field of law, language, and literature and an appreciation of the importance of James Boyd White's work in this way may strike you as odd or downright inappropriate. Are not such bold theses by way of opening statements examples of precisely the type of linguistic utterances that White has been critical of these past four decades? And has not "law and literature," if anything, consistently questioned the (ab)use and effects of propositional language in all kinds of legal texts? Of course. Nevertheless, my opening statement is a deliberate one, should you by now question my credentials to contribute to this volume. In this chapter I want to draw your attention to the fact that there are good arguments for and against both theses and that their simultaneous existence is what matters when we talk about the value of "law and literature" as we now know it and discuss the future of humanistic legal studies in general. So my theses are as accurate as they are false and in what follows I hope to elaborate on them. After all, law works by opposition and I am a legal practitioner as well as one involved in literary-legal studies. What is more, since the days of Quintilian law students have been taught to argue both sides of the case, the method of the *controversiae*, and "law and literature," if not born then raised in opposition to instrumental thought and economic reasoning, surprisingly perhaps, also has its own binary oppositions that we need to address if the field is to thrive.

The origin, then, of contemporary attention to the bonds of law and literature broadly conceived and, with it, the emergence of "law and literature" as a field of academic research can indeed be traced back to 1973 with the publication of James Boyd White's *The Legal Imagination*.[3] But, as White himself modestly wrote, "… any claim that law and humanities began in 1973 would obviously be ludicrous, for the connections between law and the arts of language go all the way back to the beginnings of law in European history."[4] And so it would seem that with the development of interdisciplinary legal studies the European roots for a reappraisal of the humanities for law, located in an era when the academic differentiation of disciplines was still a thing of the future, were forgotten along the way. Put differently, European "law and literature" from its start tended to pay homage to topics presented in Anglo-American scholarship, and White may be right here too when he wrote that the distinctly European humanistic sources belonged to "… a tradition that took itself largely for granted, and there was very little that addressed it directly".[5] Obviously, given the Whitean source of the contemporary movement, there is also good reason to call "law and literature" an American phenomenon.[6] Not only because the American renaissance of the humanist tradition built on what very soon became seminal texts, John Wigmore's "A List of Legal Novels" and Benjamin Cardozo's "Law and Literature,"[7] but also given the legal and sociopolitical constellation in the decades before 1973 and its effects on law. As far as the latter is concerned, it is important to note the critique in the legal and political consciousness of the 1950s and 1960s of the dominance of the idea of law as an autonomous discipline as championed by, for example, the legal process school (with Herbert Wechsler and Henry M. Hart Jr as prominent contributors) that also found itself under attack for its presumed tendency to ignore the question of the values and principles underlying substantive law on the view that the objectivity in law that it cherished preserved law from politics. The American interest in legal positivism, pivoting on the debate between Herbert Hart, who defended the separation of law and morals and Lon Fuller, who advocated a natural law-based legal theory, [8] also brought to the fore the legal need to seek other disciplines' help. The positivistic interpretative insistence on the separation thesis, with its tendency to out-of-context reasoning and its focus on the normative component of law, was also accompanied by a claim of neutrality, one that collapsed after the horrors of Nazi law unfolded in the wake of the Second World War.[9] The view on law as a science that considered the autarky of the discipline as a precondition for the objectivity of its results was challenged. As a counterweight interdisciplinary movements, "law and literature" among them, developed.[10] The realization that the formation of law and society is a reciprocal process made legal professionals (re)turn to the humanities because the tasks that they had to confront lay beyond those supposedly easily mediated by legal doctrine. Thus, literature entered the legal arena as an auxiliary discipline to provide the qualities that law as an autonomous discipline lacked. As further discussed later, the need felt to supplement law with supposedly external resources already contains the germ of potentially counterproductive dichotomous thought.

Fledgling "law and literature" took up the two challenges provoked by Wigmore and Cardozo. The Wigmorean focus on the literary portrayal of the legal system and its individual practitioners expanded into discussions of the normative aspects of law that resulted in a strand of research called "law *in* literature". Starting from the premise that our cultural heritage in the form of literary works holds up a mirror as far as sociolegal and political developments and values are concerned, and that it shows an external view on law and the legal profession in action, "law *in* literature" has a distinctly ethical component. "Law *as* literature" is a follow-up on Cardozo's claim that any legal professional, judges included, should develop a linguistic antenna sensitive to peculiarities beyond the level of the signifier and the signified; that is, the form of a word and its (dictionary) meaning. On the view that language is law's only tool, and that law and literature are both producers and products of culture so that they reflect as much as critique, ideally at least, the prevailing societal convictions and conventions, an investigation of the literary creation of human experience may help us understand the ways in which narratives (re)construct reality. What is more, as the authors and readers of legal narratives we also have to acknowledge that law's instrument is an institutional language that also imposes its conceptual framework on its users so that it behoves us to develop our linguistic sensibilities on this level too.[11]

Preliminary Hearing

James Boyd White's major contribution to a revaluation of the humanist legal tradition, in my view, is that what he calls the legal imagination can be looked upon as an ever-present influence upon the many trajectories of literary-legal research. That is to say, the legal imagination serves as a linchpin for most humanistic reflections of law. White has consistently argued that the essence of a legal professional's work lies in the process of dealing with authoritative texts and translating from other discourses into the law. To him, this is a literary activity that involves an, "enterprise of the imagination ... the translation of the imagination into reality by the power of language."[12] Not incidentally, the working title of *The Legal Imagination* was *Principles and Practices of Legal Expression*, for here is the connection with the original aim of "law and literature" as inspired by Wigmore and Cardozo: to provide the law student with an introduction to what doing law means (and that includes a conception of law different from the positivist approach) as well as the student of law and/or the legal professional with insights into intellectual and ethical goals including, but not limited to the development of interpretive skills and an empathetic focus on the perspectives of others. An aim, I would suggest, that scholarship in the field soon deviated from in its focus on developing theoretical claims.[13]

No solitary chapter could hope to do full justice to the wealth of James Boyd White's oeuvre. What follows first establishes some parameters of White's view on law and then concentrates on three interrelated perspectives (distinguishable but not distinct) to offer a lens with which to view current issues in "law and literature" and White's achievements, and to serve by way of backdrop to this volume's other contributions: the *paideic* importance of "law and literature" for legal education and practice, the methodological consequences of interdisciplinary positions taken and the importance of historical awareness for the future of the humanistic study and practice of law.[14]

What made *The Legal Imagination* so highly innovative in 1973 was that it connected law to what for long, because of the dominant view on law as science, had been looked upon as a literary quality only, the imagination. To White, legal practice is characterised by a constant having to come to terms with the combined representations of events in narrative form and the systematic exposition of law as a language of concepts. A legal professional should therefore have a command of the language of law in a double sense. Firstly, an understanding of and the ability to handle the institutional possibilities and impossibilities of the culture that is law. Secondly, an awareness of the impact that her choices have, because the language of law is normative in that it is a proposal to get a grip on both language and world.[15] The ability and imagination prerequisite for successfully accomplishing the translation of the case and the relevant legal texts to a new situation in the world demands insight into the fundamental difference between the narrative and the analytical forces in law. White calls this the difference between "the mind that tells a story, and the mind that gives reason," of which the former "... finds its meaning in representations of events as they occur in time, in imagined experience; the other, in systematic or theoretical explanations, in the exposition of conceptual order or structure."[16] What matters, then, is the ability to bridge these differences, in ourselves and when recognised as competing tugs in the texts we have to work with.[17] In other words, to learn to integrate the literary and the conceptual, on the understanding that "The law can best be understood and practiced when one comes to see that its language is not conceptual or theoretical—not reducible to a string of definitions—but what I call literary or poetic, by which I mean ... that it is complex, many-voiced."[18]

Hence the reason why White speaks of the constitutive rhetoric of law as "an art of persuasion that creates the object of its persuasion, for it constitutes both the community and the culture it commends."[19] Hence also why White proposes that we practise, "the art of talking two ways at once, the art of many-voicedness," and that is, "learning to qualify a language while we use it: in finding ways to recognise its omissions, its distortions, its false claims and pretensions, ways to acknowledge other ways of speaking that qualify or undercut it."[20] Not incidentally, this is also the ideal methodological starting point for our interdisciplinary ventures. Thus law should not primarily be looked upon as a system of rules or a tool of social control, but as a literary culture of argument, the essence of which is claiming meaning, as much in oral or written argument in court as in contributions to legal scholarship. All this makes law part of the humanities aimed at understanding human action, rather than the empirical social sciences aimed at explaining.

Inextricably entwined with the art of manyvoicedness is the reconciliatory counterpart of "comprehending contraries," a quality that especially a judge should foster when deciding a case, both in the process of taking the decision itself and in the textual rendering thereof. It is at the same time the experience of the extent to which the central tendency perceived in law to try and restore the disrupted balance of human relations is given adequate attention.[21] The idea of "comprehending contraries" is a redefinition of the Coleridgean thesis that a good poet is able to balance discordant qualities by means of his imagination which in itself is, ideally at least, the harmonized result of contraries and complexities.[22] It foreshadows White's later work on translation as discussed later. As far as law and legal practice are concerned, there is a direct link between "comprehending contraries" and the resistance to linguistic imperialism that White promotes in *Living Speech*, when he argues that precisely because the meaning of law depends on the way in which it is practiced we must learn to recognize when and how the dehumanizing, authoritarian "empire of force" is at work and learn how to oppose it not only in others but also in ourselves, for the empire of force too is a product of our habits of mind and imagination.[23]

Binary Oppositions or Wholeness? The Heart and the Head in Education and Practice

After William Blackstone, a writer of verse since boyhood, had entered legal practice in 1741 he soon lamented that he was forced to leave the companion of his youth in the poem "The Lawyer's Farewell to his Muse."[24] The lines used as the first epigraph to this chapter highlight not only the bifurcation Blackstone obviously experienced in his life, they are also indicative of the start of a development that made law and literature lose their original professional connections. In the Middle Ages, literary and legal life were perceived, much more than they are today, as the collective expression of a community of letters. In the fifteenth and sixteenth centuries this *studia humanitatis* strongly expanded and the integration of law and the *artes liberales* also brought about a unity of theory and practice.[25] From the eighteenth century onward law and literature went their separate ways as disciplines began to differentiate and obtained their institutional, academic forms. An external differentiation of law into economics, sociology and anthropology took place and literature became academically respectable with the foundation of Honours Schools. What is more, law's internal differentiation of private and public law accelerated as a result of the growing demand for specialized legal knowledge during and following the industrial revolution and the transformative era of technological progress in the nineteenth century. Both processes culminated in the second half of the nineteenth century with the rise of scientific and legal positivism that also brought about a separation of the supposedly hard sciences and the humanities, and, with it, the desire to ground law too as a science. Each now autonomous discipline developed its own professional language and methodology, its own culture also in the sense of conceptual frameworks and values.[26]

With this development came the tendency to oppose law and literature as hard versus soft. It is precisely this creation of binary opposition and its resulting dichotomous thought that occasioned the starting point for "law and literature"; that is, to say its desire to develop its pedagogical aim to learn how to do law differently, or "well" in a more old-fashioned way as White would call it.[27] In other words, from the dominant emphasis in legal education in the 1960s on the vocational aspect of training for the job by means of a methodology focused on doctrinal and practical issues of solving cases to a broad, humanistic education that integrates rather than separates disciplines. Preceded by William Davenport in the 1950s,[28] Charles Reich advocated a (re)turn to the humanities, on the view that "After about one year, the law school has done almost all it can to equip the student ... If courses are to be of any value, they must offer something different."[29] By contrast, legal professionals need a generalist outlook, because law deals with all aspects of people's lives and it is prescriptive. Law meets literature and the other arts in the "critique and an overview of society" that are their common concerns, according to Reich who wanted to bring questions of justice in the curriculum.[30] In a similar way White opposes a form of legal education that is solely directed at the transference of what he calls legal "doctrine in a vacuum"[31] and suggests that we look at the things that law is analogous to. On this view, too, we should not speak of "law *and* sociology or history or economics or literature, but law *as* each of these."[32] This remark contains the idea of translation as a model for interdisciplinarity that White develops in *Justice as Translation*, to which I turn shortly. Thinking in terms of integrating disciplines will necessarily redefine the academic curriculum. It will preclude any tendency to regard teaching as the mere conveyance of entities of meaning, and will redirect attention to the formation of character, professional and private, rather than the rainmaker kind of maximization of material wealth as the ultimate professional goal. It also demands a broader education for law professors to be able to teach law as a humanistic study. In short, it will mean the end to keeping law closed to outsiders that was the key to law's autonomy.

So the study of language and literature was initially promoted in order to make the much desired difference to counter to the excessive emphasis on an analytical and instrumental reading of texts as part of the case method as the main component in the legal toolbox, and subsequently teach different ways of thinking like a lawyer, encompassing other disciplines. Connected to this aim of mitigating law's traditional disciplinary tendency is also the consistent claim brought forward by Martha Nussbaum and others that the combined study law and literature may ideally join cognitive insights of morals and values in law with an empathetic understanding of the plight of those in whose lives the word of the law interferes deeply, on the view that the value of literature is that it "talks of human lives and choices as if they matter to us all."[33] The experience of viewing the world of the text and its inhabitants empathetically can be transformed into a norm for judging human relations in general, or, as Nussbaum puts it, for "our social existence and the totality of our connections."[34] Robin West offers the related view that reading literature helps us understand aspects of our own character and that our social lives demand that we recognise the needs of others. The empathic ability is therefore not only a product of, but also a precondition for, reading well. The ability to identify oneself with the other implies affective understanding as well as the capacity to act accordingly.[35] Nussbaum's plea is also one for an alternative concept of legal and economic rationality which springs from storytelling and literary imagination. Against the economic reduction of the complexity of human life to utilistic preferences she puts the capacity "to imagine the concrete ways in which people different from oneself grapple with disadvantage," and that is the heart of the literary approach that emphasises the particularity of human experience rather than an abstraction formulated on the basis of presuppositions that are hard to test.[36] Nussbaum's term to denote this capacity is fancy—that is, "the ability to see one thing as another, to see one thing in another" or "metaphorical imagination."[37] On this view, the recognition that telling stories is a way of knowing is crucial to law.

From a methodological point of view, the claim of literary jurisprudence is that narrative knowledge can help us integrate human experience and our reflection on legal interpretation. This, in turn, can promote in us a critical, professional reflection that contributes to the formation of a legal conscience of integrity or wholeness. In legal practice it alerts us to the need to recognise a diversity of rationalities when it comes to the exposition and valuation of the "facts" and the ability to present one's story and case persuasively. On the view that a judicial decision is a form of reflection of what is and should be, the visual scenes that literary works evoke may therefore also serve as a form of *ekphrasis* (a term denoting the vivid description of a work of art that elicits a direct response in the reader) to trigger resistance to the reification that results from of a one-sided attention to the language of legal concepts.

What is more, on the premise that "Law is determined very largely by the ideas of those who are practicing it, and ... their ideas are very largely governed by the quality of their education,"[38] it becomes crucial to acknowledge that the danger of legal reification of human problems looms large when lawyers fall prey to the impulse to reduce human experience to legal cliché and real people to objects under discussion, which is "an internal aspect of the problem" that is "permanently with us," as White puts it.[39] So we should learn "to understand the languages that inhabit our mind; to establish sufficient distance from them so that we can make them, and our use of them, the object of our critical attention."[40] There is good reason for doing so, if we agree with White that any concept of law should encompass a notion of justice.[41] Turning to literature and cherishing the poetic faith advocated by Coleridge (his "willing suspension of disbelief for the moment")[42] may teach us not only the necessary moment of epoché (from the Greek ἐποχή, suspension) in law and legal practice.[43] Such a turn might also to preclude challenge the divisions between thought and feeling and between the public and the private self. By such a turn we heed the warning of James Boyd White and save ourselves from the sort of overemphasis upon the analytical which was Blackstone's vice and to which he was victim.[44] Immersion in the lives and problems of others via literature can help students acknowledge the tensions that are always at work in the life of the legal professional and these also include the tension between the language of law and those of other disciplines, (e.g., statistics or psychiatry), in trial situations. Furthermore, it helps instill into students a germ for the development of the necessary professional practical wisdom from the very start of their lives as lawyers: the legal aptitude that involves ordering materials in such a way that a new proposal for the world in the form of argument and judgment can be made. Or, as U.S. Supreme Court Justice Stephen Breyer eloquently promoted the idea of empathetic imagination:

> Law requires both a head and a heart. You need a good head to read all those words and figure out how they apply. But when you are representing human beings or deciding things that affect them, you need to understand, as best you can, the workings of human life.[45]

That is why humanistic *Bildung* is not and should not be taught as a frill of the kind that law students sometimes disparagingly call "law and bananas" but as an essential component of legal education, lest legal practice remains unresponsive—as, I fear, has been the case so far—to its suggestions. Here, too, lies the project of academic "law and literature" to (re)connect legal theory and the practice of law in common law and civil law cultures. The latter code-based systems, no less than the former case-based systems, can benefit from the teaching of a critical attitude from the very start of legal education in order to encourage jurists toward improved imaginative creativity and greater ability to contextualise knowledge with regard to pragmatic and not merely doctrinal demands. The ability to enter imaginatively into any given situation is what matters, then, and with it, the disposition of *prudentia* which takes its deliberations from the circumstances of things, or *phronèsis*, as Aristotle called it.[46] Interpretation cannot thrive without practical wisdom, because legal knowledge is not a pre-existing truth. It is always a form of applied understanding, for it brings together rules that are not self-applying, and contexts that differ from case to case. Narrative knowledge, or rather a working narrative intelligence is therefore immensely important in legal practice,[47] not in the least because as practitioners we arrange events in a dramatic sequence, whether in oral pleas, written charges, or judicial decisions, and in doing so we already decide what and who is to be included or left out. Reflection on this process is essential and the same goes for our recognition of competing tugs in other people's arguments and texts. Wholeness is all, combining the narrative and the analytical to arrive at integrity in the literal sense of the word (its Latin root *integritas* meaning "being whole") both for the individual practitioner and the practice of law.

Binary Oppositions or Wholeness? Separation and Integration of Disciplines

The aforementioned argument also goes for interdisciplinarity itself. As I argue elsewhere,[48] if "law and literature" is to thrive, we will need to make it a whole as an interdiscipline—that is to say coherent and structurally a whole (i.e., integrated and intellectually sincere and conscientious). Only then will it stand a chance of accomplishing the aims with which it started. Only then can it be truly interdisciplinary as far as intellectual integration of the kind promoted by White is concerned when he wrote, "Indeed, in its hunger to connect the general with the particular, in its metaphorical movements, and in its constant and forced recognition of the limits of mind and language, the law seemed to me a kind of poetry... the activities of law and literature ... were in a deep sense the same thing, and I could not do the one without the other."[49]

This also reminds us that our disciplinary starting point determines the form of cooperation. Because law's way of being in the world starts with language, any "Law and" field needs to consider the disciplinary language views involved for they are of decisive importance for the narration in and of the texts of the cooperating disciplines.[50] To me, this speaks for our continued attention to the history of ideas. The idea that interdisciplinary scholarship is something new in that it brings together two (or more) originally separate and autonomous disciplines is a paradox when in retrospect we realise that this development took place as a reaction to the process of disciplinary differentiation that occasioned the rise of monodisciplinarity in the nineteenth century and with it, in Europe at least, the independence of national literatures. The European development coincided with the rise of nation states and their urge to distinguish themselves by means of national codifications. The growth of disciplinary autonomy was accelerated by the rapid expansion of technology and industry with their favored positivistic methodologies focused on explaining the world. This drove a wedge between the humanities and the natural and empirical sciences.

The epistemological and methodological debate that followed, or the *Erklären-Verstehen* controversy as it is called in philosophy, focused on the difference between the concept of explanation pertaining to facts and the concept of hermeneutic understanding of human action. It has had far-reaching implications for law and literature in the twentieth century, for as late as 1959 C. P. Snow still made the distinction between the two cultures, (i.e., of scientists and non-scientists), and dismissed the humanities because of their inability to contribute to solutions to global problems, a view that met with fierce oppsion by F. R. Leavis, who promoted the idea of literature as rooted in human minds that thus constitute and affirm their humanity. The effect of disciplinary differentiation and the combined emphasis on facts and literal meaning that is the heritage of positivism, also for law, are beautifully illustrated in a scene from a Dutch classic, Multatuli's *Max Havelaar* (1860), where the coffee-broker, Batavus Droogstoppel, criticises literature, and especially poetry for its lack of correspondence with the "real" world, saying

> Mind you, I've no objection to verses themselves. If you want words to form fours, it's all right with me! But don't say anything that isn't true. "*The air is raw, the clock strikes four*" I'll let that pass, if it really *is* raw, and if it really *is* four o'clock. But if it's a quarter to three, then I, who don't range my words in line, will say: "*The air is raw, and it is a quarter to three*". But the versifier is bound to four o'clock, or else the air mustn't be raw. And so he starts tampering with the truth. Either the weather has to be changed, or the time. And in that case, one of the two is false.[51]

The success of the positivist paradigm brought with it a concept of law as science that in the late nineteenth century led to a profound belief in the transparency of objective knowledge in law. In the United States, C. C. Langdell proposed a method of inductive reasoning through accumulated cases in order to distil legal concepts and doctrines that in turn could be applied deductively to new cases and thus contribute to the formation of a true science of law. This occasioned the rise of legal formalism. In civil law European countries the positivist idea that legal decision-making must necessarily opt for the guidance of the system of rules became dominant. With it came law's thrust for *Normgerechtigkeit*, as German legal theory had it (i.e., the principle that the strict application of the norm leads to a just result), and a concept of instrumental rationality on the view that, in a value-free legal science, the selection of the objectives was left to politics and the competence of the scientist would be limited to giving advice about the applicable means. The legal professional became an engineer.

Against this background it is obvious that in contemporary interdisciplinary ventures we have to address the question of the disciplinary concept we espouse. The success of disciplinary translation depends on it. This necessitates an investigation into the conceptual presuppositions as well as the interpretative strategies of the cooperating disciplines and other assumptions (shared or not). Put succinctly, for any "Law and" this means we have to decide. Does our view on law epitomise modern science with its emphasis on theoretical knowledge in which universality, objectivity, certainty, and rationality are the keywords? Or do we think of law as a hermeneutic discipline that cherishes the method of *phronèsis*, the practical wisdom rooted in the particularity of a specific situation, with as a result the acceptance of a plurality of viewpoints for debate and argumentation. In short, is a lawyer a mechanic in the sense that he "merely applies" what others have provided, or an architect, as the second epigraph to this chapter asks us to consider? Is law social engineering or is it one of the humanities?[52]

In early "law and literature," the debate between Robin West and Richard Posner on the perceived contrast between economic man and literary woman provides an insightful illustration. To Posner, it should first be noted, law is divorced from legal theory and that is why the study of any other discipline is relevant only when it uses law "in some organic sense" as is the case with economics, or so he claims.[53] Literature as in "law and literature", then, is of service to law only when it contributes to interpretation of the intentionalist kind. Now the economic goal of the individual participating in the marketplace is wealth-maximization—that is, maximization of individual preferences. On the meta-level, I suggest, this implies a methodological individualism that works from the presupposition that participants always choose rationally, and that disregards situations of dependence. Once decision-making in law is based on such supposed freedom of choice, this reveals a worldview in which human values are hardly recognised. That is the critical, political perspective that Robin West endorsed when she argued that Kafka's fiction provides us with a clear picture of the horrors of such a world in which the individual's consent to any transaction legitimates everything. To her, there is a strong contrast between the "outward descriptions imposed upon the transactions in which Kafka's characters engage and the radically different inward experience of those transactions by the parties involved,"[54] as Joseph K. in *The Trial*, Georg in "The Judgement," and the eponymous hunger-artist poignantly illustrate. The result of economic man's emphasis of individual autonomy is that "He is as incapable of error regarding his own subjective self-interest as he is incapable of knowledge regarding the subjectivity of others. Empathy is as foreign to him as rationality is familiar."[55] Hence, the need for a counterweight in the form of literary woman who, as noted earlier, by her reading of literature has developed an awareness of the complexity of the human condition.

The main point is this: in an economic environment that favours the positivistic hermeneutics that meaning is obvious, language risks becoming the supposedly neutral vehicle for the communication of information in which facts are entities in the world easily transmissible by words: the encoded perceptions of these very same facts. "Law and literature" opposes such language view because it assumes the unmediated representation of reality connected to the Cartesian idea(l) that scientific knowledge is theoretical knowledge only, easily conveyed by means of that neutral instrument called language. Such language view disregards the influence of our conceptual framework on our valuation of the world. The political relevance of the debate is obvious given our contemporary global financial and economic crises. A humanistic reconsideration of the primacy of instrumental reason in modernity therefore remains acute, for an instrumental reason enframed in a project of domination threatens our capacity to remake the conditions of our existence. As Charles Taylor claimed, we risk the growth of "a disengaged model of the human subject" at the expense of moral deliberation—that is, disengaged from our bodies, emotions, and life forms.[56] On the meta-level of interdisciplinarity, the consequence of the rationalist economic view, put bluntly, is that the language of the dominant discipline determines the form of cooperation. This leads to what White calls disciplinary imperialism, prioritizing the one language at the expense of the other.[57] The discipline connected by means of the "and" is then at best a tool or auxiliary, not a constitutive component.

In contemporary "law and literature," the flipside of the "economic man-literary woman" argument is under scrutiny. As Stephen Jay Gould claimed, the only reason that we ever developed a model of opposition between science and the humanities is our "deeply entrenched habit of ordering our categories as oppositional pairs."[58] While there may be nothing wrong with the opposition of scientific economic man (including the authoritarian man of law as science) to literary woman as a heuristic device for purposes of argumentation, we should consider whether to continue or not an antagonistic and gendered reasoning in terms of the deficiency of the one discipline compared to the superiority of the other, as scholars as varied as Jane Baron, Julie Stone Peters, Greta Olson, and Desmond Manderson have recently argued in their critiques of "law and literature."[59] The question is acute for at least two reasons. First, when we realize that the supposedly mutual incomprehension that results from the (putative) dichotomy of the scientists versus the scholars in the humanities is itself the result of the differentiation of disciplines that the advocates of a humanistic study of law ask us to reconsider. Secondly, when we discuss the future of "law and literature" and its offspring (or siblings) "law and humanities" and "law and culture," and do so from a "de-Americanized" point of view proposed by Olson, on the view that American "law and literature" scholarship has so far not done much to overcome the dichotomising.[60]

To White, by contrast, any interdisciplinary work should start from the idea that we constitute ourselves by means of the resources furnished by our culture, so that we have to remind ourselves constantly that how we express ourselves is to a large degree structured by our linguistic and cultural contexts, professional and otherwise. Thus, in using these resources we *re*create the languages that make us what we are.[61] To counter any form of linguistic or disciplinary imperialism of the kind discussed earlier, White proposes translation as a mode of thought to resist utilistic thinking and promote intellectual integration as the making of "a third, a new whole, with a meaning of its own."[62] Such integration works by seeking the homology between disciplines, by thinking in terms of fundamental commonalities rather than viewing literature as a disciplinary surplus with an additive value for law only—that is, "law *as*" rather than "law *and*" as noted earlier.[63] On this view, too, interdisciplinary research is comparable to translating texts: the construction of new meaning and the composition of a new form of language, and, with it, a new culture. The comparison is important if we consider that from time immemorial it has been the judge"s task to give words in law to what is literally unspeakable to the people who come before him.[64]

The idea of translation as integration implies that truly interdisciplinary work should aim at articulating the specificity of our acting with languages for only then can (the foundations of) both disciplines be understood in their mutual connection. To White, integrative knowledge is therefore not "the transfer of 'findings' from field to field, nor the transportation of 'method' ... but a bringing to consciousness of the nature of our own intellectual and linguistic practices."[65] To lay bare the analogies between law and other disciplines is the essence of translation. As a normative ideal it precludes any tendency to think in terms of the conveyance of entities of meaning. And since translation of disciplines is never a mechanical act, but something to be done time and again in a specific context, the imagination and, with it, practical reason play a crucial role for us to be able to understand analogies and know how to work with the materials available. The idea is behind all this is that

> There is no single appropriate response to the text of another, nor even a finite appropriate set of responses; what is called for is a kind of imaginative self-assertion in relation to another. It will be judged by its coherence, by the kinds of fidelity it establishes with the original, and by the ethical and cultural meaning it performs as a gesture of its own.[66]

For, as White astutely reminds us, "One who believes that everything can be said in a language of theory and system is an impossible fool."[67]

There is even more good reason to pay careful attention to the translation of our disciplinary narratives if we agree that scientific explanations and humanistic understandings are both forms of storytelling,[68] related though distinct: for judges who are unaccustomed to the specifics of a discipline other than their own, it can be most helpful to gain insight in the way in which other forms of cognition function when they have to decide cases in which the clash of disciplines is obvious as is the case in, for example, law and psychiatry,[69] or when they have to confront and overcome their own preconceived notions as forensic psychology suggest we all have in the forms of belief perseverance and confirmation bias. In short, even though the use of the term science seems awkward in a Whitean context, we should opt for "narrative schemes [that] may provide a science of the imagination."[70]

Back to the Future

Since 1973, "law and literature" has become institutionalised, with courses at most Anglo-American law schools,[71] a separate entry in the *Index to Legal Periodicals and Books*, specialised journals, and anthologies,[72] and, finally, an exponential growth of the number of websites devoted to the subject. In Europe, too, the humanistic study of law, aiming at opening up the law to "dialogues across disciplines," has gained momentum.[73] So it is high time to consider, also by way of conclusion, some possibilities for future research now that the humanistic study of law has once more gone global, if we recall its roots in the implementation of the Justinian Code of Roman law since the eleventh century. For a renewed legal humanism, then, one that takes as its object the plurality of aspects of the human condition, [74] the need for translation as a mode of thought remains acute. Rather than entering into fierce contestation with American scholarship or replicating it, we should engage in dialogue and reflect on our specific cultural and legal preoccupations. In short, the future lies in a comparative legal humanism—that is, a multilateral recontextualization of research topics. Contemporary pluralism in law and society strongly suggest the need for a study of unity and diversity at different levels, with attention to the traditions that brought us where we are today.

From the myriad possibilities that the humanities offer,[75] my suggestions are prompted by my conviction that given the mutual dependency of theory and practice in law jurisprudential studies should move beyond the purely academic, theoretical context and into the realm of practice. A renewed focus on doing law will give humanistic legal studies practical significance and, with that, perhaps also impact of the kind so highly desired by academic leadership.

To start with, I would like to point again to the importance of the historical perspective. Research into historical cross-sections of a field of law is admirably suited to generate new questions, nationally and internationally. This also goes for comparative law when we consider recent tendencies such as, first, the shift in civil law countries away from the traditional inquisitorial approach in trial situations toward more adversarial common-law features (e.g., equality of arms with respect to hearing expert witnesses), and secondly, the development by European courts of a European common law while, as Mary Ann Glendon already suggested, American courts seem to move toward a dogmatic stance.[76] To provide a space for cultural-legal translation is also especially important for partnerships such as the European Union in order to seek methodological integration and collaboration. In the sphere of legal language and concepts, attention to the inexhaustibility of contextual differences when concepts may have similar wordings but are nevertheless culturally and sociologically dissimilar (and that includes the discourses of gender, race, and ethnicity) is crucial. Another promising topic that ties in with current, technology-induced challenges with respect to questions of volition, authorship, and copyright in the digital world, would be the unity of law, literature, and historiography that once existed in the idea of the *auctoritas poetarum,* the authority in matters of truth and fact that Renaissance humanists ascribed to poets and historians alike.[77] Furthermore, research on the history of fictionality itself can help us to address the broader theme of the dominant epistemology and history of ideas of a specific era and reconsider the topic of how contemporary jurists seek refuge in the story in order to give their argument more weight, as their medieval precursors did before them. It can also further our inquiries into the Aristotelian opposition (in the *Poetics*) of *mythos* (narrative, story) to *logos* (dialectical discourse) that contemporary developments such as the growing importance of visuality and mediality in law prompt us to.

This brings me to my second perspective, occasioned by the influx of modern technologies in law and especially in the courtroom, that of the future of textuality in the digital age. How are judges to translate what they "see" in the pictures shown to them in evidentiary settings into the minutes of the trial session as is required in most civil law countries without jury systems? What "is" it that we actually see if we think of the influence of (popular) culture on the formation of the mental frames through which we perceive law and society, our local cultural imaginations, and scripts that are themselves narratives we live by?[78] Here, too, an exploration of differences and similarities between various legal cultures and systems, diachronicaly and synchronically, is called for. As a legal practitioner I strongly favour the idea of language as our cultural software,[79] firmly rooted as I still am in the idea of law as text. I would therefore hesitate to focus on aspects of mediality and visuality per se. My claim would be that it is precisely because of technological developments that law's textuality remains important. This also goes for the technological developments in and of the humanities themselves. As Dave Parry recently put it, "Consider the fact that we do not have 'pencil humanists' or 'typewriter humanists.' This might seem like an odd observation, but we should ask what the adjective 'digital' is doing in 'digital humanities.'"[80] While digital technologies greatly enhance the range and speed of all kinds of literary-legal textual analyses (computational and corpus linguistics, for example, can significantly contribute to the analysis of judicial decisions of supra and international courts), this does not preclude the demand for knowledge of such formal literary characteristics as genre. So the IT specialist who constructs the algorithm guiding the search cannot do without the input of the humanities traditionally conceived. Even when we would argue that our traditional human-centric view of legal codes must give ground to a machine-centric view,[81] as designers of the machines we remain responsible for their output, so code is still made by us.[82] On the view that resistance to what technocrats call nonmarketable knowledge[83] remains called for, I am optimistic about the close bond of the humanities and law on the plane of language and hermeneutic *praxis*. Their usefulness is not to be measured with a cost-benefit calculus but in terms of their contribution to law's task: doing justice.

Notes

1. First published anonymously in the 1755 Collection of Poems, edited by Robert Dodsley.
2. Walter Scott, *Guy Mannering* (London and New York: Dent and Dutton, 1954), 259.
3. For example, R. A. Posner, "Law and Literature: A Relation Reargued," *Virginia Law Review* 72 (1986): 1351, 1352, "But only since the publication in 1973 of James Boyd White's *The Legal Imagination* has a distinct, self-conscious field of law and literature emerged"; A. McGillivray, "Recherche Sublime: An Introduction to Law and Literature," *Mosaic* 27, no, 4 (1994): i, iii, "To White properly belongs the credit ... for setting Law and Literature firmly on the map of interdisciplinary study"; A. Sarat, M. Anderson, and C. O. Frank, "Introduction: On the Origins and Prospects of the Humanistic Study of Law," in *Law and the Humanities, An Introduction*, ed. A Sarat, M, Anderson, and C. O. Frank (Cambridge: Cambridge University Press, 2010), 1, 2, "The first blush of the humanistic study of law in the modern era occurred with the exploration of the conjunction of law and literature, an exploration sparked in turn by the publication of James Boyd White's seminal textbook, *The Legal Imagination* (1973)."
4. J. B. White, "The Cultural Background of *The Legal Imagination*" in *Teaching Law and Literature*, ed. A. Sarat, C. O. Frank, and M. Anderson (New York: Modern Language Association of America, 2011), 29, 29–30. As early as 1965 White wrote that he deplored the then prevailing lack of professional intimacy between law, history, and literature, fields once common to the legal profession. See, for example, J. B. White, "Review of M. P. Gilmore, *Humanists and Jurists*," *Harvard Law Review* 78 (1965): 1713.
5. White, "Cultural Background," (n 2), 31.
6. See D. A. Skeel, "Lawrence Joseph and Law and Literature" *University of Cincinnati Law Review* 77 (2009): 921, 923; A. Sarat, C. O. Frank, and M. Anderson, "Introduction," in *Teaching Law and Literature*, ed. A. Sarat, C. O. Frank, and M. (New York: Modern Language Association of America, 2011), 1, 5.
7. J. H. Wigmore, "A List of Legal Novels," *Illinois Law Review* 2 (1908): 574, and "A List of One Hundred Legal Novels," *Illinois Law Review* 26 (1922): 17; B. N. Cardozo, "Law and Literature," *Yale Review* 489 (1925), reprinted in B. N. Cardozo, *Law and Literature and Other Essays and Addresses* (New York: Harcourt, Brace & Company, 1931).
8. H. L. A. Hart, "Positivism and the Separation of Law and Morals," *Harvard Law Review* 71 (1958): 593; L. Fuller, "Positivism and Fidelity to Law— A Reply to Professor Hart," *Harvard Law Review* 71 (1958): 630.
9. The effects of the use of legalistic language and formalistic hermeneutics, or "wordiness," by French lawyers during the Nazi occupation are brilliantly analysed in R. H. Weisberg, *The Failure of the Word* (New Haven, CT: Yale University Press, 1984) and *Poethics and Other Strategies of Law and Literature* (New York: Columbia University Press, 1992).
10. For an extensive discussion of early "law and literature" and its background see J. Gaakeer, *Hope Springs Eternal: An Introduction to the Work of James Boyd White* (Amsterdam: Amsterdam University Press, 1998).
11. Beyond the scope of this chapter is the research that addresses the subject of the regulation of literature *by* law (e.g., parody, defamation, obscenity, copyright) and

that of authorship. It should at once be noted that the "law *in*/law *as*" division is mostly important for heuristic purposes. Contemporary "law and literature" shows a proliferation of topics that do not necessarily fall under one of the traditional headings. They are extensively documented in K. Dolin, *A Critical Introduction to Law and Literature* (Cambridge: Cambridge University Press, 2007); G. Binder and R. Weisberg, *Literary Criticisms of Law* (Princeton, NJ: Princeton University Press, 2000); I. Ward, *Law and Literature: Possibilities and Perspectives* (Cambridge: Cambridge University Press, 1995); R. A. Posner, *Law and Literature: A Misunderstood Relation* (Cambridge, MA: Harvard University Press, 1988, 2nd ed. 1998, 3rd ed. 2009).

12. J. B. White, *The Legal Imagination: Studies in the Nature of Legal Thought and Expression* (Boston, Little, Brown, 1973), 758.

13. See R. H. Weisberg, "Wigmore and the Law and Literature Movement" *Law & Literature* 21 (2009): 129, 138, for the claim that the Wigmorean attention to fiction exploded into a debate on textual meaning that led us up "the dubious path called 'theory.'" See also J. Gaakeer, "The Future of Literary-Legal Jurisprudence: Mere Theory or Just Practice?" *Law and Humanities* 5, no. 1 (2011): 185.

14. In what follows I draw on materials used in J. Gaakeer, "European Law and Literature: Forever Young: The Nomad Concurs," in *Dialogues on Justice: European Perspectives on Law and Literature*, ed. H. Porsdam and T. Elholm (Berlin: De Gruyter, 2012), 44; "Iudex Translator: The Reign of Finitude," in *Methods of Comparative Law*, ed. P-G Monateri (Cheltenham UK: Edward Elgar, 2012), 252.

15. For a comprehensive overview of the aims of *The Legal Imagination* see J. B. White, "Establishing Relations between Law and Other Forms of Thought and Language" *Erasmus Law Review* 1, no. 3 (2008), accessible at www.erasmuslawreview.nl .

16. White, *The Legal Imagination*, 859.

17. For the tensions at work in the process (between legal and ordinary language, law and other disciplines, opposing lawyers and ultimately law and justice), see J. B. White, "Justice in Tension: An Expression of Law and the Legal Mind" *No Foundations* 9 (2012), 1, accessible at www.helsinki.fi/nofo.

18. J. B. White, *Heracles' Bow: Essays on the Rhetoric and Poetics of the Law* (Madison: University of Wisconsin Press, 1985), xi.

19. White, *Heracles' Bow*, 35.

20. J. B. White, *Justice as Translation: An Essay in Cultural and Legal Criticism* (Chicago: University of Chicago Press, 1990), 27, 26.

21. See White, *Heracles' Bow*, 116, "The idea of "comprehending contraries" is if anything even more plainly essential to the judicial opinion, for the very idea of the legal hearing and of legal argument (of which the judicial opinion is intended to be a resolution) is that it works by opposition."

22. S. T. Coleridge, *Biographia Literaria, or Biographical Sketches of my Literary Life and Opinions*, ed. J. Engell and W. Jackson Bate (Princeton, NJ: Princeton University Press, 1983), 16–17, "This power [i.e., of the imagination] ... reveals itself in the balance or reconciliation of opposite or discordant qualities: Of sameness, with difference; of the general, with the concrete; the idea, with the image."

23. J. B. White, *Living Speech: Resisting the Empire of Force* (Princeton, NJ: Princeton University Press, 2006). See also J. Gaakeer, "Interview with James Boyd White" *Michigan Law Review* 105 (2007): 1403, 1404ff. Earlier on, the late Robert

Cover criticized White for a one-sided emphasis on law's discursive aspects on the view that a judge's linguistic doings are indissolubly bound to its results. To Cover, White underexposes the tension between the text of law and the violence of its effects, "Legal interpretation takes place in a field of pain and death ... A judge articulates her understanding of a text, and as a result, somebody loses his freedom, his property, his children, even his life." R. Cover, "Violence and the Word," *Yale Law Journal* 95 (1986): 1601, 1602.

24. For a detailed professional biography of Blackstone see W. Prest, *William Blackstone, Law and Letters in the Eighteenth Century* (Oxford: Oxford University Press, 2008). For a jurisprudential reading of the poem against the background of Blackstone's *Commentaries on the Laws of England* see M. Mauger, "Observe How Parts with Parts Unite/In One Harmonious Rule of Right": William Blackstone's Verses on the Laws of England," *Law and Humanities* 6, no. 2 (2012): 179.

25. For an elaboration of the European roots of law and literature see Gaakeer, "European Law and Literature." See also M. Leiboff, "Ghosts of Law and Humanities (Past, Present, Future)," *Australian Feminist Law Journal* 36 (2012): 3, for a connection of the German-British lawyer Otto Kahn-Freund's advocacy of the concept of *Bildung* and the importance of the humanities for legal education to Blackstone's complaint that law students did not pursue an education in the *litterae humaniores* based on the *trivium* and *quadrivium* anymore.

26. See J. Gaakeer, "Reverent Rites of Legal Theory: Unity-Diversity-Interdisciplinarity," *Australian Feminist Law Journal* 36 (2012): 19.

27. White, "Establishing Relations between Law and Other Forms of Thought and Language," "*The Legal Imagination* is a text for a course in writing (and speaking) as a lawyer.... The question is: How can they do it well, and 'well' not only in the sense suggested by a word like 'success,' but well in a deeper way, at once ethical and political. Can they find a way to use legal language that will enable them to respect themselves and the profession they have chosen?"

28. In 1954 William Davenport was asked to develop a course on legal literature at the University of Southern California Law School. The idea behind this was "making a better lawyer of the man, a better man of the lawyer," W. H. Davenport, "A Course in Literature for Law Students," *Journal of Legal Education* 6 (1954:) 569, 570. For the expansion of the project, see W. H. Davenport, "A Bibliography: Readings in Legal Literature" *American Bar Association Journal* 41 (1955): 939; "Readings in Legal Literature: A Bibliographical Supplement" and "Further Supplement" *American Bar Association Journal* 43 (1957) 813, 1018.

29. C. Reich, "Toward the Humanistic Study of Law," *Yale Law Review* 74 (1965): 1402, 1402–1403.

30. Reich, "Toward the Humanistic Study of Law," 1408.

31. J. B. White, "Doctrine in a Vacuum," *Journal of Legal Education* 36 (1986): 155 and "The Study of Law as an Intellectual Activity," *Journal of Legal Education* 32 (1982): 1.

32. White, *Heracles' Bow*, 43.

33. M. C. Nussbaum, *Love's Knowledge* (Oxford: Oxford University Press, 1990), 171.

34. Nussbaum, *Love's Knowledge*, 171.

35. R. West, "Economic Man and Literary Woman: One Contrast," *Mercer Law Review* 39 (1988): 867.

36. M. C. Nussbaum, *Poetic Justice: The Literary Imagination in Public Life* (Boston, Beacon Press, 1995), xvi.
37. Nussbaum, *Poetic Justice*, 36.
38. M. W. Bailey, "Early Legal Education in the United States: Natural Law Theory and Law as a Moral Science," *Journal of Legal Education* 48 (1998): 311, citing P. M. Hamlin, *Legal Education in Colonial New York* (New York: New York University Press, 1939), xvii.
39. White, *Living Speech*, 9.
40. White, *Living Speech*, 51.
41. See, for example, Gaakeer, "Interview with James Boyd White," 1419, "The simultaneous insistence upon law and justice produces a constant pressure to think and rethink both what justice is and what the law requires. It is an engine for opening the law to our deepest values."
42. Coleridge, *Biographia Literaria*, 6.
43. See also A. Reichman, "Law, Literature, and Empathy: Between Withholding and Reserving Judgment," *Journal of Legal Education* 56 (2006): 296, 309, "Thus, reserving judgment, combined with an empathetic mindset aquired through reading literature, may prevent legal decision-making from becoming mechanical or banal."
44. For the theme of the division between private self and public world, see also White, *The Legal Imagination*, chapter 6.
45. "Stephen Breyer on Intellectual Influences," thebrowser.com/interviews/stephen-breyer-on-intellectual-influences. See also G. Watt, *Equity Stirring: The Story of Justice beyond Law* (Oxford and Portland: Hart Publishing, 2009), 20, "Too much respect for law and a lack of humane imagination is a terrible thing in a judge."
46. Aristotle, *The Nicomachean Ethics*, trans. H. Rackham, ed. Henderson (Cambridge, MA: Harvard University Press, 2003), book 6. In drama, the comparable term for the crucial moment of recognition of what is to be done is *agnitio*.
47. See also G. Sammon, "Law, Literature and the Importance of Narrative to the Legal Education" *Cork Online Law Review* (2011): 94, 95, for the view that "... that an understanding of narrative is of vital importance to the daily professional life of a lawyer."
48. In Gaakeer, "The Future of Literary-Legal Jurisprudence," 192.
49. J. B. White, *When Words Lose Their Meaning: Constitutions and Reconstitutions of Language, Character, and Community* (Chicago: University of Chicago Press, 1984), xii (endnote omitted).
50. For example, T. Zartaloudis, "Ars Inventio, Poetic Laws: Law and Literature—The And" *Cardozo Law Review* 29 (2008): 2431, for the view that language is the "and" of law and literature in the sense that both have their foundation in the transmissibility of what happens in the world into a linguistic being.
51. Multatuli, *Max Havelaar, or the Coffee Auction of a Dutch Trading Company*, trans R. Edwards, intro R. P. Meijer (Harmondsworth, UK: Penguin, 1987).
52. See D. Howarth, "Is Law a Humanity, Or Is It More Like Engineering?" *Arts and Humanities in Higher Education* (2004) 9, 23, for the view that law is engineering and as such uses the humanities.

53. Posner, "Law and Literature: A Relation Reargued," 1359, 1360.
54. R. West, "Authority, Autonomy, and Choice: The Role of Consent in the Moral and Political Visions of Franz Kafka and Richard Posner," (1985): 384. See also R. A. Posner, "The Ethical Significance of Free Choice" *Harvard Law Review* 99 (1986): 1431, and R. West, "Submission, Choice, and Ethics: A Rejoinder to Judge Posner," *Harvard Law Review* 99 (1986): 1449.
55. West, "Economic Man and Literary Woman," 869–70.
56. C. Taylor, *The Ethics of Authenticity* (Cambridge, MA: Harvard University Press, 1991), 101–2.
57. See White, "Establishing Relations between Law and Other Forms of Thought and Language."
58. S. J. Gould, *The Hedgehog, the Fox, and the Magister's Pox: Mending the Gap between Science and the Humanities* (New York: Harmony Books, 2003), 81–82.
59. See J. B. Baron, "The Rhetoric of Law and Literature: A Skeptical View," *Cardozo Law Review* 26 (2005): 2273; J. Stone Peters, "Law, Literature, and the Vanishing Real: On the Future of an Interdisciplinary Illusion," *PMLA* 120, no. 2 (2005): 442; G. Olson, "Law is not Turgid and Literature not Soft and Fleshy: Gendering and Heteronormativity in Law and Literature Scholarship," *Australian Feminist Law Journal* 36 (2012): 65; D. Manderson, "Modernism and the Critique of Law and Literature" *Australian Feminist Law Journal* 35 (2011): 107. For a discussion of a comparable dichotomy of the theory and practice of law in legal education, see also K. R. Guest Pryal, "Law, Literature, and Interdisciplinary Copia: A Response to Skeptics" (2011), ssrn.com/abstract=1479270.
60. G. Olson, "De-Americanizing Law and Literature Narratives: Opening Up the Story," *Law & Literature* 22 (2010): 338.
61. This is the overarching topic of White, *When Words Lose Their Meaning*.
62. White, *Justice as Translation*, 4.
63. See P. Hanafin et al, eds., *Law and Literature* (Oxford: Blackwell Publishing, 2004).
64. See the late Cornelia Vismann's work on the theatrical dimension of law and the old German judge's responsibility to convert the disputed "thing" into something that could be spoken about, in *Medien der Rechtsprechung* (Frankfurt: S. Fischer Verlag, 2011), 19ff. For a reading of White's *Justice as Translation* on the view that translation too is contingent, see H. Murav, "Justice as Translation" in *Law and the Humanities: An Introduction*, ed. A. Sarat, M. Anderson, and C. O. Frank (Cambridge: Cambridge University Press, 2010), 398.
65. White, *Justice as Translation*, 19.
66. White, *Justice as Translation*, 256.
67. White, *The Legal Imagination*, 863.
68. See also M. Turner, *The Literary Mind* (Oxford: Oxford University Press, 1996), 4, "Narrative imagining—story—is the fundamental instrument of thought. Rational capacities depend upon it."
69. See White, *Justice as Translation*, 13–14, "Consider, for example, the attempt of the law to rely upon the "findings" of psychiatrists as to the "sanity" of criminal defendants.... Psychiatry thinks in terms of treatment and diagnosis and health; the law thinks in terms of guilt, blame, and punishment. There is a radical incompatibility between the discourses, between the conceptions of the human

subject and the speaker's relation to him or her, that makes any transfer of "findings" problematic, to say the least."

70. E. M. Bruner, "Ethnography as Narrative," in *The Anthropology of Experience*, ed. V. W. Turner and E. M. Bruner (Urbana: University of Illinois Press, 1986), 139, 140.

71. For early overviews see E. Villiers Gemmette, "Law and Literature: An Unnecessarily Suspect Class in the Liberal Arts Component of the Law School Curriculum," *Valparaiso University Law Review* 23 (1989): 267, and "Law and Literature: Joining the Class Action," *Valparaiso University Law Review* 29 (1995): 665.

72. For example, U.S.-based *Law and Literature* (formerly *Cardozo Studies in Law and Literature*) and *Yale Journal of Law and the Humanities*. 2007 saw the launch of UK-based *Law and Humanities*. *Law Text Culture* is transcontinental with Australian roots. The *Australian Journal for Law and Society* and the *Australian Feminist Law Journal* also regularly feature humanistic research.

73. M. López Lerma and J. Etxabe, "Law's Justice: A Law and Humanities Perspective," *No Foundations* 9 (2012): ii, accessible at www.helsinki.fi/no. European associations include AIDEL (www.aidel.it), ISSL (www.lawandliterature.org), and the European Network for Law and Literature (www.eurnll.org).

74. As Greta Olson suggests in "De-Americanizing Law and Literature Narratives," 359, we have already moved "from a binary discipline to a triadic or multiple one" as "law and culture" and "law and the humanities" show. Most congenial to me is Costas Douzinas's proposal to avoid a palliative, disciplinary approach to the humanities and reengage in *humanitas* as a broad education and *Bildung*; see C. Douzinas, "A Humanities of Resistance: Fragments for a Legal History of Humanity," in *Law and the Humanities: An Introduction*, ed. A. Sarat, M. Anderson, and C. O. Frank (Cambridge: Cambridge University Press, 2010), 49.

75. Recent developments include "law and music"—for example, B. Grossfeldt and J. A. Hiller, "Music and Law" *International Law Journal* 42 (2008): 1147; P. Butler, *Let's Get Free: A Hip-Hop Theory of Justice* (New York, New Press, 2009), and "law and film"—for example, S. Greenfield, G. Osborn and P. Robson, *Film and the Law* (Oxford and Portland: Hart, 2010).

76. M. A. Glendon, *Rights Talk: The Impoverishment of Political Discourse* (New York: Free Press, 1991).

77. An example of a cultural-historical study on the changing view on authorship can be found in F. Ost, *Furetière, La démocratisation de la langue* (Paris: Michalon, 2008).

78. For an elaboration of this argument see J. Gaakeer "Cross-roads, or Some Remarks on the Future of Law and Literature," *Pólemos* (2012): 7. For the idea of script as a cognitive category, see R. K. Sherwin, "Law Frames: Historical Truth and Narrative Necessity in a Criminal Case," *Stanford Law Review* 47 (1994): 39; for an intriguing study of visual digital technology and law see R. K. Sherwin, *Visualizing Law in the Age of the Digital Baroque, Arabesques and Entanglements* (New York: Routledge, 2011).

79. J. M. Balkin, "Ideology as Cultural Software," *Cardozo Law Review* 16 (1995): 1221, 1228.

80. D. Parry, "The Digital Humanities or a Digital Humanism?," in *Debates in the Digital Humanities*, ed. M. K. Gold (Minneapolis, University Of Minnesota Press, 2012) 429, 431, chapter 24. For a critique of the digital humanities see also A. Liu, "The State of the Digital Humanities, A Report and Critique," *Arts and Humanities in*

Higher Education 11, no. 1–2 (2011): 8, and S. Fish, "The Old Order Changeth," opinionator.blogs.nytimes.com/2011/12/26/the-old-order-changeth/.

81. For this development see N. K. Hayles, *How We Think, Digital Media and Contemporary Technogenesis* (Chicago: University of Chicago Press, 2012), chapter 5, "Technogenesis in Action"; see also Cornelia Vismann's historical analysis in *Files, Law and Media Technology*, trans. G. Winthrop-Young trans (Palo Alto, CA: Stanford University Press, 2008).

82. L. Lessig, *Code: Version 2.0* (New York: Basic Books, 2006), 6.

83. See B. de Sousa Santos, "The European University at Crossroads," ISLL Papers-Essays 1, 2010, www.lawandliterature.org/.

[2]
Towards a Critique of Narrative Reason

François Ost

My objective in this brief contribution[1] is to lay down several markers on the path toward rehabilitating narrative (*le récit*) in the face of the dominant and traditional strategy of reasoning, which in various ways disqualifies narrative. I wish to plead in favour of the importance of narrative—its genuinely constitutive importance—just as much in the imaginative constitution of peoples, plural, as at the level of the "personal novel," which each of us narrates to himself in order to build up his identity. Of all the characteristics ascribed to the human entity—laughter, which some say defines the human—language, political feeling (human as the *zoon politicon*, according to Aristotle), sapience (human is *homo sapiens*), it is this fictioning faculty which strikes me as the most fundamental one. *Homo fabulans*: the human as the animal which tells stories. Ideally, my project should lead to the formulation of a Critique of Narrative Reason. But of course, in the space of just a few pages it is not possible to do more than provide some guidelines for such an ambitious project, which is dedicated to James Boyd White, who can be considered to have inspired it.

This plea is both easy and difficult: easy because we are all surrounded by narratives on all sides, because we are accompanied by stories since earliest childhood, and because stories are generally treated with great sympathy. Hard (and uneasy) because although narrative is regarded with benevolence by the common person (contemptuously referred to by Plato as the *doxa*), it is on the other hand regarded with suspicion by our dominant model of thought, which tries to neutralise its power by lumping it in to the domain of the private and the frivolous. I must therefore begin by discussing these strategies of disqualification which cause us to "think down" narrative (i.e., to look down on it in our thinking and also to underthink it, which means failing to think about it enough). Then in a second section, I will endeavour to explain in what way narrative "gives us cause to think."

Repressions and Disqualifications of Narrative

The first disqualification is ancient and Platonic: it is based on the separation of reality and fiction. This disqualification comes from the fact that in this line of thinking, "reality" is associated with "truth" and "justice" (or, in the realm of action, with moral truth).

The second disqualification is a modern one, going back to the philosopher David Hume. It stems from the great divide between facts and norms, between describing and prescribing, between the "is" and the "ought," and from the prohibition which goes with that—that is, that it is forbidden to pass from one to the other. In this case the disqualification of narrative is a double one: as well as being denied any role either in positing a fact or prescribing a norm, in consequence of the first repression, it is also denied any role as a mediator between these two ontological realms, since any possibility of a logical passage from one to the other is prohibited.

The third disqualification is postmodern and one might say "Habermasian": in societies that present themselves as based on the Rule of Law, which respects the fundamental rights of the individual, and in societies haunted by the imperative to be transparent, and which are articulated around multiple spaces of "rational" dialogue and discussion, all claims are supposed to be expressible freely and completely, without residue and without repression. All demands for recognition and claims to identity are thus supposed to conform to and to fit in with the procedures of dialogue and judicial process which modern societies place at the disposal of individuals and groups. Everything happens, then, as if the space of narrative were dried out and sucked up by the modes of argumentation—legal ones above all—which are supposed to do justice to the claims of individuals for recognition.

Of course, narrative never disappears, not under any of these three regimes; but it remains neglected—"underthought"—on account of these successive disqualifications. Plato, who follows the proud procession of the passage from *mythos* to *logos*, (i.e., the claimed emancipation of thought from the pre-logical categories of myth), relegates narrative to the dawn of societies (Homer, Hesiod) and to the earliest years of childhood (the fables told to children). These stories are thus simultaneously accepted (they played a part in the education of children and Greek society remains immersed in them) and reviled.

In modern times, the "great divide" (to borrow from Bruno Latour)[2] between being and having-to-be leads to two things: on the one hand, the formidable enterprise of explaining the world by means of science, based on *a priori* laws, which can be established and predicted using theoretical hypotheses and deductions combined with science-laboratory experiments; and on the other hand the writing of political constitutions and law codes, which are inspired by a positivist philosophy of law, which claims to have freed itself from the approximations and guesswork of so-called natural law. In both cases— the scientific enterprise and the establishment in written form of "positive" law— narrative is relegated to the prehistory of reason, which is associated with superstitions and the false prestige of appearances. And yet, to be sure, these societies never stop telling stories and telling themselves stories. The novel, the genre par excellence of triumphant individualism, prospers, but only in the space of "entertainment," out in the margins of the great adventure of modern reason, the maker of Progress.

In the present period, the juridical procedures and rational apparatus used by our society for channelling demands and claims have of course not stopped the flow of the narrative drive, no more than any of the preceding regimes. On the contrary, narrative is proliferating in contemporary society, now that it is largely freed from the constraints of genres and forms and very substantially freed also from the academic figure of the "author." Storytelling is taking over all spheres of activity (e.g., commercial advertising, where selling a brand amounts to telling the epic story of the company; electoral propaganda and the *celebrification* of the candidates; the proliferation of religious sects each peddling its own narrative of revelation...).

Such is the paradox that surrounds narrative: omnipresent since the dawn of humanity, it remains underthought and even disqualified in the dominant Western tradition, always relegated to the margins of reason (to the stammerings of infancy, to society's obscurantist prehistory, to the dubious domain of the *fait divers*, to the narcissistic staging of reality TV, to the mad ramblings of sectarian discourse).

Thus a vast philosophical field opens up, demanding that we reevaluate the place of storytelling in the adventure of reason and the formation of societies. This would involve reevaluating the role of fiction in the face of what is conventionally termed "reality" and "truth" and "justice" (which was the first separation and Plato's first repression). It would then involve revisiting the great "modern separation" denounced by Latour and showing how narrative carries out mediation functions that are the mediations of life itself— mediations which are obviously established every second between the facts and the norms which analytical reason strives to keep separated. It would involve, finally, investigating the ability of narrative to take account of the Unsaid, or even the Unsayable, which the rational procedures of democratic communication do not manage to account for; and yet without giving in to the dubious facility of storytelling.[3]

This last observation contains a warning which traces out a second axis of the philosophical field, which is opening up: after the rehabilitation of narrative must come its critique—something like a "Critique of Fabulising Reason." A task as delicate as it is necessary, to elucidate the relations which each society (or even: each individual) maintains with "his" fictions; a task that is under constant threat of "repression," on the level of individual narratives, and by "censorship," on the level of society (once again, Plato gives us the example)—and a task which is nevertheless indispensable since the act of telling stories is an activity subjected to all sorts of constraints that must be brought to light and sometimes accepted. Thus it is not a question of substituting narrative, in an idealised and absolutised form, for the other productive processes of reason, but a question of thematising their respective articulations. Paul Ricoeur's aphorism, "the symbol gives us cause to think" (*le symbole donne à penser*)—the symbol does this, yes, but so does narrative – can serve as a kick-off for this reflection (see section 2).[4]

Within the limits of this article, I shall content myself with discussing the first of these repressions of narrative. Hume's repression would assume that we deploy, following Ricoeur especially, the dialectic of "describe" and "prescribe"—a dialectic in the heart of which the act of narrating plays the role of mediator. As for the third repression (which for the sake of simplicity and brevity I have described as "Habermasian"), it could be discussed on the basis of what Jean-Marc Ferry calls *reconstructive ethics*,[5] whose objective is to take on board, by means of the resources of narrative, that proportion of the Unsayable (of the "differend," as Jean-François Lyotard would call it) to which the official juridical and communicational procedures cannot do justice (examples of which could be found in the work done on restorative justice, and notably on Truth and Reconciliation commissions).

The dominant inherited Western thinking is marked by the tyranny of the *real*. Which is also the reign of the present (of presence), of the a priori and of the given, and also of the stable form (the essence or idea):

a certain idea of purity and of perfection (the opposite of the composite and of that which is grasped only in its becoming). Therein we have a framework for thought and action, which conditions our most elementary and hence most fundamental representations. This *real* is indeed associated just as irresistibly with *truth* and *justice*. It's as if we were to be imperatively required to conform to this framework, on pain of error, of madness, of infringement, or of sin, were we to deviate at all from it, and all the more so if we were to contest its very validity. Of course it is impossible to deny the existence of the composite, of change, of impurity, but these things are implicitly dealt with by the dominant thinking using a whole system of classifications and hierarchies whose effect is to subordinate them to the real, to the form and idea of truth and justice, endowed finally with stability. In a definitive way, this framework of representation aims to bring back the whole set of the given within the reassuring and unchanging limits of the *same*. Its logic is that of the tautology, as empty as it is incontestable: *A=A, dura lex, sed lex*. or, in today's prevalent language, "business is business."

It is understandable that, in this context, narrative should be held in deep suspicion. This is because it opens up the space of the *as if*, which instantly cracks the constraining framework of the "real-true-*a priori*." An immense and virtual field opens and spreads out as soon as the tale-teller utters the words *once upon a time...* At once something imaginary gets into action, seeming to set in motion the process of becoming, throwing our certitudes into doubt, exciting the appetite for the *possible*. And so the official version of our world becomes the target of a generalised *subversion*.

Plato, the archetype of the dominant thinking, in his *Republic*,[6] banishes from the city all poets and dramatists. The guardians of the republic judge in effect that their art is corrupting, that it mixes the true with the false, that it portrays the same characters sometimes as great and sometimes as small, that it evokes chimeras and phantoms, and does not respect the distinction between good and evil. In a state governed by wise laws, there can be no place for this sort of art that feeds the bad element in the soul, that element which has truck with the things of the senses and with pleasure. In the *Laws* (VII, 817),[7] the lawgivers of the colony of Magnesia likewise oppose the entry of the tragedians into the city, or rather, they let them in only on one condition and in exchange for their submission to a severe censorship: the authorities alone will decide whether "the work is morally respectable and fit to be heard by the public." Knowing the formidable power of fiction, these lawgivers are determined to keep the poets at a distance in order to preserve the integrity of the law and of justice.

Such, then, is the repression which sets in right from the start: narrative is the victim of the radical split between reality and fiction. Narrative is not given right of citizenship. Not that it then stops haunting this city. Basically we are looking at a very classical situation here: repression and the (problematic) return of the repressed. But what if, as we should ask, the problem resided not so much in narrative itself but rather in the starting framework? Such is the question that is necessarily presupposed by any endeavour to rehabilitate the act of narrating.

This canonical framework assumes something like a "freeze-frame" image, in which time is artificially immobilized in order to make it yield to the grip of reason. As if reason, in order to elaborate its work of establishing the truth, of positing the form and definition of the idea, had to arrest the course of development and contemplate things *sub specie aeternitatis*. This is the strategy of "all things being equal," which is deployed by all analytical reason. In order to be intelligible, things must be defined (i.e., very precisely delimited, separated, closed-off, immobilised). More generally, the real must be protected from the virtual and the possible. Only on these conditions can language claim to correspond (as a calque corresponds) to the real which is its target; only on these conditions can language "speak" things in their truth, and "speak" actions in conformity with justice.

It is very significant that Plato concluded his long critique of tragedians and poets, those authors of fallacious narratives, with discourse on the theme of the immortality of the soul. (*The Republic*, X, 608c). What's at stake in this whole discussion—the positing of what I have called the "canonical framework" of the "real-true-a priori" in opposition to narrative fiction—is to conjure with the passing of time and thus to become immortal, and, by inscribing the labour of reason under the auspices of divine eternity, to guarantee at least the infallibility of our mental representations.

Yet this desire, legitimate though it is, is nonetheless deceptive: time does pass, the human is mortal, reality is composite and changing, language apprehends it only very imperfectly, truth is problematic, and justice is controversial.

And all the while, humans go on telling stories. Is it not time to reconsider these stories from a different perspective, rather than merely dismissing them as the nonsense tales of infancy, or subjecting them to a troubled and anxious censorship? To reconsider them from a different perspective, because these stories, by taking account of the weight of passing time, precisely, and by going beyond the narrow frame of definition of a given real, and by expanding it to include the enticing virtualities of the possible—these stories liberate us from the tyranny of truths that are never anything other than successive versions of the official orthodoxy, and they give us access to the highly promising domain of sense. Sense: that is, in two senses—sense as "sense of direction" and sense as "meaning"; one could say, an intelligibility in motion. To put it yet another way: a truth that is mobile, relative, caught in the movement of time. Or again: a reality-in-process of becoming, altered by time and movement and the unpredictable action of the *other* upon which we have no direct purchase. In this way we escape from the sterile samishness of tautology, at the risk of being adulterated by the advent of the other. Something, indeed, is arriving, an event is making history, a story which our histories have a duty to signify. A different constellation is thereby proposed, articulated around the notions of the possible, of becoming, of story/history, and of sense.

This, then, is the choice on offer: either the orthodox truth (which in the politico-juridical realm means: legalistic justice) *sub specie aeternitatis*, or else the adventure of sense in the element of passing time leading to death. In a desperate effort to give itself unchangeable certitudes, Western reason overwhelmingly opts for the former, denying itself the resources of sense suggested to it by narratives which were there before it came along. Because this proudly arrogant analytical reason cannot deny that humans have always already told stories that give sense to existence. But from these theogonies (Hesiod), these myths of origin (found in all societies studied by ethnologists and anthropologists), these heroic epics (Homer), these primitive fables, these law-giving utopias, Western reason turns away in horror.

Let us reread once more the passages from *The Republic* in the light of these earlier observations. What appears in every line is the overdetermination of a fixist metaphysics by a rigid governance, this metaphysics being itself fed by a fear of adulteration. "*Reason itself prescribes* to us to banish from our State all art of this nature" (X, 607). An art that deceives us by imitating the multiple and by arousing empathy toward various feelings—a trick art that is like those mirrors that reflect all appearances rather than the one unique form, created by God (X, 506e). Thus, explains Plato, "the maker of tragedies is three degrees removed from truth and from the king" (X, 598). Three degrees because being a mere imitator, he is neither the creator of the very form of the imitated thing nor the creator of one of its concrete avatars. So it is not surprising, adds Plato, that Homer should be neither an educator nor a political guide, capable of discriminating between a good and a bad city. Likewise Plato sets himself the task of watching over and sorting or filtering the fables told to children. For example, we must not tolerate the line from Homer that speaks of "*Zeus, dispenser of good and bad things*", or this passage from

Aeschylus: "*God makes crime arise among mortals when he wants to ruin a house entirely*" (II, 380). (By this reckoning, we would have to excise from the Bible the Book of Job, which is one of its great marvels, along with the Song of Songs.)

Struggling against this subversion by narrative, the lawgivers dictate that God should be represented *just as he is* (II, 379b), that the citizen be valorised as a model of virtue and *equal unto himself* (X, 604d), and that we should protect ourselves against the appearances of the real (e.g., the object which in water appears to be broken), and that this should be done "*by measurement, calculation and weighing*, which are excellent safeguards against these illusions" (X, 602b-3).

Are we to think that the message is unequivocal, that the lesson is clear? It is not so simple ... because what else is Plato doing himself, other than telling stories? The cave parable, the utopia of the City of Magnesia, the narrative of the banquet, the imaginary dialogues with Socrates—and did Socrates, his hero, even exist? Plato is a philosopher-storyteller, and assuredly not the least of them. Besides, is this not equally the case with the lawgivers whom he puts on stage? After they have kicked out the poets and tragedians, here we have their confession: "We shall compose, ourselves, a tragic poem to the best of our ability, the most beautiful and the most excellent one possible; our whole political organization consists in an imitation of the most beautiful and most excellent life!" *Coup de théâtre*! We thought poetry had been denigrated and degraded to the rank of sensory pleasure, and now we see it elevated to the rank of Constitution of the State. "We are your competitors," admit the lawgivers, "being the authors of the most magnificent of dramas: the one, precisely, whose stage director could only be an authentic code of laws" (*The Laws*, VII, 816–17). On Plato's use of the narrative and the dramatic form we can refer to James Boyd White's excursion on "*The Phaedrus*: Philosophy, Rhetoric, and Love" in *The Edge of Meaning*.[8]

In order to move forward, we must therefore think against Plato and with Plato. Against Plato, who claims to reason independently of narrative; and with Plato, who philosophises like the great mythographer that he is. I propose to proceed by way of a meditation on this aphorism of Paul Ricoeur: "the symbol gives us cause to think."[9] By conjugating together the symbol (metaphor, narrative) and thought in the form of a relation of giving, a token of reciprocal fecundity, it seems to me we have good chances of succeeding.

The Symbol (or the Narrative) Gives us Cause to Think

If the symbol "gives" us cause to think, it is because, like narrative, it comes first of all. That is not contested even by Plato. The difference is that its priority here takes the form of a seminal donation, from an establishing or foundational source and not from a deceptive preliminary gesture. What we must come to understand, in order to do justice to this initial donation, is the properly constitutive character of these originary narratives. They are "constitutive" in the sense in which Searle and the theorists of language speak of "constitutive rules," in opposition to merely "regulatory rules." A constitutive rule is one that "causes to exist" that which it refers to, whereas a regulatory rule does no more than to regulate a preexisting reality.[10] To decide that France is a republic and Belgium a constitutional monarchy, to decide that gold is money and the individual a citizen—these are examples of constitutive rules or decisions. To decide that cars drive on the right is an example of a regulatory rule.

A constitutive utterance is a product of that "socio-historic imagination" of which Cornelius Castoriadis speaks, forming the conceptual and normative matrix of an entire culture.[11] In the confused magma of empirical impressions and sensations, this constituting imaginary, which speaks in narratives, selects, with a virtually infinite diversity as reflected in the variety of languages, of rites and practices, the facts which are pertinent and the values which are significant in the eyes of this initial script, schema, or scenario. Functioning like a cinematic montage that draws upon an enormous number of "rushes," the socio-historic imaginary of peoples (plural) makes for itself its own history whose successive episodes it will never finish writing. In this way, they are constitutive in the sense in which White refers to the "constitutive rhetoric" of law and legal language that comprises "the art of constituting character, community, and culture in language."[12] No matter what may be the later avatars of the labour that a culture performs on itself (sometimes violently rejecting certain panels from its heritage)—just as language never stops self-transforming—it is always *on the basis of* this initial donation that its conceptual elaborations are made and that its normative options are shaped. Literally, we learn to think—George Steiner goes further and even says that we learn to speak—in the element of originary narratives. What's involved here is something like the "internal point of view" proper to the group, a point of view that irrevocably determines how it orients itself in the world. What would our conception of languages be if we had never heard tell of Babel? What would our conception of time be if we had not received the myth of Kronos eating his children? What would our conception of perversion be if we had not heard tell of Sodom and Gomorrha? Greek myths; biblical parables; the fables of La Fontaine; the myths of Don Juan, Faust, and Robinson Crusoe; the utopias of More; Bacon, and Fourier; timeless fairy tales collected in modernity by Perrault, Andersen, and Grimm: there we have the rich loam in which our culture is embedded.

Without our even noticing it, at least in the first phase and for want of a patient labour of self-elucidation, these narratives select the themes of interest, the characters worthy of attention, the values to pursue or reject; a vocabulary that is implicitly put into circulation, a tried-and-tested temporal structure (it is a fascinating observation to note that the way in which different peoples situate themselves on the scale of time varies greatly), genders are imposed (why do certain languages use the neuter gender, whereas in others it is unknown?), schemas of action and reaction are put forward. Unconscious dichotomies—bearers of limits and thus of unwritten norms—are naturalised: I am thinking especially of the division of the sexes, the distinction between generations, and the separation of the living and the dead that make up the whole material of Greek tragedy.

As Ricoeur writes: "not only is imagination itself without rules, but it constitutes the generative matrix of the rules."[13] I repeat: each civilisation, each culture will operate in the wake of a ceaseless critical labour upon this heritage (in which phases of institutionalisation alternate with phases of critical deconstruction, still according to Castoriadis's observation); nonetheless, it is *starting from* this quasisubliminal frame and not *outside of* it that each civilisation is constructed.

What is true on the collective level turns out to be true on the scale of our individual histories likewise. Each of us, in order to face his existence, to lay claim to his own identity and take his place in society, constitutes for himself a "personal novel." Largely unconscious, deceptive or illusory in many ways, it is nevertheless constitutive of our fragile ego that puts itself at risk in the view of others. Seen from the side of the writer or storyteller, the narrative operates as a heuristic instrument of discovery or even of constituting the self; viewed from the side of the reader or listener, this narrative produces those same effects, this time by putting into play mechanisms of empathy and identification with regard to the author or his characters.

It is this life narrative, at times chaotic and at times even delirious, but oh-so-constitutive, that the suffering patient will perhaps tell to the therapist and which, together, they will try to reelaborate in order to reconstitute a personality: here, too, the narrative "gives us cause to think."

On another stage, the juridical scene, it is also the life narrative that attempts to clear for itself a path to the courtroom, notably by the intermediary of the lawyer, and which will have such difficulty making itself heard through the chinks and loopholes of juridical qualifications and procedures: literature is full of these stories that try, at times desperately, to get themselves heard by the magistrates. I quote two examples among many others: George Simenon's *Letter to my Judge*, in which a doctor sentenced for the murder of his wife explains to the judge that he is not really the one who was present at the trial, nor was he really the one who was convicted; and Stendhal's *Scarlet and Black*, which lets the author rewrite the plea for the defence of Julien Sorel (alias Antoine Berthet) in its entirety, because his lawyer "in the world" had not reached the true personality of the accused.[14]

Thus the narrative *gives*. It now remains to show that it gives us cause to *think*.

A matrix of mental representations, the constitutive imaginary is at the source of the elaboration of concepts, and thus, by successive stages, of the labor of constructing theoretical reason in its double face, speculative and nomothetic; a matrix of implicit valorizations, this same imaginary is likewise at the source of our elaboration of norms, and thus, by successive stages, of the labour of enunciation of practical reason in its double face, moral and juridical.

I shall here just allude briefly to many sources, with regard to the labor of theoretical reason, because otherwise it would lead me into conducting a vast epistemological inquiry that has no place here. Might I just be permitted to make do with several intuitions that remain to be elucidated and enlarged upon at a later time. I maintain that the imagination plays a heuristic role (a role of "setting in motion"), which is essential to scientific discovery and the formulation of the laws which derive therefrom.

At the origin of the scientific "paradigms" discussed by Thomas Kuhn, we find the action of vast "world views," translated into a network of metaphors that orient the research in a decisive direction, which is sometimes the origin of a "scientific revolution."[15] Besides, what is a "paradigm" other than a well-chosen example which illustrates the theory—an example, a profound experiment, a memorable event—in law a "leading case" that makes jurisprudence and which, far from applying a preexisting law, is rather the narrative that allows the law to be deduced?

Thus, each great scientific discovery is supported by or rests upon the intuition of a possible world translated into a kind of speculative narrative embryo. Of course, in the next instant, theoretical reason, of the calculating variety in particular, takes up the story, and is soon followed by the testing and measuring equipment of the laboratory—but these things never do more than enact the script suggested by the narrative intuition of the researcher: "*and what if we said that?...*" One would have to reread Ladrière and Bachelard, Latour and Prigogine in particular, to strengthen this hypothesis. Likewise, one would have to study anew and more closely the role played by the transcendental imagination in the Kantian critique (notably the famous paragraph 49 of the *Critique of Judgment*: in this passage, entitled "the faculties of mind that constitute genius," the creative imagination is liberated from the tutelage of the concept and from its role in determinant judgment; here, it gives us cause to think and to understand). One would also have to meditate upon the recent works of Michel Serres.[16]

I therefore pose the question: what imaginary animated Darwin and his war between the species, or Newton and his universal force of attraction, or Einstein and his theory of relativity?

A fortiori, it seems to me that I can maintain also that the great advances in the human and social sciences are due to the imaginative fecundity of certain pioneer researchers. It suffices to cite a few names: Freud and Jung, who one day decided to let our most intimate nocturnal narratives speak (and also, let it be said in passing, a lot of ancient and modern stories), thus lifting a corner of the veil on that immense "possible world" of the unconscious that accompanies us like a shadow without our ever (one can certainly say this) becoming conscious of it; Lévi-Strauss, who constructs structural anthropology on the basis of the scrupulous deciphering of the plentiful myths of the populations he studied; Auguste Comte, who invents the fable of the "three ages of humanity"; and Marcel Mauss, who works out his own ambitious theory of the gift based on the narrative of the *potlatches*.

I would add—and this is more than a mere detail—that these pioneer narrators devote a lot of attention to the writing of their theory, thus bearing witness to a "style" of their own that is not unrelated to the interest that their works arouse. The same remark applies, by the way, to the writing of the philosophers: this is a domain still largely unexplored, and a very promising one, the examination of the content and "style" of a philosophy. Indeed, it is precisely the sort of work that has been pioneered by James Boyd White.[17]

But if narrative plays a heuristic role at the level of scientific invention and theoretical speculation, the same goes for the formulation of moral ideas and their translation into the form of rules of law. Here again, narrative is primary and constitutive: literature, the laboratory of the human, carries out all sorts of experiments on evaluative judgements that are like the propadeutic of ethics-in-situation.[18] I am thinking of the founding narratives of the giving of the law—more precisely the Jewish narrative of Sinaï and the Greek tale of Protagoras. But one could also evoke the modern stories of rationalist authors like Hobbes, Locke, or Kant, who no doubt believed they had freed themselves from the prestige of the fable. Now, what do they do then, other than to tell us stories, when they speak to us about a dangerous state of nature from which we must absolutely flee, and about a reassuring civil state that we achieve each time that we are able to agree a social contract amongst ourselves or with the Leviathan. A Leviathan? Isn't that a legendary biblical character? A social contract—isn't that a pure product of political imagination?

One could also evoke a contemporary author like John Rawls, author of a very ambitious *Theory of Justice*,[19] undoubtedly a work that is jealously possessive about the rationality and objectivity of its argument. But what does it rest upon other than a fable about a negotiation conducted under a veil of ignorance: it was said that men, desirous of finding the fairest rules for a well organised society, met together to negotiate in a situation such that they each had no knowledge as to whether the others at the meeting were rich or poor, young or old, men or women, sick or well; and *it would also be said* that these men were all respectful of the promises made, all were *self-interested*, and all shared the same aversion to risk. Well now! Doesn't this sound like the start of a fairy tale intended for the executive board of an American charitable foundation? The story is a poor one, no doubt, and not very exciting, but it is still a story, and Rawls's whole construction rests on these initial presuppositions.

The great normative texts that frame and commit human societies—I am thinking of the constitutions and the great international treaties about fundamental rights—are not necessarily so shy or ashamed about their narratives: they open with protocols that speak of the "political novel" of the nation, itself understood as a "narrative community."

Authors like Michael Sandel[20] and Charles Taylor[21] have shown very well in this regard how closely a political community is linked to a shared imaginary story/history, and how much its identity, its memory, and its capacity to make projects owes to the interpretation of the world provided by its founding narratives. In this regard, one can never emphasise enough the importance of certain canonical authors, such as for example William Shakespeare, in the case of the creation of the English nation.[22] Ian Ward does not hesitate to write that a play like *Henry V* holds a greater importance than a treaty of constitutional law: placed at the heart of the narrative construction of the English cultural community, the work determines a whole tradition of thought.[23] The constitutions and treaties/treatises written by jurists are, from this point of view, the digest of the story/history of political morality of the community. "Constitutions are just so many examples of narratives which tell the story of men and give a sense to their individual and collective life," writes D. Rousseau, who goes on as follows: "Constitutions are the mythologies of modern societies."[24]

The history of the great *Declarations of the Rights of Man* is very revealing in this regard: in the preamble to each one of them, we find a narrative, sometimes very developed, sometimes limited to a few lines, evoking what is going to count henceforth as a strong moment of the community (a revolution, a declaration of independence, etc.) or what attaches it to an immemorial founding past.

Judge for yourself. The Bill of Rights of 1689: the detailed circumstantial narrative of the abdication of James II and the meeting of the assemblies at Westminster, a declaration "as their ancestors have always done in similar cases in order to assure their ancient rights and liberties." The U.S. Declaration of Independence (1776): a long political narrative that begins in these terms: "when in the course of human affairs it becomes necessary for a people to dissolve the political ties which bind it to another ...". [25] The *Declaration of the Rights of Man and of the Citizen* (1789): "the representatives of the French people, constituted in a National Assembly, considering that ignorance, forgetfulness or contempt for the rights of man are the sole causes of public ills and the corruption of government ..." The Universal Declaration of Human Rights (1948): "Considering that ignorance and contempt for the rights of man have led to acts of barbarism which cause revulsion to the conscience of humanity ..." The new South African Constitution (1983): "The present Constitution builds a historic bridge between the past of a society that was profoundly divided, marked by untold struggle, conflict, sufferings and injustice, and a future founded on recognition of the rights of man, on democracy and on a life peacefully lived side by side, and on chances for development for all South Africans, regardless of race, colour, beliefs or sex."

Notes

1. A version of this essay first appeared as F. Ost, "Towards a Critique of Narrative Reason," *Law and Humanities* 7, no. 1 (2013): 55–67.
2. B. Latour, *We Have Never Been Modern*, trans. C. Porter (Cambridge, MA, Harvard University Press, 1993).
3. C. Salmon, *Storytelling. La Machine à Fabriquer des Histoires et à Formater les Esprits* (Paris: Editions la Découverte, 2007).
4. Paul Ricoeur studies closely the articulation between a narrated story (fiction) and a learned scholarly history (scientific), in *Temps et Récit* vol. I (Paris: Seuil, 1983).

5. J-M Ferry, *L'Éthique Reconstructive* (Paris: Les Éditions du Cerf, 1996), 59–61, 93, 104–8. This ethics might begin to respond to the lack/denial/refusal of recognition raised/generated by incommensurable claims, as studied by J. F. Lyotard in *Le Différend* (Paris: Les Éditions de Minuit, 1983).
6. Plato, *Republic*, trans. R. Baccou (Paris: Garnier-Flammarion, 1966), 370 *et seq*.
7. Plato, *Laws*, trans. A. Castel-Bouchouchi (Paris: Gallimard [Folio, Essais], 1997).
8. J. B. White, *The Edge of Meaning* (Chicago: University of Chicago Press, 2001). See, especially, the text and references accompanying page 135 n.1, and, further, 137 n.3.
9. P. Ricoeur, *Le Conflit des Interprétations. Essais D"Herméneutique* (Paris: Seuil, 1961).
10. J. R. Searle, *Les Actes de Langage. Essais de Philosophie du Langage*, trans. H Pauchard (Paris: Hermann, 1972).
11. C. Castoriadis, *L'Institution Imaginaire de la Société* (Paris: Seuil, 1975).
12. J. B. White, *Heracles' Bow: Essays on the Rhetoric and Poetics of the Law* (Madison: University of Wisconsin Press, 1985), preface, x.
13. Ricoeur, *Temps et Récit*, vol. I, (Paris: Seuil, 1983), 132.
14. J. Verges, *Justice et Littérature* (Paris: PUF, 2011), 175 *et seq*.
15. T. Kuhn, *La Structure des Révolutions Scientifiques* (Paris: Flammarion, 1972).
16. M. Serres, *Ecrivains, Savants et Philosophes Font le Tour du Monde* (Paris: Les éditions du Pommier, 2009).
17. White (n 7).
18. F. Ost, *Raconter La Loi. Aux Sources de L"imaginaire Juridique* (Paris: Odile Jacob, 2004), 13 *et seq*.
19. J. Rawls, *Théorie de la Justice*, trans C. Audard (Paris: Seuil, 1987).
20. M. Sandel, *Democracy's Discontent: America in Search of a Public Philosophy* (Cambridge, MA: Harvard University Press, 1996).
21. C. Taylor, *Sources of the Self: The Making of Modern Identity* (Cambridge: Cambridge University Press, 1989).
22. F. Ost, *Shakespeare, La Comédie De La Loi* (Paris: Editions Michalon, 2012).
23. "Littérature et Imaginaire Juridique," *Revue interdisciplinaire d"études juridiques* 42 (1999): 161.
24. D. Rousseau, "Question de constitution," in *Le nouveau constitutionnalisme. Mélanges en l'honneur de Gérard Cognac* (Paris: Economica, 2001), 6.
25. J. B. White has offered challenging reflections on the U.S. Declaration of Independence and the U.S. Constitution. See, for example, J. B. White, "Constituting a Culture of Argument: The Possibilities of American Law," in *When Words Lose Their Meaning* (Chicago: University of Chicago Press, 1985), chapter 9.

[3]

Imagining Rhetoric, Approaching Justice

Willem Witteveen

According to ancient definitions, rhetoric is an art. It is the art of speaking well, of being able to persuade an audience.[1] For Cicero and Quintilian, for instance, the art of rhetoric is an essential part of the education of future citizens who will, on this basis, be able to play a leading role in the Roman republic. The art of rhetoric is developed from within social institutions designed in such a way as to make meaningful communication and the formation of judgment possible. In the Athenian democracy of the fourth century BC, the term for "art" is *technè*, a word combining notions that would later be separated: *technè* is a craft, an art form, a technique, a professional tool. It is a form of life even, which one can enter by learning the rules of the game and by being socialized in the practices and situations where persuasion takes place. There were three major contexts: the political assembly, the law courts, and occasions for public rituals (such as speeches during the Olympic Games and public funerals). What would be appropriate and effective as well as ethical in these contexts varied somewhat, reflecting the understanding that persuasion is such a central task of communication between human beings that there cannot be one overriding model of an idealized speech situation. Fundamental precepts—such as the idea that all persuasive activity is audience directed—have to be adapted to ever changing contexts and practices. In time new arts would be developed from the ancient models, such as an art of writing diplomatic letters to people in power, or an art of holding a sermon to an audience of believers, or an art of engaging in critical discussions on the meaning of a canonical text. However far these later arts would move away from the original ideas—and there were and are continual adaptations and innovations going on—the kernels of understanding developed in the heart of the rhetorical tradition remain visible to the trained eye. The notion, for instance, of audience-directed communication (from which much follows) is evident in all later approaches to persuasion.

The Demise of the Art of Rhetoric

In the circumstances of today's world, rhetoric is no longer an art. We still use the word, of course, and we understand that persuasion is a central activity, especially for law and politics, and that it can be studied and trained. But the old ideas seem to have become trite. The life has seeped out of them. We read that Cicero favored decorum (in the sense of dignified speech) in a speaker and mutter "of course" under our breath, overlooking the psychological and strategic significance of this simple advice. Such notions no longer work to highlight what is and what is not important in rhetorical situations and practices. The current understanding seems to be that modern sciences in specialized fields—ranging from politics and law to communication studies and marketing—have made the classic, unified knowledge of rhetoric irrelevant. And the centrality of the three ancient contexts has dwindled. Politics has lost much of its preeminent status as the privileged place where binding decisions are made. Law has become instrumental mostly, a technique of regulation and governance. And public rituals have become orchestrated as media events, far removed from the dynamics of rhetorical situations designed to attribute praise or blame. So, for someone new to the art of persuasion, there is no coherent view available. If, as is said, rhetoric concerns all attempts to influence an audience by word or by (symbolic) deed and to make it accept the view of the speaker or doer, in this broad sense everybody seems to be a rhetorician. All citizens have some experience with the acts of persuasion, on the sending and the receiving end of the communication process.

There is very much rhetorical activity going on in the world. Far too much, in fact, to get a grip on this ubiquitous presence. One's own involvement in rhetoric makes it even harder to reflect in a detached manner on this crucial aspect of one's social existence. And where people are seen to be studying the art of rhetoric in order to be effective in public communication—an example is the way in which speeches by prominent American politicians are prepared by speech writers who have studied classical rhetoric—this evokes an attitude of weariness with observant citizens: "Isn't it all a bag of tricks?" As far as rhetoric manifests itself, it is perceived as a form of manipulation, as an exercise in strategic argumentation at best. It is seen to be superficial, unrelated to the core of principled thoughts supposed to be guiding one's speech. These criticisms are often justified, but those critics turning away from organized and reflective rhetoric seem not to realize that their complaints are the ancient ones which have been with us since Plato: that rhetoric is not an art but a knack and that there is no depth under the brilliant surface.

Reflective Rhetoric

The contemporary view is superficial. What it fails to acknowledge is that self-consciousness of the rhetoric one employs in connection with others is a prerequisite for high level participation in core democratic practices.[2] Such "reflective rhetoric," as we might term it, is needed for effective engagement with political issues in a way that is authentically representative of voters and it is needed in order to debate the merits of a legislative proposal in the way a true legislator should. It is also needed in arguing a case in court as an effective and responsible lawyer and in deciding issues of law and justice the way an independent and impartial judge should perform that duty. Reflection on rhetoric is needed for citizens and professionals alike when they attempt to make these practices into meaningful and useful ones. Rhetoric is one of the arts that make it possible for people engaging in public deliberation and judgment to say the magical word "we." Our ability to express our connectedness to an imaginary community with a fictive common good can only be recovered by engaging in rhetorical practices and being at home in rhetorical situations. Rather than relegate the art of rhetoric to the past or denigrate it by reference to the doctrines of modern sciences, we must reimagine rhetoric as an art for citizens and professionals alike. Hidden in classic texts there is a lost world of rhetoric that has shaped our own notions and practices. We can hope to recover this lost world by using our imagination.[3]

Where to begin? Rather than trust modern studies of classical rhetoric, it is advisable to turn to the originals, and thus to the writings of Plato and Aristotle for Greek rhetoric and to Cicero and Quintilian for Roman rhetoric. There is an interesting fracture in this list, as Aristotle, Cicero, and Quintilian develop a democratic or republican rhetorical art, which trusts citizens to use the resources of rhetoric in order to make the political community flourish, while Plato establishes an anti-rhetoric, the upshot of which is that he places his trust in philosophers or specialized governors and legislators to take over all of the important tasks of governing. Plato mistrusts the mass of citizens as well as the sophistic orators pandering to them. In view of the prevalent distrust of rhetoric and rhetoricians in our own day, it is perhaps as well to begin with Plato's early efforts to resist demagoguery. Of course his antidemocratic approach makes him especially interesting to modern readers, for we will be deeply suspicious of his vision for an almost totalitarian state and will discern a strategic rhetorical motivation in his anti-rhetoric.

My own reading of Plato's *Gorgias* has been deeply influenced by James Boyd White and perhaps it is good to shift to a more personal narrative register for a moment to make clear how this came to pass. In 1980, I was a junior teacher at the Department of Constitutional and Administrative Law of Leyden University. I had graduated from political science, where I had learned to be empirical and ethically and emotionally uninvolved in the object of my study. As a result, I found it difficult to switch to the normative discourse and internal perspective on law practiced by my colleagues. They seemed to believe that, already by speaking the language of the law, they could directly intervene in the world without regard to the kind of factors that, in an empirical analysis, would be an obstacle to such a direct intervention. If the Dutch constitution recognized a human right, for instance, even in vague language ("right to a clean environment"), this meant it actually existed and no research into the actual social practices conditioning the exercise of this right would be needed for that conclusion. (Later I would discover their attitude was in fact both more sophisticated and grounded in a Hartian or Dworkinian approach to law.) What bothered me was the lack of consideration of why it was that legal language could be so powerful in affecting the culture of a community. How did the language of the law persuade both its competent users and those not versed in the intricacies of legal speech? Was it a mere act of power, dressed in words? It was at this point that I discovered there had in the past been an art of rhetoric, concerning all available means of persuasion (as Aristotle writes). A colleague of mine had been to Chicago, where he had taken a course in law and literature with James Boyd White. We wrote to him and received a draft paper on the significance of Plato's *Gorgias*. White made it clear that Plato, through Socrates's engagement with three rhetoricians, did not intend merely to demolish the sophistic uses of rhetoric as a spurious craft, but intended to force both his interlocutors and himself to think through the meaning of the words used in conceiving of public life. Rhetoricians work with the materials of the culture as a given and do not reflect on the meanings embedded in crucial terms such as *agathos* and *kalos* (good and noble) versus *aischros* and *kakos* (bad and shameful).

Rhetoricians do not read the dangerous assumption enshrined in this terminology, namely that "good" equates to what is effective and "bad" equates to that which does not work. Justice and injustice are thereby rendered relative to practical power. Socrates confuses his interlocutors and also his readers in order to make them see the problem of conventional terms such as these. He sets off a dialectical search for new, shared meanings of what it means to act rightly or wrongly, apart from considerations of effectiveness alone. This is an almost therapeutic move. The dialogue between philosophizing partners leads away from harmful practices and towards new forms of life. "In showing us how it makes a language the dialogue shows us how it defines a life."[4] In studying the *Gorgias* in conjunction with White's essay, I started to glimpse the possibility that rhetoric could be more than just a bag of tricks. It could again be a reflective art drawing the practitioner of law towards an understanding of what speaking the language of law could do for a people living in a community deemed to be democratic and subject to the rule of law. In his Montesquieu Lecture, given more than twenty-five years later at Tilburg Law School, where I then worked, White returned to the issue presented by Plato's *Gorgias*. Plato was aware that the conventional language was not the right way to think and also that he could not address this issue directly because he "had no place outside his language from which he might see and criticize it."[5] It was to combat this difficulty that the art of dialectical questioning was developed as an alternative to rhetorical speech making. Our own legal and political language is not any better than the conventional language of Socrates' time.[6] "We too find our languages undone, taken apart, lying in pieces at our feet. Plato's relation to his language, then, is that of: user, critic, destroyer, remaker."[7] This, I feel, is still the challenge for constitutional law discourse.

Dialogue and Justice

The *Gorgias* not only demonstrates the method of dialectics as a way of achieving better language through dialogue, the text is also about justice and injustice. One way in which it engages with these issues is in the relationship between philosophizing friends, as manifested in the dialogue. This turns out to be a failed collective undertaking, however. Indeed, when it comes to practicing dialectics the text shows us as readers that Socrates's attempts are a deep failure. The discussion with Gorgias himself leads to a bland admission by the old sophist that when his students do not know what justice requires he will teach them justice. He clearly has not fathomed the deeper meaning of Socrates's queries.

Polus, the young and unruly pupil of the master, is unable to question Socrates in a meaningful way so Socrates has to take over and, when Polus does not manage to produce sensible answers, mocks him with a satirical description of true and false arts. Callicles, as an imaginary adroit Athenian politician, is wise to the sophistic tricks that Socrates employs, but he does not want to practice the new art of dialectics either, seeing it as a power game stacked to his disadvantage. He even withdraws from the dialogue and so forces Socrates to give the answers to his own questions himself. The *Gorgias* culminates in a long poetic speech by Socrates in which he unilaterally declares what he thinks about justice and injustice. In doing so, he behaves just like the sophist Gorgias, who is said to excel in long speeches. Dialectics at the end of the dialogue has regressed into a form of rhetoric. This means that over the issue of the nature of justice and injustice no real agreement between the interlocutors has been reached. The positions remain opposed. Callicles holds, like Thrasymachus in *The Republic*, that justice is defined by those in power as everything that is in accordance with their needs and interests; justice is an empty word that can and will be filled with any meaning emerging from the powers that be. Socrates holds that nobody really can be certain of his interpretation of justice, but that minimally it has to be accepted that the greater good is to avoid injustice; power is never to be involved in doing justice or avoiding injustice, rather attention to the real needs and interests of other people in relation to oneself. The discussion is not closed but reframed and kept open.

It is time for a fresh start. If our times evidence widespread confusion about rhetoric as a practical art in the service of a well-functioning polity aspiring toward democracy and the rule of law, there is no less confusion about the nature of justice. Not only are there many incompatible academic theories about what the ideal of justice means and how it can be embodied in the world, but beyond the disputes going on in the ethical branch of political theory there is conceptual puzzlement in society at large, extending towards debates held in legislatures and cases brought to court where justice or injustice in some form or other is at stake. Moreover, some of the same developments that have led to a low opinion of the art of rhetoric seem to be influential in creating and sustaining this conceptual puzzlement. There is the same uncertainty generated by the proliferation of specialized disciplines, all purporting to cover more than an aspect of justice and claiming a preferential position toward the others. Should we turn to ethics, to political theory, to criminal law, to social scholarship, to economics, to game theory, or to biology even? There is no integration equivalent to anything resembling a neo-Aristotelian or neo-Kantian framework.[8] This is exacerbated by the loss of meaning provided by the political organs of society, which are seen more as arenas for power struggles than as the places where debates lead to interpretations of the General Will, somewhat along the lines of Rousseau's social contract theory. The instrumental utilization of law, mentioned earlier, also plays a role. And the way the media convert ethical controversies into melodramatic soap operas does not help either. All in all, the prevailing attitude is superficial if not outright cynical: like Callicles proposes, issues of justice are seen as issues of power.

Justice in Rhetorical Situations

How can the voice of Socrates again be heard in the debate? One way is to follow his example in approaching the issue obliquely rather than head on. By imagining rhetoric as an art we will be approaching justice as a particular set of virtues and ethical relationships which are manifested in communication.

For a start, let us take a closer look at the fundamental precept of all rhetorical writings about the importance of the audience in organizing and directing persuasive efforts towards their goal. Perelman and Olbrechts-Tyteca state: "It is indeed the audience which has the major role in determining the quality of argument and the behaviour of orators."[9] From the phase of invention, when relevant arguments are first collected, through the phases of composition and stylistic elaboration and up to the memorization and actual delivery of the speech, an orator will have to be constantly aware of what the audience knows, what the audience expects, what it feels, and how it will probably react. Beyond this elementary insight, we can note that in the classical handbooks a particular model of the rhetorical situation evolved. The model seems to be that of the interaction between pleaders and judges in a court of law. While this is not a normative model in a strong sense (there will always be many deviations), the model points at a construction value for the design of rhetorical situations and institutions: they must be structured in such a way that they allow partisan, even strategic, interaction, and also provide the decision-makers with the information they need in order to assess the issue from all sides and take a balanced decision with a high communicative quality. This is the dynamic found behind codes of procedure for courts, but also at the base of rules of conduct for other rhetorical institutions and situations, from parliamentary debates to academic discussions requiring a jury decision. And then within this large variety of rhetorical situations the conditions are met for establishing a certain kind of justice as well. Stuart Hampshire argues that justice as procedural fairness, which uses the conflict between competing views to articulate all relevant information that may be used in judgment, is the fundamental requirement for justice in free and democratic societies upholding the rule of law.[10] From a very different angle—research in social psychology—Tom Tyler arrives at the same position when he concludes on the basis of empirical evidence that the reason why most people obey the organs of the law is that they experience the process of judgment by the authorities as procedurally fair, giving them the chance to be heard in a meaningful way.[11]

But procedural justice as fairness is not the only kind of justice coming into view as we attempt to imagine the conditions under which rhetoric can flourish as an art. It is often seen that the professionals who participate in court procedures are acquainted with all three positions: that of pleader, counter-pleader, and judge. Lawyers often work both for the prosecution and the defense, and they can also be part-time judges (the Dutch legal system exemplifies this switching between professional roles). By experiencing over the years how the system works from all available angles, these lawyers and orators come to possess a particular virtue that is essential for the operation of legal institutions generally and this is: *perspectivism*.[12] Perspectivism means the ability and willingness to defer one's judgment until all sides have been heard and all positions have been fairly represented in the mind of the person working towards a decision. Deferral of judgment is necessary because the case will from the beginning inevitably be framed in some way, and our knowledge is then as yet no more than a prejudice which needs first to be challenged before it can be safely relied upon. Perspectivism requires respect for persons one does not like (even for those one abhors), because someone does not need to be nice or decent in general terms to have justice on their side in a particular matter. Most of all, the virtue of perspectivism requires a self-reflective attitude on the part of the person working toward a conclusion and a willingness to explain the grounds on which the conclusion rests. The perspectivist orator approaches issues in the spirit of Popper's ideal of falsification, regarding his ideas as provisional opinions which may well be proven wrong or be shown to be inadequate.

It is interesting to remember that Socrates's method of dialectics as the philosophers' game, in which you ask questions of others which will be answered truthfully and, in your turn, are prepared to answer honestly questions asked of you, is not sustained in the practice of argumentation portrayed in the *Gorgias*. Instead, a battle of wills ensues in which Socrates is the better combatant. He also has the more attractive ethos. Gorgias is shown as an old man out of touch with reality, Polus is downright stupid and undisciplined, Callicles is power-hungry. Only

Socrates is sympathetic in his unrelenting pursuit of truth and truthfulness and the reader will forgive him his sophistic tricks since they all aim to articulate his grand vision. Socrates, one tends to think, is beyond the virtue of perspectivism, but still willing to practice it by being prepared to change his mind (though none of the interlocutors ever succeeds in bringing this about). And when we read his final speech with its eloquent evocation of the importance of not being unjust, we see to what content the forms of perspectivist discourse lead: taking responsibility for oneself and for others in awareness of the limitations placed on all human understanding:

> All the other theories put forward in our long conversation have been refuted and this conclusion alone stands firm, that one should avoid doing wrong with more care than being wronged, and that the supreme object of a man's efforts, in public and in private life, must be the reality rather than the appearance of goodness.... It would be shameful for men in our present condition, who are so ignorant that we never think the same for two moments together, even on the subjects of the greatest importance, to give ourselves the airs of persons of weight.[13]

The perspectivist justice emerging from a reimagination of the art of rhetoric has wider ramifications. Taking the point of view of the other into account is what Adam Smith in his *Theory of Moral Sentiments* calls "sympathy." Only the resonance of imagining the plight of the other can provide the required emotional basis for ethical judgments. For Smith and a line of theorists inspired by his work, justice is not a grand theory derived from abstract principles in a neo-Kantian vein, but a set of virtues and duties rooted in recognition of what makes a person human. Justice is not to be strictly fixed in abstract general rules and principles, but to be found in practices viewed through the prism of flexible norms which help in achieving judgments on new cases continually coming up from the practices of social life. Justice is in the details. We need to picture it, to make it visible for our eyes. And in that ambition the techniques of rhetoric are again of great use, such as the method of *ekphrasis* (the art of vivid description).

Visualizing Justice and Injustice

In the rhetorical approach to public life, justice has to do with virtues shown by citizens and professionals in the performance of their duties rather than with encompassing schemes or abstract systems. Cicero writes in *On Duties* not of the general constitution of the great Roman republic that he serves, but about the attitudes and skills needed in citizens who can, through their way of life, keep the ideal of the republic alive. In all his rhetorical writings he portrays certain just individuals who for him embody the ideal and he shows them in dialogue, talking with each other about concrete legal and political issues. His famous dialogue *On the Orator* shows us two important rhetoricians (Licinius Crassus and Marcus Antonius) who are typically decent and highly esteemed members of the polity, in a company of friends debating politely about the art of rhetoric itself. This text, while giving a lot of information, is not a technical handbook at all. It is an exercise in *ekphrasis*, portraying the just statesman.

In the later rhetorical imagination of the Renaissance, justice is personified, as is injustice. Most famously this is done by the painter Giotto in frescoes on the walls of the Capella della Scrovegni in Padova. While Cicero placed his personifications of good orators in the company of a circle of discussants, the frescoes by Giotto portray idealized versions of the just and unjust ruler. Power has been concentrated in one person rather than being an aspect of citizen interaction. When we enter the Capella della Scrovegni today, we notice that on opposing walls the seven virtues have been placed facing their corresponding vices. Together they form a cycle of vignettes under the rows of paintings of biblical scenes. As viewers we are able to see these seven oppositions as a continuing tale of the good and the bad life. On the left, facing the entrance that the Scrovegni family would have seen when first upon entering their chapel, is Prudence, opposing Stupidity. Then consistent Courage is seen facing wavering Timidity. Thirdly, Temperance is facing Anger. Justice is in fourth position opposite Injustice. Faith in fifth place is distinguished from Idolatry. Christian Benevolence in sixth position opposes Jealousy. Finally, Hope is confronting Desperation. Of these fourteen figures, one is male (Injustice); the others are women. Judith Shklar is surely right in singling out the depiction of Justice and Injustice as an eloquent painting. She provides a wonderful *ekphrasis* of it, emphasizing the vice of passive injustice, not acting when its aid is called for:

> The face of Giotto's Injustice is cold and cruel with fanglike teeth at the sides of the mouth. He wears a judge's or ruler's cap, but it is turned backward and in his hand is a nasty pruning hook, not a sceptre or miter. As he has sown, no doubt so shall he reap, for some of the trees that surround him are rooted in the soil beneath his feet where crime flourishes. Around him is a gate in ruin, but under him we see the real character of passive injustice. There is a theft, a rape, and a murder. Two soldiers watch this scene and do nothing, and neither does the ruler. The woods, always a dangerous place, are unguarded; they are the place where the sort of men who prosper under passive injustice can be as violent as they please. They have a cruel tyrant to govern them, but he and they deserve, indeed engender, each other.[14]

Shklar next turns her gaze to Justice. The structure of the painting is similar to that of Injustice. Here we see portrayed scenes of a tranquil state where people live at peace. There are hunters and dancers and people enjoying music, but no references to labour and industry. Shklar notes that the woman ruling over them is strangely uninvolved, aloof:

> Justice is a calm and majestic woman who looks right at us, not at either the heaven or hell of the Last Judgment. She may not be a real person at all, as Injustice certainly is with his supine face. Her face is benign. But apart from that it is expressionless, as one might expect of the impartiality appropriate to a personification of justice. We can certainly feel afraid of Injustice, but Justice radiates no emotional appeal.[15]

Shklar finds it troubling that Justice is so aloof and she wonders why there are no people portrayed engaging in acts of citizenship, like debating or ruling themselves. She feels that the ideals of the republican tradition have vanished from the world of these Christian symbols. Maybe this is not quite true. We should look at the whole story of the virtues and vices. On the left of Justice is the vignette of Prudence. She is shown as a woman in a white robe standing behind a lectern that is plain but well-proportioned. On the lectern there is an open book. In her hand Prudence holds a pen; apparently she is writing something. But her eyes are neither on the open book nor on us, the viewers. She gazes into a small round mirror she is holding in her left hand. Thus we see here a woman who is observing herself while she is writing. Maybe she is in the process of composing a speech, and are her reflective looks in the mirror meant to convey a sense of competence and subtlety, of how she adroitly moves back and forth between standpoints in her work of finding, composing, and formulating her argument. Prudence is a woman in whom the Ciceronian ideals of citizenship virtues are clearly present. Let us now turn our gaze to Stupidity (*Stultitia*) on the opposite wall. This picture adds color to the serene picture of the reflective woman writing her text. Stupidity is frivolous. She wears a short white dress with flaps like wings at the back. Clearly she is pregnant, but this does not seem to concern her at all. In her hand she holds a large stick that she is in the process of swinging left and right. Her other hand is raised as if in speech, but her eyes are gazing out over an invisible audience into the distance where nothing is visible. On her head she wears a band with feathers in them, a token of her frustrated desire to fly away.

Is Prudence portrayed as someone lacking emotional appeal? Is she like Justice, in the interpretation of Judith Shklar, not involved with people and their experience? We see a woman who has turned her gaze inwards but the mirror she uses is also a reference to the outside world as it is an open space potentially reflecting all that is held before it. We may imagine the prudent ruler to turn the mirror of her mind not only inwards but outside into the world as well. Otherwise, what would there be to write about, what speech to compose, what book to prepare for what kind of audience? Where books come into view, there is a suggestion of readership, and thus of one of those instances of the audience that rhetorical theory has always cherished. Prudence is not acting in the moment she is glimpsed on the walls of the chapel, but we can imagine her as someone who is about to act in a way that keeps the reflective capacities of her mind intact. Maybe it is not too far-fetched to look for more evidence in the other vignettes of the virtues. What matters in relation to the virtue of Sympathy is in what way the personified virtue is looking at us, viewers. Justice is looking straight at us, but maybe she is also looking through us, guessing our secrets. Faith and Temperance also look straight ahead, admonishing us to have faith and be moderate in our thoughts and actions. Courage is not looking at us but at an imaginary enemy approaching behind us—she has seen it coming and raises her stick and shield. That leaves Charity and Hope. These two ladies look to the right of us, in exactly the same way as Prudence does. The faces of these three figures are very much alike and different from the faces of the other virtues. We can take them to be sisters. Charity looks to her left because in the air there is a holy person handing her a fruit. In her left hand she holds a plate of the same fruits; obviously she is on the point of lovingly distributing the received holy food. And Hope is looking to the right as well to another holy figure holding up a crown for her. She has wings and her feet have already left the ground. Complementing Prudence, the images of Charity and Hope show a set of virtues commending citizens and professionals alike to be reflective in all their social roles and functions. In this they must be sympathetic to the needs of others and constructive in working for a better future already announced by manifested symbols.

It is likely that Judith Shklar arrived at her interpretation of the images of Justice and Injustice not only by studying books about these works of art, but as a result of at least one actual visit to the Scrovegni Chapel. Walking in a space that in rows of panels evokes the narratives of the Bible through pictures of crucial scenes, she has engaged in an act of interpretation which is familiar to the practitioners of the field of "law and literature." My own interpretation is based on a similar endeavour to connect art and life. However, as a result of the chapel's complete reconstruction in order to protect the fragile frescoes, there is now a curious constraint on this way of interpreting art: visitors may not be longer in the chapel than fifteen minutes. This is insufficient for adequate scrutiny of the artwork. So, when you want to be thorough you have to go out again, buy another ticket, await your turn, and cherish your next fifteen minutes of Giotto. The unintended consequence is to heighten the intensity of the experience of visiting the chapel. This is perhaps no bad thing, for intensity of gaze must be a precondition for understanding the meaning of the personifications of the virtues and vices. Thus, unwittingly, we visitors perform a hermeneutic circle.

Law-Jobs

When we are done, a disturbing question must be addressed. Can our imagination of the rhetorical motives and public deliberations that went in to these artistic personifications of virtues and vices still be of relevance in our attempt to approach justice? Can the art of the past relate to the challenges of our current social and political world? The kind of systematic answer demanded by ethical political theory cannot be given, for a great deal depends on the personality of the interpreter. Stating general findings is difficult. The better approach is to focus, instead, upon the personal characteristics of people operating within the legal system and to pay attention to their style of operation. No matter what kind of system the legal institutions have become, they will still have to be operated by humans. The way they perform their roles or make the system function, matters as it always did. Take, for example, Karl Llewellyn's theory of law-jobs. Llewellyn's theory is an influential and important scheme for classifying the organization of the state and its functions. He mentions four functions that can be found in any functional group: disposition of trouble-cases; preventive channelling and reorientation of conduct and expectations; allocation of authority; organization of the group as a whole so as to provide cohesion, direction, and incentive. This is a way of speaking intended to open our eyes to the importance of such classical functions as judging, legislating, constitution-building, and organizing. But these four jobs can be performed only when there is a fifth one present: the job of juristic method. It is defined as "keeping both law-stuff and law-personnel up to the demands of *all* the law-jobs."[16] Interestingly, Llewellyn comes to this notion after studying extensively the way the Cheyenne Indians operate in "cases of trouble," in a famous fieldwork expedition with his anthropological colleague Hoebel. He had to step outside of his own legal order to find an order that could shed light on it. The comparative method, placing systems next to each other, which before this work would have seemed too far removed from each other to warrant inferences, generated for Llewellyn the idea not only of the law-jobs but also his celebrated notion of the Grand Style in appellate judging. Juristic method may start out as legal method, but it moves beyond that:

> Juristic method sums up at once man's achievement and man's quest in matters legal. It is the search for serviceable forms and devices. But it is also the quest for their skilful use. It is also the seeking to keep vital and vigorous under any form, any formula, any "rule", its living reason, its principle.[17]

Juristic method is therefore not mere technique but something elusively akin to style. It matters a great deal with what mentality the law-jobs are conducted through juristic method:

> Legal method may be skilful, it may be ingenious, splendid of technique, and varied; but where its purpose is to serve a litigant or client only, and not Justice, it is only legal. Juristic method is the problem and the technique of *solution, for the Entirety*, and the problem of keeping the machinery of the law abreast of the needs of the Entirety.[18]

Llewellyn here capitalizes Justice, personifying the ideal in the performances of justice he observed with the Cheyenne chiefs. He also underlines the reference to the Entirety, to the needs and welfare of the whole community, as the animating principle leading beyond legal techniques. Many of his later concerns were with describing the leeway that is necessary in legal language if judges are to be able to practice their skills with consummate wisdom. But we could also argue in a different direction, asking what particular virtues the jurist employing his knowledge in furtherance of the ideal would have to cultivate, or which vices she would have to avoid. A wise decision-maker in a case of trouble could derive inspiration from confronting mental images of Justice and Injustice and connecting these central insights to contemplation of what Prudence requires in the circumstances of the case or on how to avoid Stupidity, while remaining Patient, Temperate, and Hopeful.

Justice as Translation

One reason why it is nowadays not only desirable but imperative to focus on the virtues and vices of the jurist as decision-maker employing a professional rhetoric, is that in the context of the modern and postmodern bureaucracies of governance so much comes to depend on it. The people of the law may work as judges or as lawyers or as legal advisors within or outside large organizations, but in all their different contexts and rhetorical situations they will have to come to terms with the alienation of the language of the law from ordinary language, and the distance between social ideals framed in law-speak from the concerns of members of the public. Unlike Cheyenne chiefs they do not personally know the human beings they have to deal with and decide upon. Unlike the appellate judges envisioned by Llewellyn they do not work in organizations that leave them much leeway to be prudent and even wise professionals. Instead, they are subject to influences in their organizations that increasingly enforce logics external to the law: of power, money, science, status, control. That the jurist has become a bureaucrat is one very good reason to argue for a return to the tradition of rhetoric as a way of approaching justice while avoiding injustice.

Plato in the *Gorgias* attempted, in James Boyd White's interpretation, to break open the inauthentic and inadequate language of the Athenian polity in order to replace it with a richer, more humane, and philosophically adequate language. If this was a failed attempt, at least it stimulated a dialogue on rhetoric as an art in the service of justice that continues to this day, with Aristotle, Cicero, and Quintilian arguing against the Platonic deconstruction. If our legal and political language is debased as well, failing to be the ideal medium of communication between humans, it is not possible to try and get rid of it and replace it with a better vocabulary. Differentiated social systems, each with their own internal rationality—think of the various logics of economics, science, bureaucracy, the media, for example—controlling the life world are simply too strong and pervasive for that.[19] There is no Esperanto for a just world. But there are things we can do when we imagine ourselves to be rhetoricians performing the duties of law and justice. We are not powerless, even when each of us has but little power. We can redescribe the task of the jurist as one of translation. James Boyd White has shown how this redescription activates ideals of an ethical nature while acknowledging the impossibility of perfect or often even of adequate translation between the people whose needs and interests are adjudicated by systems of law. "At the centre of law is the activity of translation," White writes, adding:

> The central truths of translation are the central truths of human interaction ... It means the perpetual acknowledgment of the limits of our minds and languages, the sense that they are bounded by the minds and languages of others. It is in these ways that the activities I call "translation"—making texts in response to others while recognizing the impossibility of full comprehension or reproduction—becomes a set of practices that can serve as an ethical and political model for the law and, beyond it, as a standard of justice.[20]

Notes

1. "Let rhetoric be the power to observe the persuasiveness of which any particular matter admits," Aristotle, *The Art of Rhetoric* 1356a, ed. H. C. Lawson-Tancred (London: Penguin

Books, 2004), 74. In Rome, the famous *Rhetoric ad Herennium* defines the task of the public speaker as "to discuss capably those matters which law and custom have fixed for the uses of citizenship, and to secure as far as possible the agreement of his hearers" (I.1.2), referring to the three genres of epideictic, deliberative, and judicial speech. (Cicero, *Ad Herennium,* trans. H. Caplan (Cambridge, MA: Harvard University Press, 1981), 5. After discussing a number of these definitions, Quintilian simply concludes that the best definition is that rhetoric is the science of speaking well (II.xv.38). (Quintilian, *Institutio Oratoria,* trans. H. E. Butler (Cambridge, MA: Harvard University Press, 1980), 319.

2. W. C. Booth, *The Rhetoric of Rhetoric* (Malden, MA: Blackwell Publishing, 2004).

3. A good example is M. Billig, *Arguing and Thinking: A Rhetorical Approach to Social Psychology* (Cambridge: Cambridge University Press, 1987).

4. J. B. White, *When Words Lose Their Meaning* (Chicago: University of Chicago Press, 1984), 104.

5. J. B. White, *When Language Meets the Mind: Three Questions* (Nijmegen: Wolf Legal Publishers, 2007), 19.

6. One problem, noted by White, is that we increasingly talk economics when we should be talking politics or law instead.

7. White, *When Language Meets the Mind*, 20.

8. R. Geuss, *Philosophy and Real Politics* (Princeton, NJ: Princeton University Press, 2008), 98–101.

9. C. Perelman and L. Olbrechts-Tyteca, *The New Rhetoric* (Notre Dame, IN: Notre Dame University Press, 1969), 24.

10. S. Hampshire, *Justice is Conflict* (London: Duckworth, 1990).

11. T. R. Tyler, *Psychology and the Design of Legal Institutions* (Tilburg: Wolf Legal Publishers, 2007).

12. The locus classicus is of course, Nietzsche, *On Truth and Untruth,* trans. T. Carman trans (New York: HarperCollins, 2010). My own brand of perspectivism is influenced more by Kenneth Burke, however. See K. Burke, *A Grammar of Motives* (Berkeley: University of California Press, 1969).

13. Plato, *Gorgias,* ed. W. Hamilton (Harmondsworth: Penguin Books, 1987), 148–49.

14. J. Shklar, *The Faces of Injustice* (New Haven, CT: Yale University Press, 1990), 46.

15. Shklar, *The Faces of Injustice,* 103.

16. K. N. Llewellyn and E. Adamson Hoebel, *The Cheyenne Way* (1941) (Norman: University of Oklahoma Press, 1987), 293.

17. Llewellyn and Hoebel, *The Cheyenne Way,* 307.

18. Llewellyn and Hoebel, *The Cheyenne Way,* 309.

19. N. Luhmann, *Law as a Social System* (Oxford: Oxford University Press, 2004).

20. J. B. White, *Justice as Translation* (Chicago: University of Chicago Press, 1990), 258.

[4]

It's Not All About Pretty

Human Rights Adjudication in a Life and Death Situation
Julen Etxabe

"How wonderful it is to find someone whose language speaks to you..."[1]

"Two voices is the minimum for life, the minimum for existence."[2]

It is not easy to convey in a few words the impact that James Boyd White's *Justice as Translation* had on me. Ostensibly this is a book about judicial excellence and the quality of judicial opinions, arisen out of a concern for our increased inability to speak intelligently about questions of value: either because the task is perceived as outdated and reliant upon old-fashioned ideals; or because these judgments are seen as matters of taste and subjective preferences, over which no public discourse can be had; or because such issues are viewed as outside the scope of legal scholars aspiring to be scientific. I could, in a few words, explain what White has to say about all these questions and offer a short summary of the book, but none of this will obviously help convey my meaning.

What the book offers—what it asks from (and what it actually happened to) my conception of judicial opinions and myself as a legal scholar—is a transformation; the sort of full torsion of the body of which Plato spoke in the cave. Thus, it is no coincidence that the book begins with a citation of William James, for whom "what is called our 'experience' is almost entirely determined by our habits of attention."[3] *Justice as Translation* modified my habits of attention and hence my experience—my ways of looking, thinking, feeling, and valuing law.

As a guiding question, White borrows a sentence from John Dewey, another great American pragmatist (and theorist of art, education, and democracy) who said that "democracy begins in conversation."[4] What if, wonders White, we were to assess judicial opinions as conversations in which democracy begins (or ends)? What would it mean for us as legal scholars, teachers, citizens, or practitioners of law to test law and legal reasoning with this question in mind? How would our own practices of reading and assessing judicial opinions change? What would it mean for us and our object of study to look at the law in this way?

Admittedly, the questions both puzzled and intrigued me. After all, I had been trained in a tradition where judicial opinions stood for a particular rule or outcome, to be assessed by the coherence and consistency of their reasoning. In this way, we learned to abstract the operative principle of judicial opinions and discard the rest as legally irrelevant (i.e., *obiter dicta*). To be sure, we could criticize an opinion for its lack of coherence and certainty, since these were understood to be common standards of rationality. But judgments of value were to be avoided as detracting from the objectivity, impartiality, and neutrality of legal analysis, and external to a law believed to be unitary, complete, and rounded like a system. All this, to my mind, sounded highly implausible (and I doubt that my teachers *really* believed it), but it still was presented to me as a regulative ideal, necessary for the advancement of legal science.

What *Justice as Translation* proposes is a clean break, for:

> In every opinion, a court not only resolves a particular dispute one way or another, it validates or authorizes one form of life—one kind of reasoning, one kind of response to argument, one way of looking at the world and its own authority—or another. Whether or not the process is conscious, the judge seeks to persuade her reader not only to the rightness of the result reached and the propriety of the analysis used, but to her understanding of what the judge—and the law, the lawyer, and the citizen—are and should be, in short, to her conception of the kind of conversation that does and should constitute us.[5]

> When we turn to a judicial opinion, then, we can ask not only how we evaluate its 'result' but, more importantly, how and what makes that result to mean, not only for the parties in that case, and for the contemporary public, but for the future: for each case is an invitation to lawyers and judges to talk one way rather than another, to constitute themselves in language one way rather than another, to give one kind of meaning rather than another to what they do, and this invitation can itself be analyzed and judged. Is this an

invitation to a conversation in which democracy begins (or flourishes)? Or to one in which it ends?[6]

Such a way of looking at the work of judges is not just different or new, but transformative of the old, in the sense that it calls upon us to open up our senses toward a full range of aesthetic, ethical, and political dimensions entailed by every judicial opinion. White's rich and rewarding practice of close reading is not circumscribed to the operative part of the decision, but takes the judicial opinion as a *compositional whole*, as one would approach a piece of music, a painting, or a poem.[7] In doing so, the reading becomes richer and more probing than the mere exposition of the court's reasoning—and critique of "weaknesses." This equally differs from a kind of hyperrealism that reduces the opinion to an epiphenomenon or façade. In White's view, the political and ethical dimensions of an opinion are not "hiding beyond the appearances of language," but are rather imprinted in, or, more accurately, *enacted by* it—including its silences and omissions. What White offers is not a "method" that one could mechanically follow, but a series of recurring questions through which we might arrive at our own judgments, which are always language-bound and culture-specific. To read judicial opinions in this way is hence not to aspire to an ultimate position of neutrality on matters of value, but to be ready to make judgments (however tentative and partial) about the most important aspects of our lives as individuals and as members of a polity.

Not everyone can be expected to share my experience with the book, which I will not try to defend here.[8] What the critics demand instead, and I hope to do in what follows, is to show the possibilities it affords in a real context, here, the adjudicatory practices of the European Court of Human Rights (hereinafter the ECtHR or the court). The case I have chosen concerns Mrs Dianne Pretty, at the time of the proceedings, a 43-year-old woman suffering from an irreversible neuro-degenerative disease, who had unsuccessfully pleaded to obtain dispensation from the UK law banning assisted suicide.[9] After seeking in vain to obtain prosecutorial immunity for her husband to assist in her death, and failing to win her case also before the House of Lords,[10] she applied to the ECtHR to find a violation in her rights under the European Convention of Human Rights (hereinafter the convention).

Pretty v UK begins with a brief explanation of the procedure and circumstances of the case, followed by a long citation of the opinion of the House of Lords—a lengthy judgment delivered by Lord Bingham—as well as other voices and arguments.[11] In turn, Lord Bingham is also obliged to interpret the convention and engage directly with the court's jurisprudence, because the applicant relied directly upon the convention. It may be tempting to say that these voices are in dialogue with each other, but this is both to say too little and too much. It is too little, because unless we describe more precisely the *kind* of dialogue they are engaged in, a general appeal to "dialogue" is too vague and risks being fetishized (after all, not all dialogues are based on mutual respect and can turn into "dialogues of the deaf"). It is too much, insofar as the risk here is to elide the inevitable tensions, frictions, and misunderstandings of the real conversation. This is why we need a more nuanced approach to the rich polyphony of voices that constitute the opinion—an advice that I take from Desmond Manderson's recent book[12]—since the relationships established in and by the decision are the best indication of whether this is an opinion in which democracy begins, or not.

Rather than as a logical chain of legal propositions, then, I would like to explore this opinion as a text where the drama of life and death unfolds.[13] The case is obviously dramatic and thus a good candidate to test the profundity (or lack thereof) of what critics often dismiss as simple matters of "style"—hence the play of words, not meant as frivolous, in my title. Further, the opinion can also be taken as exemplary of the kind of human rights adjudication proper to the ECtHR, not as a forum of principle, or as balancing of interests as it is generally understood,[14] but rather as an institutionally entangled, nonhierarchical form of judgment, where democracy is being defined, as well as enacted, through the intertwining of its many voices. Therefore, in translating White's way of reading into a different context, I aim to go beyond showing its suitability as a general method of analysis, wishing further to reveal something distinctive about human rights adjudication in the context of the European Convention of Human Rights.

Constructing the Judicial Authority: Defining the Judicial Ethos

Lord Bingham, who delivers the leading opinion of the House of Lords,[15] begins in this remarkable fashion:

> No one of ordinary sensitivity could be unmoved by the frightening ordeal which faces Mrs. Dianne Pretty, the appellant. She suffers from motor neuron disease, a progressive degenerative illness from which she has no hope of recovery. She has only a short time to live and faces the prospect of a humiliating and distressing death. She is mentally alert and would like to be able to take steps to bring her life to a peaceful end at a time of her choosing. But her physical incapacity is now such that she can no longer, without help, take her own life. With the support of her family, she wishes to enlist the help of her husband to that end. He himself is willing to give such help, but only if he can be sure that he will not be prosecuted under section 2(1)

of the Suicide act 1961 for aiding and abetting suicide. [...] Mrs. Pretty claims that she has a right to her husband's assistance in committing suicide and that section 2 of the 1961 Act ... is incompatible with the European Convention of Human Rights.[16]

The paragraph is notable in exposing the emotional undertones of the case and eliciting a human reaction of sympathy. The death awaiting Mrs. Pretty is described as humiliating and distressing, opposed to the peaceful end at the time of her choosing. Her physical strains are opposed to her mental alertness; her own incapacity, to her husband's willingness to provide the assistance she needs. Her decision is no mere impulse or avoidance, but comes after reflection and with the support of her family. In this setting, the threat of criminal sanction appears as an obstacle standing between the individual and her wishes. Shouldn't the European Convention of Human Rights protect her?

And yet, if asked to imagine how the argument might continue, few would be surprised to learn that, Mrs. Pretty's personal situation notwithstanding, the conclusion is that the UK law is not in breach of the convention when denying her petition. In effect, after the passage quoted, Lord Bingham begins immediately to take distance and to clarify that "[t]he committee is not a legislative body. Nor is entitled or fitted to act as a moral or ethical arbiter."[17] Hoping to turn a potentially endless debate into a manageable discussion, Lord Bingham distinguishes the "legal" from the myriad ethical and moral considerations surrounding the issue of euthanasia, for these are "questions on which widely differing beliefs and views are held, often strongly."[18] As defined by him, "[t]he task of the committee ... is not to weigh or evaluate or reflect those beliefs and views or give effect to its own, but to ascertain and apply the law of the land as it is now understood to be."[19] The rest of the opinion is a demonstration of this twofold "understanding"; namely, what it means to understand the law and how one can say to have understood it—which compels him to adopt the impersonal voice (i.e., "understood to be").

Lord Bingham invites us to a specific kind of discourse. He is implicitly telling us: "what you are about to observe is how legal argument is supposed to work, which has its own forms of procedures and operations. For it to function properly, some of the arguments must be left out, which gives us a better chance of success." In his mind, judges, as the rest of human beings, are imbued with ordinary sensitivity, beliefs, and emotions, but *as judges*, they ought not to be "moved" by them. The implication is hard to miss: whereas common sentiment would naturally tend to empathize with the plight of Mrs. Pretty, the case at hand requires him to "resist" this proclivity.

This raises an interesting question, for, if the point was at all times to reach the conclusion, why does Lord Bingham begin with so charged emotional language? In other words, what exactly is the role of the first paragraph in Lord Bingham opinion? Is it a polite manner of getting her out of the way in order to arrive to what *really* matters? Should we then dismiss his words as irrelevant, or, worse, cynical? One way White would invite us to inquire further about this question is to ask what would happen if the paragraph had been omitted; that is, how would the opinion be read differently if nothing had been said about Mrs. Pretty's predicament. Surely in that case, Lord Bingham could have been perceived as lacking the human warmth necessary for the application of law, which obviously does not exclude a self-serving rhetoric. But whether the judge really *means* it or not, the paragraph brings the central issue into focus: whatever else is true about it, we are reminded that this is not a hypothetical debate on abstract rules and principles, but one which has real implications on the life of Mrs Pretty and her closest relatives.

Having defined his role and authority, Lord Bingham goes on to analyze each of the separate articles of the convention, articles 2 (right to life), 3 (prohibition of degrading or inhuman treatment), 8 (protection of private and family life), 9 (freedom of expression), and 14 (prohibition of discrimination). In each of these articles, the arguments on behalf of the applicant are the best he can think of, and yet the answer of the House of Lords is invariably negative, defending his opinion that the convention does not grant the right to die, and that, in any case, the law that criminalizes assisted suicide is not in breach of the convention. For reasons of space, I will center on articles 2 and 8—the former because it shows the style of reasoning of Lord Bingham, and the latter because it is the only point of disagreement between the English and the European judges.

The Erotics of Conceptual Talk

The relevant sections of article 2 of the ECHR state:

1. Everyone's right to life shall be protected by law. No one shall be deprived of his life intentionally save in the execution of a sentence of a court following his conviction of a crime for which this penalty is provided by law.
[20]
2. Deprivation of life shall not be regarded as inflicted in contravention of this Article when it results from the use of force which is no more than absolutely necessary: (a) in defense of any

person from unlawful violence, (b) in order to effect a lawful arrest or to prevent the escape of a person lawfully detained, (c) in action lawfully taken for the purpose of quelling a riot or insurrection.

Article 2 presents not a few interpretive dilemmas: How to interpret the fact that it uses the language of property ("to be deprived of") and is addressed mainly against the state? Does this mean that individuals are "owners" of their own lives and may decide to forgo their "title"?[21] To what extent do the exceptions of section 2 affect the interpretation of the article?

On behalf of Mrs. Pretty counsel submits that article 2 protects not life itself, but the *right* to life. The purpose is therefore to protect individuals from third parties (the state and public authorities). Further, it recognizes that it is for the individual to choose whether or not to live and so protects the individual's right to self-determination. Accordingly, a person may refuse life-saving or life-prolonging medical treatment, and may lawfully choose to commit suicide. The right to die is hence not the antithesis of the right to life but its natural corollary, and the state has a positive obligation to protect both.

It is difficult to imagine a better argued case for the applicant. In these brief lines, counsel for Mrs. Pretty offers a compelling reinterpretation of the scope and core protected value of article 2, and, drawing from the fact that individuals may lawfully choose suicide and also refuse life-prolonging treatments, concludes that the right to die must naturally follow.

How does Lord Bingham respond to the challenge? After declaring that the starting point must be the language of the article, he states that "the thrust of this is to reflect on the sanctity which, particularly in Western eyes, attaches to life." In his view, "[a]n Article with that effect cannot be interpreted as conferring a right to die or to enlist the aid of another in bringing about one"s own death."[22] Lord Bingham acknowledges that some convention rights confer both positive and negative aspects (e.g., freedom of expression, freedom of religion...), but other rights cannot be said to confer a right to do the opposite of what they are intended to protect (e.g., the prohibition of slavery, the prohibition of torture and inhuman or degrading treatment) and he takes the right to life to belong to the latter category.

Lord Bingham further points out that no convention authority supports Mrs. Pretty's contention. He cites extensively from the case of *Osman v United Kingdom* (1998),[23] the case of a stalker who ended up killing two people, where the court affirmed the positive obligations of the state to adopt reasonable measures to protect life. Lord Bingham acknowledges that this case is very different, since the victims of that crime did not have any wish to die, but the approach was entirely consistent with his own. He also cites two other cases (*X v Germany*[24] and *Keenan v United Kingdom*[25]) where prison authorities were under the duty to protect people under their care. Once again, Lord Bingham acknowledges the limits of the analogy, since Mrs. Pretty is not incarcerated, but this does not entail that the state would have a duty to recognize her right to die.

Finally, Lord Bingham presents Mrs. Pretty's claim as inconsistent with two distinctions of English law, which are not a simple matter of "semantics"[26]: first, between the taking of life by oneself or doing so with the help of another; second, between the cessation of life-prolonging treatment and those other actions intended solely to terminate life. In sum, he concludes that Mrs. Pretty has failed to establish that the UK is in breach of the convention.

Lord Bingham's style of reasoning is highly abstract and analytical, driven by the apparent desire to exhaust all possibilities: to this end he browses precedents and discerns their implications, provides analogies while acknowledging their limits, and borrows from the conceptual tools afforded by his legal tradition. All this confers upon his conclusion certain flair of inevitability. To paraphrase what White writes in another context, in Lord Bingham we find a "mind of great fastidiousness and care" that has gone over virtually all applicable materials, only to decide that they are not helpful to Mrs. Pretty.[27]

However, even though Lord Bingham declares that "the starting point must be the language of the Article", he proceeds as if the language could be pierced in order to reach the reality behind it, the absolute and unqualified "sanctity which, particularly in Western eyes, attaches to life".[28] Lord Bingham does not explain what this sanctity entails (nor why it is more significant in the West than in other parts of the world), but everything else follows from it. The sanctity of life works in this way as a conclusory and inarticulate premise that presupposes already that which is the task of the analysis to demonstrate, namely, whether (or not) the Mrs. Pretty has a right to forego her life without fear of criminal sanctions.

Lord Bingham places his reliance on a concept beyond language, an extralinguistic reality called "life" that it is the duty of the state to protect, but no such "concept" can be derived from a reading of article 2, which originally permitted the death penalty, which relies on the language of property to refer to life, and which provides a series of exceptions in which life can be lawfully taken. The same can be said about the common law distinctions which are said to exist "beyond semantics." The use of precedents can also be questioned, since none of the people in them had properly a desire to die;[29] and the state's duty to protect life is curbed precisely by the respect for human dignity and freedom.[30] In truth, Lord Bingham disregards the language of article 2, relying instead on his preconceived notion of its "sanctity," nowhere defined, nor clarified, and which ironically debases life to a bare biological function unaffected by the meaning individuals attribute to it.[31]

To be sure, Lord Bingham's logic has undeniable appeal. Consider this: If you were to oppose Lord Bingham, you would have to work as hard as he works himself, mounting the herculean task he undertakes, running through all the precedents and carefully sorting them out, in the hope of offering a more cogent, alternative interpretation. But not even then could you be sure to persuade Lord Bingham. One is left with the impression that his mind is made up. Such is the belief in the power of his analytical skills, his confidence in having understood and mastered all the relevant materials, and to have come to the correct conclusion: that there are no circumstances, exceptional as they might be, in which he might consider a different outcome—save explicit change in the legislation.

As a result, even though Lord Bingham concedes at various moments that he might be wrong in his analysis, there is little room for real disagreement in it. His reasoning aims to impose itself even upon those who would disagree as to the merits, enacting a form of "coercive logic" that seeks to defeat the opponent.[32] Arguably, the ethical and political community enacted in his writing is not democratic or dialogical in character, but rather monological and authoritarian, subject to a logic that demands submission. If asked about the conversation he invites for the future, Lord Bingham closes off all avenues for an alternative interpretation of article 2.

Who is Speaking?

This conclusion becomes apparent when we pause on the manner in which this voice resonates with the European court. After a brief reminder of its jurisprudence—which enjoins the state not only to refrain from the intentional and unlawful taking of life, but also to take appropriate steps to safeguard the lives of those within its jurisdiction—the court is "not persuaded that the right to life involves a negative aspect."[33] Unlike other articles of the convention that imply some measure of choice in their exercise (e.g., the freedom of association), "Article 2 of the Convention is phrased in different terms" and "it is unconcerned with issues to do with the quality of living or what a person chooses to do with his or her life."[34] As a result, "Article 2 cannot, without a distortion of language, be interpreted as conferring the diametrically opposite right, namely a right to die; nor can it create a right to self-determination in the sense of conferring on an individual the entitlement to choose death rather than life."[35]

Hearing this language, one does not have the impression that the court is grappling with a case of high moral stakes; one that deserves the closest attention by an international court. There is no issue of real complexity, no real debate over which people might disagree, often profoundly. There seems to be, in fact, no real decision: the court speaks as if the case were easy and uncomplicated, a mere application of language imagined to be transparent and in need of no interpretation. This clear and unambiguous language determines that the right claimed by Mrs. Pretty is a mere "distortion," "diametrically opposite" to the right to life.

When we consider the way that Lord Bingham's voice features in the opinion of the European Court, we find that it appears not as the enriching voice of diversity, but as a colonizing force that supplants the independent analysis of the court. Lord Bingham does not mean his interpretation to be exhaustive, or even preferred, but merely not incompatible with the approach of the court. The danger is that, once the European Court confers upon it its own mantle of authority, a reading that is merely suggestive turns into the authoritative meaning of article 2.

Therefore, even though the European Court brings in and engages with Lord Bingham's different voice, there is no real dialogue between the two: nothing that would offer an occasion for contrast; for mutual adjustments, for disagreement. Instead what we find is a form of *legal ventriloquism*, where the House of Lords is allowed to speak and think for the European Court of Human Rights. To the extent that the European Court does not enrich but rather impoverishes the conversation around the right to life, this is not an opinion in which democracy begins.

Finding a Voice among Many: An Entangled World

The conclusions have to be qualified in light of article 8, concerning the protection of private and family life. As if it had suddenly recovered its voice, the court makes a startling departure from precedent and assures that, even though "no previous case has established as such any right to self-determination, the notion of personal autonomy is an important principle underlying the interpretation of its guarantees," which extends to behavior perceived to be harmful, dangerous, or even of life-threatening.[36] In this case, the applicant "wishes to mitigate that suffering by exercising a choice to end her life with the assistance of her husband," but "is prevented by law from exercising her choice to avoid what she considers will be an undignified and distressing end to her life." Thus, having stated that "the very essence of the Convention is respect for human dignity and human freedom,"[37] "the Court is not prepared to exclude that this constitutes an interference with her right to respect for private life as guaranteed under Article 8 § 1 of the Convention."[38]

The conclusion seems radically to shift from the abstract language of conceptual clarity, to the perspective of the individual who is facing what *she* considers an undignified and distressing end. This opens up a different kind of dialogue, a different political philosophy in fact, where the state's duty to protect finds a limit in the principles of human dignity and personal freedom of individuals. These principles carve out a space for self-determination where what matters is not the content of choice (whether individuals decide to die rather than to live), but that individuals are able to make and define their own life-choices. The court's language enacts a pluralist society where people are expected to choose different ends, not all compatible with the public "perception of the good."

In order to understand this considerable transformation and, indeed, to understand it as part and parcel of the same judicial opinion, it is necessary to attend to the rich dialogue of voices around article 8, first, with respect to the applicability and interference of the right of private life (8 § 1) and, then, regarding the possible justification of the state interference (8 § 2). This brings us back to Lord Bingham, for whom the answer is uncomplicated. Simply put, the right to private life is not engaged at all because the alleged choice of the applicant would extinguish the very benefit which article 8 supposedly protects; even if it were engaged, he surmises, the interference would at any rate be justified.

It must be Lord Bingham's commendable commitment to the legal process that compels him, before reaching the conclusion, to examine "the most detailed and erudite discussion"[39] known to him on the topic, the case of the Canadian Supreme Court in *Rodriguez v Attorney General of Canada*.[40] In this way, we are introduced to yet another group of voices that speak from their own jurisdictional context. The main debate concerns section 7 of the Canadian Charter of Rights and Freedoms, which ensures that no one shall be deprived of the rights of life, liberty, and security "except in accordance with the principles of fundamental justice." Writing for the majority, Justice Sopinka considered that personal autonomy was engaged, for the applicant's problems were due to governmental action and not to her physical disabilities. Consequently, it was necessary to determine whether there had been any deprivation thereof that was not in accordance with the principles of fundamental justice. His conclusion was that "given the concerns about abuse ... and the great difficulty in creating appropriate safeguards ... it cannot be said that the blanket prohibition on assisted suicide is arbitrary or unfair."[41] In arguing so, Sopinka relied on a substantial consensus among Western countries and assured that attempts to fine-tune this approach by creating exceptions tended to support the theory of the "slippery slope."[42]

It is noteworthy that Lord Bingham includes also the dissent of J. McLachlin, according to whom "Parliament has put into force a legislative scheme which does not bar suicide, but criminalizes the act of assisting suicide. The effect of this is to deny to some people the choice of ending their lives solely because they are physically unable to do so." Consequently, "it does not accord with the principles of fundamental justice that [the applicant] be disallowed what is available to others merely because it is possible that other people, at some other time, may suffer, not what she seeks, but an act of killing without true consent."[43]

The extraordinary thing about this whole citation is that for Lord Bingham the Canadian precedent is not even relevant, for the Canadian judges rely on a provision with no close analogy in the European Convention that protects only privacy. In his view, privacy can only extend to the protection of personal autonomy while individuals are living their lives, but not to the choice to live no longer. This suggests that Lord Bingham sees himself immersed already in a dialogue he anticipates with the European Court, and is responding to their potential disparity of criterion, aiming to fill the spaces of dissent even before they open up.

Additionally, the inclusion of these voices provides him with the opportunity to editorialize—that is, to shape and channel the way the European Court will read and interpret the case. Thus, even though Mrs. Pretty places reliance on the dissent, Lord Bingham reminds his audience that "a majority of the court regarded that right as outweighed on the facts by the principles of fundamental justice."[44] Obviously, he has confidence in his own power to steer and command an interpretation, hoping that, beyond small discrepancies, the reviewing organ will accept the interpretation he is proposing.

The Exuberances of Citation

White suggests that every citation can be a source of "exuberances";[45] namely, an uncontrollable supplement of meaning that overflows the attempts fully to contain it. Indeed, once the judges of the Canadian Supreme Court are willing to extend the protection of autonomy to the decision of life and death, Lord Bingham's insistence on denying that private life is at all engaged appears somewhat artificial, considering the similar structure of both Documents. The European Court does not abide by Lord Bingham's formalism and assumes that, even though the Canadian provision is framed in different terms, "comparable concerns" arose in both cases.[46] Without dodging the issue under technicalities, the Court seems willing and ready to engage with the central issue of the case.

Likewise the European Court cites approvingly the concurring opinion of Lord Hope of the House of Lords, who thinks that "the way she [Mrs. Pretty] chooses to pass the closing moments of her life is part of the act of living, and she has a right to ask that this too must be respected."[47] Suddenly, an opinion other than Lord Bingham's is being heard, showing that he is not the only voice within the House of Lords and that he actually has less than its full authority.

With the support of the Canadian judges and Lord Hope, the ECtHR comes out of its earlier ventriloquism to engage now in proper institutional dialogue with the other participants. Thus, for the first time, we hear the distinctive voice of the European Court confronting the convention in its own right, exercising the power to read and explain its own jurisprudence, where the absence of prior explicit language of self-determination is no obstacle to understand it as implicit interpretive principle. In this light, the court reads its own case law concerning the refusal to certain medical treatments as indication that private life is interfered with, even when it leads to inevitable death.

They see this situation as analogous to Mrs. Pretty's, who wishes to exercise a choice to end her life. As stated by Lord Hope, this choice is not external to life, but belongs in the kind of decisions human beings face in the course of living, and the least one can expect from others (particularly from the state) is a measure of respect. This is furthermore consistent with the core values of the convention, the very "essence" of which, they say, is the respect for human dignity and freedom. In this way, Mrs. Pretty's choice itself is dignified, enabling her to preserve some sense of dignity *during* and *for* her life.

Mrs. Pretty's decision is made more comprehensible still by placing it in the context of modern medicine. As the court writes, "in an era of growing medical sophistication combined with longer life expectancies, many people are concerned that they should not be forced to linger on in old age in states of advanced physical or mental decrepitude which conflict with strongly held ideas of self and personal identity."[48] The thought of "forcefully" "lingering on" in "decrepitude" is unlikely to be desired by or to anyone; indeed, it is far more likely to be found amongst the deepest fears of "many people." Mrs. Pretty's predicament, as her choice earlier, is turned communal: a situation that can affect us all.

With this the court arrives to the heart of the matter, which is the threat of criminal sanctions standing between Mrs. Pretty and her decision. As the court sees it, "the applicant in this case is prevented by law from exercising her choice to avoid what she considers will be an undignified and distressing end of her life," in alignment with the individual perspective that Lord Bingham was at pains to discount. And hence, naturally, "the Court is not prepared to exclude that this constitutes an interference with her right to respect for private life."[49]

The Court as a Language-Maker: A Self-Reflexive Jurisprudence

The second and final stage of the argument must examine whether the interference can be justified under the requirements of article 8 § 2.[50] What is discussed is not the legitimacy of laws prohibiting assisted suicide. The issue is whether the 1961 act, in failing to allow exceptions for a case like Mrs. Pretty's, and adopting instead a blanket ban irrespective of circumstances, violates the necessary proportionality of the law.[51] Lord Bingham calls the argument "beguiling," but cites the authority of Dr. Samuel Johnson, who argued that "laws are not made for particular cases but for men in general," and that "to permit a law to be modified at discretion is to leave the community without law."[52] Lord Bingham opposes the "seductive" nature of Mrs. Pretty's arguments to the "sobriety" of law, tying himself to the mast of its bonds and strictures.

And yet his commitment to the sobering rule of law does not prevent him from displaying an alternative, sentimental scenario: "It is not hard to imagine that an elderly person, in the absence of any pressure, might opt for a premature end to life if that were available, not from a desire to die or willingness to stop living, but from a desire to stop being a burden to others."[53] To Mrs. Pretty's concrete situation, an imaginary, non-adjudicated case is opposed which has nothing to do with her different predicament.

To be sure, there may still exist valid reasons to maintain the protections afforded by the law, which is why the European Court is on the horns of dilemma. Here we encounter one of the *aporias* identified by Jacques Derrida: a tension between doing justice to the individual case and preserving the generality of law.[54] Whereas Lord Bingham simply ignores the *aporia* by subsuming the individual under the general, a court of human rights requires additional arguments to confront it, for it cannot rely on an abstract generality to deny justice to the individual case.

The ECtHR begins with an interesting avowal:

> It is true that it is not this Court's role ... to issue opinions in the abstract but to apply the Convention to the concrete facts of the individual case. *However, judgments issued in individual cases establish precedents ... and a decision in this case could not, either in theory or practice, be framed in such a way as to prevent application in later cases.*[55]

In a revealing exercise of self-reflexivity, the court sees its own opinions as modeling the conversations to be had in the future, where law is not something external to the court's activity, but the very language the court now creates. The *positionality* of the court vis-à-vis the law changes: whereas Lord Bingham positioned himself as an observer of a law that exists independently of his "understanding" of it, here the court becomes an active participant in the making of law.

Paradoxically, the court's acknowledgment of being a maker of law is accompanied by resolve to make no active practical contribution in the present. Worried that words uttered on behalf of Mrs. Pretty can eventually be "misquoted," the ECtHR decides to quieten its voice lest such words be used for less deserving cases. In my view, this evinces mistrust rather than prudence and restraint: the court does not put faith in other actors being able to sort out complications as they arise in future cases, which does not call into being a community of readers with the skills and capacities that the court claims for itself. As a result, the court fails to resolve the case as the case would require if considered on its own, and the apparent desire to deliver justice to Mrs. Pretty is silenced.

Finally, the European Court subjects the UK system to scrutiny in terms of proportionality. It observes that between 1981 and 1992, in twenty cases where "mercy killing" was an issue, there was only one conviction for murder and another for life imprisonment, while lesser offences were substituted in others, and most resulted in probation or suspended sentences. In light of this, the court concludes that it does not appear arbitrary to prohibit assisted suicide, while providing for a system of enforcement and adjudication that allows due regard to be given to the circumstances in each particular case.[56]

There might be different ways to read this. On the one hand, it appears that the court is more comfortable with an ensuing control of administrative practices, than with a prior assessment of the legislation, which gives wider latitude to the authorities than might be otherwise desirable. On the other hand, one welcomes the fact that the court is willing to scrutinize not only the law-in-the-books, but also how the law has been implemented in practice.[57] Admittedly, this apparent attention to law-in-action does not modify the situation of Mrs. Pretty, who is not afforded legal protection (a cynical reader may even wonder whether the court is inviting Mrs. Pretty and her husband to "try their luck" with the system). But it is also possible, if I were to impersonate the court, to read an implicit warning of the kind: "Do not think that because we find no violation in this case we will never do so, for instance, if criminal sanctions are excessive, if 'mercy killing' is treated exactly as murder, if there is no possibility of tempering the punishment, or to take account other exigent circumstances." Even if the court tries to restrict its current ruling, different actors in different contexts will inevitably expand its future meaning.

The Shape an Opinion Makes: Many-Voicedness and Human Rights Adjudication

So where does the meaning of this opinion reside? As White time and again has repeated, the meaning of the opinion lies not in its result, but in what that result is *made to mean*, in the interactions and conversation it establishes—with and between the parties, with other institutional actors, among the various voices in and of the opinion, with the society at large—and in the ethical and political community it enacts and makes possible for its readers.[58]

Once we turn away from the concrete result and begin to listen more closely to the music that the opinion makes, we find that a rich polyphony of voices emerges. This polyphony constitutes the life-form of the decision. To listen to these voices is required, in fact, even to understand the more "technical" aspects of the decision: one would search in vain to find the meaning of article 2 by reading what the court says about it in this case, if one did not also seek to hear Lord Bingham's reading of the same Article, and if one did not attempt to contrasting both voices with what the court says in regards Article 8. Thus, there are important aspects of the decision raised by voices other than the European Court. For example, Lord Hope and the Canadian Supreme Court awake the ECtHR from its previous stupor in order to confront its own jurisprudence and role as a court of human rights.

An opinion is thus a complex web of interconnected narratives that respond, enrich, undermine, and dissent from one another. The meaning lies in the interaction of all these voices, in their mutual responses, and also in their silences, in the arguments they do not answer and are let to stand, unaddressed. These voices are often in tension with each other and, sometimes, also with themselves, as for example the court's disparate readings of articles 2 and 8, and the tensions between the first and second sections of this article. Here's where White's judicial many-voicedness—the art of writing "two ways at once"—meets Bakhtin's heteroglossia.[59] To analyze the opinion in terms of its many voices makes us more receptive to its changes of tone and modulations, to its shifts and transformations, to its ambiguities and contradictions, to its possibilities of being, and of being otherwise.

This focal point enables us to contrast a particular voice against the framework within which it operates. For example, we can assess how the jurisprudence of the ECtHR figures in Lord Bingham's opinion and, vice versa, how Lord Bingham's voice appears in the court's, first as the leading voice, and then suddenly as one among many, having less than full authority of the House. Likewise the Canadian case features differently in Lord Bingham's and the court's respective narratives: in the former's it is a case from which one can gain erudition and sophistication, but one that is not relevant in the end; in the latter's it is a case to rely on through analogical thinking, for the concerns are substantially comparable.

To read the judicial opinion in this way is not to wish to dilute all political concerns into matters of "style"; rather, it is to treat those matters as deeply embedded in ethical and political commitments. For example, Lord Bingham's exhaustive, professional talk privileging conceptual clarity discloses a monological and authoritarian bent that ignores the individual and the singularity of the case. In contrast, the anti-formalism of the court allows it to confront the substantive issue without hiding behind conceptual abstractions. Each voice validates a different conversation, and hence a different future, for the law.

Finally, we might also better comprehend the institutional entanglements in which the court participates, and the position of the court vis-à-vis other institutional actors, individual citizens, social organizations, third-party interveners, legal communities, and societies at large. In this setting, the jurisdictional task of the court and of human rights adjudication is to be understood not in terms of competing principles, or a balance of interests, but rather as a negotiation of institutionally entangled, deeply contextual, judgments. The court must negotiate its interpretation of rights with interpretations spoken by other voices, and assess also the societal impact of its decision, while inquiring self-reflexively about its role as a maker of legal language with a wide area of influence. This may partially explain why the European Court finds itself unable to follow through with its apparent desire to deliver justice to Mrs. Pretty and chooses instead to legitimize the domestic practices.

What the Text Leaves Out

White has often reminded us that there is always something that every text "leaves out," which is why we must be vigilant in choosing our texts. However, he has also shown us that, occasionally, a text is able to create the conditions to transcend its own limitations. To conclude, I would like to locate this possibility not outside, but deep inside the opinion, embodied in the powerful minority dissent written by Justice McLachlin in the *Rodriguez* case. According to the dissent, the effect of a "legislative scheme which does not bar suicide, but criminalizes the act of assisting suicide ... is to deny to some people the choice of ending their lives solely because they are physically unable to do so." Nor it does accord "with the principles of fundamental justice that [the applicant] be disallowed what is available to others merely because it is possible that other people ... may suffer, not what she seeks, but an act of killing without true consent."[60]

As we have seen, Lord Bingham tries to submit the dissent to the logic of majorities and minorities, but he proves incapable of restraining it: once the force of the argument has been heard, it cannot be unheard. The minority dissent points to the fact that this case is different to all the others considered by Lord Bingham in at least two respects: in none of the others did the applicant seek voluntarily to die, and in the present case the law is discriminating against Mrs. Pretty on account of her physical disability. Accordingly, Mrs. Pretty's case is to be treated as those who commit suicide voluntarily, and not as those who, vulnerable or not, do not give their consent to it. The dissent introduces a wedge into the watertight logic of Lord Bingham and protests against the assumed generality and equal application of the law.

The example of the Canadian dissent pushes the European Court to engage with a societal reality beyond the strict boundaries of the 1961 act and to demand that the reasons for criminalizing assisted suicide be less "general" and more "specific." (Rather than defend the abstract generality of law, the court tries to assess the concrete proportionality of the law as currently implemented in the UK.) However, the court still finds itself unable to grant relief to Mrs. Pretty, for fear that this will open the door to unwanted claims in the future. In this way, the dissent confronts the court with the limits of its own language, beyond which they do not dare to speak. And yet the dissent turns the abstract issue of the right to die into the different one of discrimination, where the state action is itself promoting it. (As White would stress, a person need not accept that there is an absolute right to die in order to agree with this different point.) Like an unfinished note, then, the dissent resonates with conversations to be had in the future, when it will be less and less acceptable to use arguments based on vulnerability to oppose those who, like Mrs. Pretty, are not vulnerable at all.

Notes

1. J. B. White, *Justice as Translation: An Essay in Cultural and Legal Criticism* (Chicago: University of Chicago Press, 1990), 36n.
2. M. Bakhtin, *Problems of Dostoevsky's Poetics* (Minneapolis: University of Minnesota Press, 1984), 252.
3. White, *Justice as Translation*.
4. White, *Justice as Translation*, 91.
5. White, *Justice as* Translation, 101–2.
6. White, *Justice as Translation*, 102.
7. See, among many, J. B. White, *Heracles' Bow: Essays on the Rhetoric and Poetics of the Law* (Madison: University of Wisconsin Press, 1985).
8. For example, Sanford Levinson found his own experience "more vexing than enjoyable," "Book Review: Conversing About Justice," *Yale Law Journal* 100 (1990–1991): 1855, 1861. More viscerally, M. V. Tushnet responded "as most people respond to fingernails raking across a blackboard," "Book Review: Translation as Argument," *William & Mary Law Review* 32 (1990–1991): 105, 105. A more welcoming experience, closer to my own, is described by E. Mertz, "Creative Acts of Translation: James Boyd White's Intellectual Integration," *Yale Journal of Law & Humanities* 4 (1992): 165.
9. *Pretty v The United Kingdom*, Application 2346/02, Judgment of April 29, 2002 (hereinafter *Pretty v UK*).
10. *The Queen on the Application of Mrs Dianne Pretty v Director of Public Prosecutions and Secretary of State for the Home Department* (2001) UKHL 61 (hereinafter *R [on the application of Pretty] v DPP*).
11. The opinion also includes the arguments of the Voluntary Euthanasia Society as well as of the Catholic Bishop's Conference of England and Wales.
12. D. Manderson, *Kangaroo Courts and the Rule of Law: The Legacy of Modernism* (Abingdon: Routledge, 2012).
13. This is more than just a metaphor, for a few weeks after her case was denied in court, Diane Pretty died as a result of her illness. For an analogy between judicial opinions and tragedy, see James Boyd White, "Human Dignity and the Claim of Meaning: Athenian Tragic Drama and Supreme Court Opinions," *Journal of Supreme Court History* 27 (2002): 45.
14. For the former, see G. Letsas, *A Theory of Interpretation of the European Convention of Human Rights* (Oxford: Oxford University Press, 2007). For the latter, S. Sotiaux and G. Van der Schyff, "Methods of International Human Rights Adjudication: Towards a More Structured Decision-Making Process for the European Court of Human Rights" *Hastings International & Comparative Law* 31 *Review* (2008): 115.
15. The judgments of the House of Lords do not permit to identify a leading opinion, but I will take Lord Bingham's as the leading one, since the ECtHR cites it verbatim in paragraph 14 of the decision in *Pretty v UK*.
16. *R (on the application of Pretty) v DPP*, paragraph 1.
17. *R (on the application of Pretty) v DPP*, paragraph 2.
18. *R (on the application of Pretty) v DPP*, paragraph 2.

19. *R (on the application of Pretty) v DPP*, paragraph 2.
20. When the convention was first drafted death penalty was still contemplated, but subsequent protocols have practically abolished it (the notable exception being Russia), though the original text remains.
21. For various ways to understand the analogy between the right to life/die and property rights see S. B. Chetwynd, "Right to Lie, Right to Die and Assisted Suicide," *Journal of Applied Philosophy* 21 (2004): 173.
22. *R (on the application of Pretty) v DPP*, paragraph 5.
23. *Osman v United Kingdom* (1998) 29 EHRR 245.
24. *X v Germany* (1984) 7 EHRR 152 (force-feeding prisoners on hunger strike).
25. *Keenan v United Kingdom* (App n° 27229/95, 3 April 2001) (an alleged schizophrenic who had committed suicide in prison).
26. *Pretty v UK*, paragraph 9 (citing Lord Donaldson of Lymington MR in *In re J (A Minor) (Wardship: Medical Treatment)* [1991] Fam 33 [46]).
27. White, "Human Dignity and the Claim of Meaning," 53.
28. White, in "Human Dignity and the Claim of Meaning," alerts against the attitude of eschewing the tangible reality of text toward an ideal plane where concepts are supposed to lay bare (31, 33). In his view, "what lies beyond language is real alright, but it is not communicable, certainly not in the language of concepts" (35).
29. Lord Bingham acknowledges this explicitly in *Osman* (note 23) but fails to mention it in the other two examples.
30. In *Keenan* (note 25), a prisoner with schizophrenia was allegedly driven to suicide by the penal authorities, and the court said that the state duty to protect life must yield before human dignity and individual autonomy (paragraphs 92 and 93 of the judgment).
31. Likewise, the manner of approaching death—the ability to write the closing chapter in her life's book—is given no consideration. See R. Dworkin, *Life's Dominion: An Argument About Abortion and Euthanasia* (London: HarperCollins, 1993).
32. White, *Justice as Translation*, 29.
33. *Pretty v UK*, paragraph 39.
34. *Pretty v UK*, paragraph 39.
35. *Pretty v UK*, paragraph 39.
36. *Pretty v UK*, paragraphs 61 and 62.
37. *Pretty v UK*, paragraph 65.
38. *Pretty v UK*, paragraph 67. Article 8 § 1 of the ECHR states: "Everyone has the right to respect for his private and family life, his home and correspondence."
39. *R (on the application of Pretty) v DPP*, paragraph 19.
40. *Rodriguez v Attorney General of Canada* (1994) 2 LRC 136.
41. *Rodriguez v Attorney General of Canada*, 189.
42. For a sustained criticism of the judgment, see L. Weinrib, "The Body and the Body Politic: Assisted Suicide under the Canadian Charter of Rights and Freedoms," *McGill Law Journal* 39 (1994): 618. Slippery-slope arguments are inherently problematic, for the consideration of the instant case is subordinated

to an imaginary, speculative, scenario. Obviously, the argument can also be questioned on empirical grounds; see R. G. Frey, "The Fear of a Slippery Slope," in *Euthanasia and Physician-Assisted Suicide: For and Against*, ed. G. Dworkin, R. G. Frey, and S. Bok (Cambridge and New York: Cambridge University Press, 1998), 43–63.

43. See *R (on the application of Pretty) v DPP*, paragraph 22.
44. *R (on the application of Pretty) v DPP*, paragraph 23.
45. White, *Justice as Translation*, 235 (referring to Spanish philosopher Ortega y Gasset on translation).
46. *Pretty v UK*, paragraph 66.
47. *Pretty v UK*, paragraph 64. The court's citation has been interpreted by UK courts as an "endorsement" of Lord Hope on this issue. See *The Queen (on the Application of Debbie Purdy) v DPP* [2009] EWCA Civ 92 [2009] (Ward, J., paragraph 47).
48. *Pretty v UK*, paragraph 65.
49. *Pretty v UK*, paragraph 67.
50. Article 8 § 2 of the ECHR states: "There shall be no interference by a public authority with the exercise of this right except such as is in accordance with the law and is necessary in a democratic society in the interests of national security, public safety or the economic well-being of the country, for the prevention of disorder or crime, for the protection of health or morals, or for the protection of the rights and freedoms of others."
51. For a relevant (and controversial) case striking down national legislation with the argument that Parliament failed to make relevant distinctions, see *Hirst v UK* (App n° 74025/01, 6 October 2005) (holding that the ban of voting rights for prisoners irrespective of their prison sentence violated the electoral rights of article 3 of protocol 1 of the ECHR).
52. J. Boswell, *Life of Johnson*, 3rd ed. (Oxford: Oxford University Press, 1970), 735 and 496 (as cited by Lord Bingham in *R (on the application of Pretty) v DPP*, paragraph 29).
53. *R (on the application of Pretty) v DP* , paragraph 29.
54. J. Derrida, "Force of Law: The 'Mystical Foundation of Authority'" *Cardozo Law Review* 11 (1990): 919, 961–63.
55. *Pretty v UK*, paragraph 75.
56. *Pretty v UK*, paragraph 76.
57. The court tries to navigate the *aporia* (between the generality of law and the particular case), first, by extending the definition of law to the practices of implementation and enforcement, and then, by showing that the individual claims for justice have been generally attended by the law.
58. See White, *Justice as Translation*, and White, *Heracles' Bow*. Also, White "What's an Opinion For?" in *From Expectation to Experience: Essays on Law & Legal Education* (Ann Arbor: University of Michigan Press, 2000), 35–42.
59. White, *Heracles' Bow*, 116.
60. See note 45 and accompanying text.

[5]

Slow Reading and Living Speech

James Boyd White on What a Constitutional Law Opinion is For
H. Jefferson Powell

The first time that I engaged deeply with James Boyd White's work, it had nothing to do with the law: I read his book on learning to read the seventeenth-century poet George Herbert, *"This Book of Starres."*[1] I love poetry, and in the religious tradition that Herbert, White, and I share, Herbert is viewed as a saint. I knew about Jim White of course, as the leading practitioner of "law and literature," and so when I came across his book on Herbert I felt something like an obligation to buy it. I did so, however, without much conviction that I would ever do more than crack the cover and read a few pages, for I knew that Herbert's poetry, whatever its technical brilliance, expressed the sort of saccharine piety that is everything I don't like in religious writing. It seemed extremely unlikely that Prof. White, however distinguished a legal scholar he might, could have anything interesting to say about the early modern equivalent of the verses you find on a greeting card.

I don't know with certainty how long it took me to realize that however boring Herbert might be, Jim White is a great and challenging thinker and writer—I was probably hooked by the time I finished the preface, in which Jim describes "the reading of any book of poetry, or prose too, as a kind of language-learning, and of writing as a kind of language-making."[2] What White seemed to be saying resonated deeply with my own experience of the law, and of the theology in which I was trained before I became a lawyer. Equally exciting, if a little difficult to credit given my view of Herbert, was White's remarkable claim that for him the result of reading Herbert attentively had been "to shift the way I perceive and live in the world, a transformation of the self."[3] It was without doubt only my engagement with Jim that kept me going.

I don't recall exactly when my skepticism about White's subject vanished, though I vividly recall the particular theme in White's "slow reading" (as he described it[4]) that opened my eyes to Herbert's towering genius as a poet and, for that matter, a religious thinker: it was the way in which White's writing patiently led me to see that far from being saccharine or superficial, or even merely technically adept, Herbert's poetry draws one within the mind and heart of a person wrestling with the deepest issues of identity and meaning, and that in part the poems do so by the way in which Herbert gives voice to conflicting thoughts, emotions, and passions. I had thought Herbert expressed a bland and even smug religiosity that implicitly denied the complexity of life and faith: Jim White showed me, convinced me by his own sensitive and passionate readings of Herbert's poems, that Herbert had grappled with unfailing honesty with his experiences, and expressed his struggle above all through the revelation, not the denial, of tensions and doubt as well as commitment and belief.

Reading *"This Book of Starres"* started me on a wonderful, now almost twenty-year-long spiritual journey with George Herbert, and for that gift I shall always be deeply grateful to Jim White. (I should note, however, that my copies of Herbert's collected poems get opened far less than either of my two copies of White on Herbert, which give me Jim's commentary as well as Herbert's poems.) But White's book about learning to read Herbert was also my real introduction to his approach to reading serious texts in any genre, an approach that has profoundly influenced my own understanding of the law, and of my role as a lawyer and a teacher of law. Several aspects of what White wrote about Herbert—though he makes many of the same observations in other writing about other authors and genres—have been important to me.

First, and perhaps most importantly, as I've already suggested, central to the way that *"This Book of Starres"* transformed my view of Herbert was White's patient demonstration that, as he put it, Herbert's is "a poetry of voices … in which the speaker is not in any simple sense the poet himself;" the voices "are mainly internal ones, different versions of himself," and thus in frequent tension or even sharp disagreement with one another.[5] "Slow reading," in White's sense, centrally demands an openness to or search for the points of tension, fracture, or contradiction in the text, understood not as evidence of confusion or illogic on the writer's part but as entry points into the kind of thinking that any serious writing will embody. The impulse to gloss over or harmonize discordant elements in a serious piece of writing, including legal writing, is thus a mistake, at least if we give into it too quickly: we can learn more by asking what it is we can learn from the points of strain in thought or expression that the writer herself has left in place. Both in my own writing and in the classroom, I have tried to emulate White's practices of reading in this regard.

Law, and perhaps especially American constitutional law (which is my own area of specialization), might seem uniquely ill-suited for the application of the White "slow reading" approach. After all, in an obvious way it is intrinsic to the very processes of constitutional decision that voices contrary to that of the decisionmaker are silenced or at least rejected as wrong, the views of dissenters deemed unpersuasive, other concerns overridden by those that the decisionmaker finds more salient. It is unsurprising, surely, that constitutional opinions, whether set forth by the judgments of the United States Supreme Court or in the pages of scholarly publications, are very often stated in a dogmatic or even imperious tone that hardly allows for other voices except as examples of error. White wrote of Herbert that for him "'belief' ... is not a simple credal affirmation, reducible to doctrinal terms, but a field of contest and uncertainty, including various forms of disbelief."[6] But isn't the very point of a statement of law to resolve contest, eliminate uncertainty, provide affirmations that can be reduced to doctrinal terms?

As an illustration of the way in which I believe Jim White can help us deepen our understanding of an opinion on constitutional law, I'd like to consider Justice Robert Jackson's famous concurring opinion in *Youngstown Sheet & Tube Co v Sawyer*, the case in which the Supreme Court decided that it was unlawful for President Truman to seize the American steel industry to avert a potential shutdown of production during the Korean War.[7] The Court has long since come to treat Jackson's concurrence as the central opinion among the six filed by the justices in the *Youngstown* majority, displacing in most invocations of that case's meaning even the formal opinion of the Court written by Hugo Black. As William Rehnquist once wrote for the Court, both lawyers and justices have come to agree that Jackson's concurrence "brings together as much combination of analysis and common sense as there is in this area [of the scope of presidential power]."[8] Most of the time, however, the attention given Jackson's opinion is narrowly focused on the couple of pages in which Jackson sets out what the Court now terms the "familiar tripartite scheme [that] provides the accepted framework for evaluating executive action."[9] The other nineteen or so pages of Jackson's concurrence, an opinion Jackson drafted and revised personally and that constitutes a closely reasoned and passionately eloquent statement by a justice highly regarded by most, regularly go unnoticed. The reason for this lopsided focus of attention is easy to see: the "familiar tripartite scheme," abstracted from the rest of Jackson's opinion, can be read as a dogmatic affirmation of constitutional truth, a doctrinal formula that reveals no uncertainty on the author's part and brooks no opposition on the reader's. As a result, read in a very non-Jim White fashion, this small fragment of what Jackson actually composed is immensely valuable to the lawyer writing a brief, the law clerk drafting an opinion, or the student or scholar organizing the subject: plugged in at the appropriate point, the "tripartite scheme," like any bit of black letter, puts an end to doubt and the search for understanding by pronouncing what the rule is. The implicit or explicit message is that the reader of such a pronouncement has but only to obey.

The problem with this common treatment of the *Youngstown* concurrence is that it is almost as bad a reading of Justice Jackson's opinion as my pre-White view of Herbert as sentimental versifier misunderstood that great poet's work. Even the passage that we have turned into a black letter, tripartite rule undercuts the common reading of its words. Jackson notoriously described the "actual test of [presidential] power" when the executive acts neither with nor against an act of Congress as likely to depend on "the imperatives of events and contemporary imponderables"—language that looks to the dogmatist like an inexplicable lapse in performance, as if the Nicene Creed's third article began "We believe in the Holy Spirit, whatever that may be." Given the intense care with which Jackson crafted the opinion, the idea that he simply dropped the ball at a crucial point is, I suggest, highly implausible. Furthermore, if we go back to Jackson's opinion as he wrote it, and give his work the kind of "slow reading" Jim White proposes and practices, we can see that the bigger and basic mistake lies in reading Jackson as if his goal were to provide a statement of constitutional dogma to be accepted and applied without question. Of course Jackson intended to provide a reasoned exposition, one complementary to that provided by Justice Black's very different line of thought in Black's opinion for the Court, of why the *Youngstown* majority was right to come to its judgment that President Truman had acted unlawfully. And there is no reason to doubt that Jackson hoped that future constitutional lawyers would take seriously his thoughts in coming to their own conclusions about whatever problems they might have to address. But Jackson's opinion is something far greater than a strangely-prolonged presentation of the black letter rule that can be stated (or restated!) in less than a page into which we have turned it. White's "slow reading" is the key.

You'll recall White's observation that George Herbert's is "a poetry of voices," none of which are simply to be equated with Herbert himself, in the singular: what a slow reading of Herbert enables us to hear are what are distinct and "mainly internal voices" that present "different versions" of Herbert by expressing the tensions, conflicts, and doubts that were intrinsic and valuable aspects of the man, that enabled him to be a great literary artist, and a subtle and profound religious thinker with much to say about human existence even to those who do not share his faith. In a similar fashion, Robert Jackson's opinion in *Youngstown* (indeed, his judicial work generally) is a "jurisprudence of voices." There is a deep coherence to what Jackson wrote—elsewhere I have referred to his *Youngstown* vision, an account of the American constitutional order and the place of law and of lawyers within it that is compelling precisely because it makes ultimate sense of both American arrangements and the moral choices those arrangements require.[10] But Jackson achieves coherence and expresses vision not through the suppression of tension and doubt but precisely through the ways in which he makes plain to himself and to the reader the presence of conflict and the unavoidable uncertainties that accompany, or should accompany, momentous constitutional decisions.

Consider the first paragraph of Jackson"s opinion:

> That comprehensive and undefined presidential powers hold both practical advantages and grave dangers for the country will impress anyone who has served as legal adviser to a President in time of transition and public anxiety. While an interval of detached reflection may temper teachings of that experience, they probably are a more realistic influence on my views than the conventional materials of judicial decision which seem unduly to accentuate doctrine and legal fiction. But as we approach the question of presidential power, we half overcome mental hazards by recognizing them. The opinions of judges, no less than executives and publicists, often suffer the infirmity of confusing the issue of a power's validity with the cause it is invoked to promote, of confounding the permanent executive office with its temporary occupant. The tendency is strong to emphasize transient results upon policies—such as wages or stabilization—and lose sight of enduring consequences upon the balanced power structure of our Republic.[11]

For the legal dogmatist looking for unquestionable black letter this is a bizarre way to begin an opinion meant to lay down the law. For a slow reader, in contrast, Jackson begins his effort to reach and explain the proper resolution of a great constitutional question by introducing us to three distinct perspectives.

We first meet Robert Jackson the attorney general, whose service "as legal adviser to a President in a time of transition and public anxiety" lies in the past but who will be a lively and vital presence throughout most of the opinion. As a high officer of the executive branch, charged in some large measure with enabling the president to pursue his policies but also with ensuring that the claims of the law are heard, this voice admits the tension inherent in advising a president faced with national crisis: "comprehensive and undefined presidential powers hold both practical advantages and grave dangers for the country." At subsequent points in the concurrence, Jackson the attorney general will concede that a legal advisor to the president can come under great pressure to lay claim to "inherent and unrestricted presidential powers," claims that play well in "political controversy" but not in court, and he will even reject the attempt of the government lawyers to invoke as authority the "self-serving press statements" he himself issued in defending Roosevelt administration actions.[12] But read carefully, in the way Jim White teaches, the *Youngstown* concurrence enables us to understand that assertions of presidential authority involve constitutional duty as well as political expediency: Jackson the attorney general comments, for example, reflecting on the question of what powers belong to the president as commander in chief, that "just what authority goes with the name has plagued Presidential advisers who would not waive or narrow it by nonassertion yet cannot say where it begins or ends."[13]

In the second sentence of the concurrence, we first hear Robert Jackson the present judge, tasked with deciding the legality of a presidential action presented to his court and both troubled and puzzled by the question. It is this Jackson who reflects, in the first-person singular, that his pre-judicial experiences as a lawyer for the president "probably are a more realistic influence on *my* views than" legal doctrine, despite the fact that as a judge he has had the advantage of "an interval of detached reflection" between advising and defending President Roosevelt and sitting in judgment on President Truman. The judge's detached reflections, this voice recognizes, have not eliminated the risk that the experience voiced by Jackson the attorney general may make the judge unduly indulgent in determining the legality of a presidential decision out of a sympathy rooted in experience for the exigent sense of concern for the national welfare that no doubt motivated Truman. Indeed, Jackson the judge intimates, it is not only former attorneys general whose exercise of the judicial function is likely to "suffer the infirmity of confusing the issue" of legality with the question whether the president's policy preferences are benign or desirable. But the task of distinguishing legal validity from political approval, however difficult, is not impossible: if the decisionmaker (judge or advisor) will only acknowledge the difficulty, "we half overcome mental hazards by recognizing them." Both voices have recognized these mental hazards: as a result there is reason to hope that the Supreme Court can decide the case before it without falling into either blind acceptance of a presidential decision in time of war or a reflexive distrust of the claims of the executive branch.

In the final sentence of this opening paragraph, I believe we hear for the first time a third voice, one more impersonal than that of either the attorney general or the judge: "The tendency is strong to emphasize transient results upon policies-such as wages or stabilization-and lose sight of enduring consequences upon the balanced power structure of our Republic." Here at last we find a statement that might satisfy a reader searching for legal dogma: taken out of context the sentence has the abstract and Olympian tone that judges (and other legal writers) often affect, a tone that implies that the reader is being presented with a *Diktat* from on high rather than a thought for her consideration. But in this opinion (as elsewhere) what Robert Jackson asks of his reader *is* reflection rather than mindless obedience—it was Jackson, you may recall, who famously disavowed for the Court any infallibility except in the brute sense that the Court is effectively beyond correction. ("We are not final because we are infallible, but we are infallible only because we are final."[14]) If we give the great Steel Seizure concurrence the slow reading à la Jim White that it invites, what I believe we hear in this sentence and later is Jackson's mind in yet a third register, looking not only backward to the experiences of the attorney general, or at the present duty of the judge who must decide, but forward, to the role that Jackson's words will play in the future for presidential advisors, and judges, and citizens, who will address problems that Jackson himself cannot foresee. It would be easy, and more satisfactory from the standpoint of the searcher for legal dogma, if we could at least treat this third voice, when we hear it over the course of the opinion, as Jackson's *final* word, and the more overtly personal voices as internal cogitations that have made their way, somewhat mysteriously and even unfortunately, onto the pages of the published opinion. But Jackson—on a slow reading—will not let us do that. Not even literally: the final words in the opinion are the judge's ("We follow the judicial tradition instituted on a memorable Sunday in 1612 [by] Chief Justice Coke").[15] More importantly, I believe that his opinion is constituted throughout by the conversation Jackson conducts by speaking distinctively through all three voices even if they converge on the judgment that Jackson announces in the heading of the opinion ("Mr. Justice JACKSON, concurring in the judgment and opinion of the Court"[16]) but only alludes to at its end.

This isn't the occasion on which to give Justice Jackson's entire concurrence in *Youngstown* the sort of slow reading that Jim White teaches us to do in his book on George Herbert and in many other places as well ... although such a reading of Jackson would be extremely rewarding. But we shouldn't leave Jackson without asking what to make of the famous bit of his opinion, "the familiar tripartite scheme," when we put that fragment back into its setting. We hear, I believe, the voice of Jackson the attorney general introducing the three categories that make up what the Court refers to as a scheme. Jackson imagines himself President Truman's advisor (just as he was in fact President Roosevelt's) and suggests that "a President [who] doubt[s] his powers" or worries that "others may challenge" his actions may find it useful to consider his decision in the light of "a somewhat over-simplified grouping of practical situations."[17] The three categories, in other words, are proposed in the first instance as a tool for deliberation *within* the executive branch, in discussions among the president and his advisors, before Jackson adopts them as a judge evaluating the legality of the steel seizure from the outside perspective of the Court. The puzzling description Jackson gives his middle category that I quoted earlier—the legality of some decisions depends on "the imperatives of events and contemporary imponderables"—is a deliberate observation about the difficulty of giving the president sound legal advice in conditions of uncertainty rather than an odd lapse into imprecision on the part of a judge who is not ordinarily wooly headed. When we hear the other two voices in the opinion pick up on the categories, as we immediately do, they are responding to a line of reasoning shaped by the practical and political concerns of the president's advisors and not just by what Jackson has termed "the conventional materials of judicial decision." Subsequent use of the categories by advocates, scholars and judges has turned them into precisely that—a conventional bit of black letter—a fact that is unsurprising but quite ironic.

I hope I have given some small indication of how fruitful the slow reading Jim White commends can be when it is applied to an opinion like Justice Jackson's concurrence in *Youngstown*. Its value is both analytical—we can make better sense of what Jackson meant—and pedagogical. My own introductory constitutional law materials give my first year students a substantial proportion of his opinion, and when I teach *Youngstown* I try to lead my students in studying the opinion through a process of slow reading. Just last fall one of my students commented that she thought Jackson's opinion was faulty because he made it possible for her to wonder whether he and the other justices in the majority had been right. I responded that her observation was directly on target—she was entirely right to read Jackson in that fashion—but that for myself it was Jackson's success in unveiling the uncertainties and difficulties in his own position as well as in the president's that made his concurrence a great opinion. And I do this, or try to, not just with Jackson and *Youngstown* but throughout the course and with respect to many of the opinions that my students and I read together. In teaching, in advocacy, and in responsible legal decisionmaking, White's slow reading is an enormously valuable practice—and not just for lawyers like me who love poetry! It is the age-old temptation of the advocate to pick out the useful phrases and ignore the thinking embodied in the words of an opinion. Our own era's taste for supposedly algorithmic forms of reasoning can reinforce our desire to deny the existence of difficulty and suppress our awareness of doubt, to pretend that by using the "right" intellectual technique we can avoid tension and uncertainty in our decisions. But as Charles Fried recently observed, "the search for security and objectivity in [such techniques] is a will-o'-the-wisp," and wise legal judgments depend on the exercise of "not just keenness of mind but prudence," the exercise of practical wisdom in decision in the presence of conflicts that cannot be eliminated by deductive logic.[18] Jim Whites work is a powerful antidote to these pathologies in the practice of law whatever our role in that practice.

If I have been at all successful, up to this point I have told the happy story of a brilliant and creative thinker who has a tremendous amount to contribute to law, and more particularly to the area of law that is my own specialty, American constitutional law. I have no doubt this story is true, but perhaps its truth is limited: Jim White is brilliant and creative but for reasons I shall now lay out, it isn't at all clear what and how much he can contribute to constitutional law. Not to leave anyone in suspense, let me say at once that the problem lies not in White's work but in constitutional law itself. I've tried to show how valuable White's slow reading can be for the constitutional lawyer by talking about Robert Jackson's opinion in *Youngstown*, but doing so (I must now confess) was a form of intellectual sleight of hand. Jackson is dead, which is sad enough on its own, but what is more, everything about Jackson's concurrence that makes it amenable to slow reading is, one might well argue, equally dead. Jackson wrote his Steel Seizure opinion with very little help from his clerks, one of whom was the young William Rehnquist; Jackson's notes and drafts are available, and reveal the care, intelligence, and even passion that Jackson invested not just in his judgment in the case but equally in the precise wording of his opinion; Jackson himself is often thought to be among a tiny handful of first-class writers in the history of the American bench. (G. Edward White's great essay on Jackson as a judge focuses much of its attention on the relationship between style and thought in Jackson's work.[19]) If there were only three or four other notable poets in English literature, Jim White's book on George Herbert would still be a great interpretation of Herbert, but its value for the general study of literature might seem considerably narrower than I believe it is. But perhaps there are only three or four other notable writer-judges in American constitutional law. Or, only slightly less dismally, however many such judges there were in the past, in essence they are no more: our modern practices have driven them to the brink of extinction.

My assumption is those who are familiar with contemporary constitutional law in the United States will scarcely need me to explain why I make this unhappy assertion, but for others and the record, let me state my reasons. First, it is generally believed, and apparently with good reason, that in recent decades the vast majority of federal judges (including the members of the United States Supreme Court) have left most of the chore of drafting opinions to their law clerks. My point is not to give credence to the occasional suggestion that clerks in their mid-twenties are determining the law of the land—in the sense of what the ultimate decisions are—while the putative judges are off on a frolic and detour: I don't believe that. But a judge who leaves the task of drafting an opinion to someone else, no matter how detailed her instructions, no matter how careful her editing, is simply not wrestling with the opinion, either in its reasoning or its expression, in the fashion that Jackson did superbly in *Youngstown*, and indeed that at one time all judges did, however well or poorly. Justice Louis Brandeis once said that "the reason the public thinks so much of the Justices of the Supreme Court is that they are almost the only people in Washington who do their own work."[20] If the justices' work involves not just determining outcomes but explaining those outcomes and shaping the language of the law for the future—as Brandeis certainly thought it was—then most recent justices no longer do much of their own work. It isn't at all clear what value there is in applying Jim White's technique of slow reading to documents that are in very substantial measure not the work of their putative authors but instead the output of a "writing" process more akin to the production of a committee report than to the creation of a poem.

The source of my second reason for worry that we can't usefully bring Jim White's approach to bear on constitutional law opinions is a book entitled *Living Speech* by one James Boyd White(!).[21] In that book, White identifies "living speech" as "speech that is deeply meant ... that comes from the center of the person, and is addressed to the center of its audience; speech worthy of real attention; speech upon which both individual and shared life can be built."[22] Speech, in short, of the kind that we find in a Herbert poem and a Jackson opinion. (White in fact discusses several Jackson opinions as exemplifying living speech.) In contrast, White evokes powerfully the pervasiveness in contemporary life of "dead language," "the reiteration of clichés, formulas, slogans,"[23] the language of advertising, propaganda, publicity, sentimentality, expression that is "empty, strategic, manipulative,"[24] that seeks to control the recipient without offering her any access to the actual thoughts and intentions of the generator of the expression. About the law, White writes, with painful accuracy:

> Lawyers are all too familiar with this sort of speaking and writing, of which a certain kind of brief can be taken as an example: one that pieces together rules and quotations, makes distinctions, argues to conclusions, but without ever making it the work of the individual mind ... [The writer's] effort is not actually to think through the legal problem and express his thought in legal language ... but to sound like someone doing those things: to sound like a lawyer, not to be one. The reader of such a brief is offered not the work of a mind with which he or she can engage, but something very different ... none of which is truly meant.[25]

The point of course is not that all legal language must present the lawyer's private opinion on the best reading of the law—someone writing a brief, for example, is an advocate whose role is to present the most persuasive reasons supporting her client's position rather than to express her views of the law in the abstract. A judge writing an opinion expressing a judgment that he believes compelled by erroneous but controlling precedent is in a somewhat similar position. But in any legal context, we can see the difference between the living speech of a lawyer actively engaged with the legal issues she must address and one who is just going through the motions. It is the former, not the latter, who is effective, even as an advocate: Justice Brandeis once commented that Robert Jackson should be "Solicitor General for life" in recognition of the way that Jackson brought the same investment of mind and thought into his work as the government's advocate (where his conclusions were predetermined) that he would later display in his judicial opinions.[26]

Unfortunately, I think it is fair to say that a great many U.S. Supreme Court opinions in recent decades have been prime exemplars of dead speech. (White gives examples in his book.) This problem is undoubtedly related to the practice of clerkly ghostwriting, and other factors, perhaps including such lowly factors as the seductive ease of electronic research and the copy-and-paste function, are at work as well. But the problem of dead language in the constitutional opinions of the high Court is distinct from its causes and might not disappear even if all the justices started doing their own work in the sense of drafting their own opinions. I referred earlier to our time's attraction to what I called allegedly algorithmic lines of argument. In the courts and in the academy, those who advocate forms of constitutional decisionmaking that promise, or at least appear to promise, a means of eliminating the role of judgment in difficult cases often seem to be in the ascendancy. "Lawyers' work," we are assured, has to do with "texts and traditions [that] are facts to study," and reaching the proper decision in a constitutional case neither requires nor (when the judge understands her role correctly) permits the sort of creative wrestling with normative issues that Justice Jackson undertook in *Youngstown*.[27]

It is Jackson, and not our contemporary constitutional dogmatists (who disagree in ideology but not in their commitment to dogmatic certainty), who stands in the American constitutional tradition. The great Benjamin Cardozo said of Chief Justice Marshall that "he gave to the constitution of the United States the impress of his own mind; and the form of our constitutional law is what it is, because he moulded it ... in the fire of his own intense convictions."[28] On Cardozo's view of constitutional law, we should hope and expect for constitutional opinions that are living speech in Jim White's sense and that we can profitably approach through his slow reading. But Judge (and later Justice) Cardozo, and if Cardozo was right Chief Justice Marshall, too, were heretics by the standards of today's warring, would-be orthodoxies: what White calls dead language is probably a virtue from those varying perspectives because their shared use of dead speech eliminates from constitutional law the role of the individual mind and normative judgment they so abhor. Jim's style of slow reading—it might be thought—is of little use for a constitutional lawyer in an era of ghostwritten opinions produced under the aegis of judges many of whom seek, as a matter of principle, to treat constitutional decisionmaking as an investigation into facts rather than a wise judgment about norms. That is not my view, but we cannot grasp what White's contribution may be unless we first acknowledge how uncongenial to his vision the current scene truly is.

Jim White's book on *Living Speech* is remarkable in many ways, not least because it is in fact four or five books happily coexisting in one fairly slender volume: a moral philosophy of human communication, a social critique of contemporary American society, a study of judicial opinion-writing, a proposal to reorient First Amendment thought, and (not least of all) a fascinating and thoroughly persuasive interpretation of Dante's *Divine Comedy*. I won't even try to explain how one book can do all that! What is important for this paper is that it is through White's treatment of Dante's great poem that I get a glimpse of how I think his overall approach to reading texts might find purchase in the apparently hostile world of contemporary constitutional law.

As White notes in *Living Speech* when he first introduces Dante, on its face the *Divine Comedy* might seem to portray and indeed celebrate the ultimate "empire of force:" "Dante's theological emperor, the Deity, is omnipotent and has used his power, especially in creating the Inferno, to define and maintain the moral coherence of the universe as he has imagined it into existence."[29] Dante's would be a universe, it seems, of absolute power enforcing a theological "ideology working out its iron logic without hitches or gaps or cracks, a system of thought and imagination in which there [is] no place for you, except as a subordinate." The eternal punishment of the damned in the Inferno could only be the ultimate expression of a world that is "perfectly authoritarian."[30] In such a world, speech cannot ultimately be the mode through which the living thoughts of the speaker evoke the active response of the hearer and so build a shared life, because in the end the only speech possible is dead speech, the unquestionable decrees of a universal despot and the respectively servile or despairing utterances of those who cower or rebel in equal helplessness before him.

There have certainly been Christians who have understood the universe in these terms, and no doubt when they took note of Dante they construed the *Divine Comedy* accordingly. What Jim White does over the course of *Living Speech* is to argue, convincingly, that this is not *Dante's* understanding of the universe or the meaning of his poem, that in fact Dante employs his poetic and intellectual gifts "to keep the highly juridical world that he imagines into existence in this poem from becoming an empire of force ... by ... mak[ing] necessary the presence and place and judgment of the reader ... one who must be satisfied in his or her own mind, and not simply rest on a set of authoritative declarations."[31] As White writes near the end of his book:

> The effect of this is to compel the reader to assert his own judgment about the matter, thus constituting him as an independent mind, forcing him to think things through in a way for which he will himself be responsible. The poem thus seems written to express and celebrate orthodox Christian views, but to resist authoritarian and empty ways of conceiving of them.[32]

Authoritarian speech, by definition, is dead speech: it offers no genuine explanations, it can only command or manipulate the hearer, who is thereby reduced, whether knowingly or not, to the object of (at least) verbal force. What Dante did in the *Divine Comedy*, White shows, was to take a theological language that might seem inextricably authoritarian—an omnipotent Deity, inexorable decrees—and make it into a commendation and exemplar of living speech that "constitutes the reader as an independent mind" and invites the reader to address "the problem of justice [that is] at the center of our own experience of the world."

It was not an option for Dante (I mean an existential option) to reject the "orthodox Christian views" including the punishment of the damned and relegation of Virgil to an eternity of "desire without hope."[33] Dante was well aware of the way that this orthodox language could be understood in authoritarian terms, as what White would term empty or dead speech. (See White"s discussion of Guido da Montefeltro.[34]) But he refused to understand the language of orthodoxy in this fashion or to use it that way himself. Instead, Dante took the orthodoxy he had inherited and made of it the means by which he leads the reader to perceive that as human beings we ought not submit without question to divine decrees regardless of their apparent injustice, but instead we should view "the question of justice as a real and valid one, the nerve of human life ... to which it is our task to respond as well as we can, as it is our task to respond to life itself."[35]

American constitutional law does not concern itself directly with the ultimate questions of existence posed by the *Divine Comedy*, but the issues it does address are important enough, and I believe that Jim White's reading of Dante suggests the stance constitutional lawyers might take toward the dead speech that makes up much of contemporary constitutional law. The language of Supreme Court opinions, whether written by a master like Jackson or promulgated under the name of a less engaged justice, is central to constitutional law; indeed, the use of those opinions in reasoning and argument is a defining characteristic of constitutional law as American lawyers have practiced it historically. Great opinions such as Jackson's in *Youngstown* invite and reward White's slow reading, and model for the rest of us how we ourselves should write and reason in the law. White's approach is valuable, however, even when applied to the more common examples of dead speech that clutter the volumes of the United States Reports because it allows the reader to unmask the presence of the formulaic and unthinking, and to see more clearly what substantive issues a poor opinion obscures or with which it fails to wrestle. Not, I hasten to add, that we ought to rest easy with current judicial practice: I think the rest of us ought to be far more critical than we are of judicial practices such as the overuse of clerks. Instead of seeking mindless commitments to "interpret not make law" from Supreme Court nominees the Senate Judiciary Committee ought to ask of nominees the meaningful commitment to imitate Jackson and draft their own opinions.

American constitutional lawyers need not and ought not wait upon the wholesale conversion of justices and senators to living speech. It is open to the rest of us to take the materials of constitutional argument—the Court's opinions but other sources of argument as well—and treat them as the raw materials for a style of constitutional debate and decisionmaking that would treat the exercise of prudence and judgment as unavoidable, legal argument as an invitation to think together even if we do not in the end agree, and the uncertainties and tensions that attend any difficult legal issue as matters to be confronted directly rather than concealed or denied. The often-decried tendency of the modern Court to splinter, thus producing a sometimes bewildering array of concurrences, part-concurrences and dissents, need not be seen as an unmitigated vice from the perspective of the slow reader. Separate opinions make it more difficult for the legal dogmatist to find *the* black letter rule in the decision, but for a lawyer whose habits of reading are informed by Jim White they often expose by their external disagreements the lines of contention and uncertainty that a great judge like Robert Jackson incorporated into the substance of his opinions.

This last may seem entirely too quixotic, so I want to conclude with a specific proposal for my fellow teachers of constitutional law—I do not think Jim White, a great teacher and a very serious one, will think it inappropriate to end on a pedagogical note. The introductory constitutional law course in U.S. law schools, which most schools and teachers seem to think should be a survey of the field, is increasingly unable to accomplish that goal because there is simply too much constitutional law to cover. The area of constitutional law that is most often at issue in the courts, constitutional criminal procedure, exited the introductory course decades ago, and the First Amendment now seems to be following it, but at some point the ruthless exclusion of entire areas of the law will make it absurd to see the course as a survey. The proper solution, I believe, is to recognize with Jim White that the fundamental educational need is to learn how to read, whether what we want to read is George Herbert's poetry or the Supreme Court's decisions. Our objective in the introductory course should not be to run through some unavoidably incomplete list of constitutional topics but to bring the students into engagement with meaningful practices of constitutional argument and judgment in constitutional decision. In doing so, as Jackson's concurrence illustrates, we need to reconsider the common habit of stripping constitutional opinions down to their doctrinal "core"—even an inadequate opinion may offer more for thought and discussion in what a thoughtless editor might dismiss as "dicta" than can be found in the bits excerpted in the headnotes.

The unsatisfactory nature of many of the high Court's opinions should not stop the teacher from inculcating in her students the habits of slow reading that Jim White advocates: as I learned long ago from his book on Herbert, slow reading proceeds in large measure by seeking out the lines of stress and contradiction in what one reads. A ghostwritten and thoughtless opinion patched together out of quotations from earlier cases may not be admirable work, but read in White's fashion the very ways in which it employs (or lapses into) bombast or cliché will often reveal, however unwittingly, the fault lines in the position the opinion advocates and suggest the questions that a serious engagement with the issues before the Court—and the class—must consider. When approached as a course about learning to read judicial opinions, constitutional law need be neither a slide-show presentation of ideologically driven outcomes nor an exercise in pretending that the justices always make sense: instead, it can introduce the students to the skills and habits of slow reading and living speech that will make them better lawyers and, I even hope, better citizens. It is all too easy to find constitutional law, and the task of teaching it, depressing. It is one of Jim White's many contributions that he can make both the subject and the teaching a source of inspiration.

Notes

1. J. B. White, *"This Book of Starres": Learning to Read George Herbert* (Ann Arbor: University of Michigan Press, 1994).
2. White, *"This Book of Starres,"* xvi.
3. White, *"This Book of Starres,"* xvi.
4. For example, White, *"This Book of Starres,"* xxi.
5. White, *"This Book of Starres,"* 11–12.
6. White, *"This Book of Starres,"* 20.
7. 343 U.S. 579 (1952).
8. *Dames & Moore v Regan*, 453 U.S. 654, 661 (1981).
9. *Medellin v Texas*, 552 U.S. 491, 524 (2008).
10. See generally H Jefferson Powell, *The President as Commander in Chief: An essay in constitutional vision* (Durham, NC, Carolina Academic Press, 2013).
11. *Youngstown* (note 7), 634.
12. *Youngstown* (note 7), 647.
13. *Youngstown* (note 7), 641.
14. *Brown v Allen*, 344 U.S. 443, 540 (1953) (concurring in the result).
15. *Youngstown* (note 7), 655 n27.
16. *Youngstown* (note 7), 634

17. *Youngstown* (note 7), 635.
18. C. Fried, "On Judgment," *Lewis & Clark Law Review* 15 (2011): 1021, 1045. Citing Aristotle, Professor Fried commends, as "the best means for teaching and acquiring [the] virtue" of prudential judgment, the study of "persons who to a high degree exhibit the virtue" and includes Robert Jackson on a very short list of judges with that virtue (1045). Jim White's slow reading can be an invaluable part of such study.
19. G. Edward White, *The American Judicial Tradition: Profiles of Leading American Judges*, 3rd ed. (Oxford: Oxford University Press, 2007), 184–91.
20. J. S. Rosenthal and A. H. Yoon, "Judicial Ghostwriting: Authorship on the Supreme Court," *Cornell Law Review* 96 (2011): 1307, 1307.
21. J. B. White, *Living Speech: Resisting the Empire of Force* (Princeton, NJ: Princeton University Press, 2006).
22. White, *Living Speech*, 16.
23. White, *Living Speech*, 16.
24. White, *Living Speech*, 164.
25. White, *Living Speech*, 15.
26. V. A. Graffeo, "Robert H. Jackson: His Years as a Public Servant 'Learned in the Law,'" *Albany Law Review* 68 (2005): 539, 542.
27. The quoted language is from *Planned Parenthood v Casey*, 505 U.S. 833, 1000 (1992) (separate opinion).
28. B. N. Cardozo, *The Nature of the Judicial Process* (New Haven, CT: Yale University Press, 1921), 169–70.
29. White, *Living Speech*, 17. The expression "empire of force" comes from Simone Weil. The first sentence in the introduction to *Living Speech* comments that "in an important sense this entire book is an extended essay on the single sentence … taken from Simone Weil's wonderful essay on the *Iliad*: "No one can love and be just who does not understand the empire of force and how not to respect it." White, *Living Speech*, 1. Weil's essay is entitled "L'Iliade, ou le poème de la force" and was originally published in *Cahiers du Sud* (December 1940–January 1941); the translation of the quoted sentence is White's.
30. White, *Living Speech*, 21.
31. White, *Living Speech*, 25.
32. White, *Living Speech*, 201. White is specifically discussing the way in which the *Divine Comedy*, which in accordance with contemporaneous theological opinion locates the great Roman poet Virgil in the limbo reserved for righteous pagans, "make[s] us feel, repeatedly and acutely, that Virgil's treatment is unjust." (White, *Living Speech*, 202–3). Dante deliberately raises this issue for the reader, implicitly driving the latter toward reaching her own judgment, unlike the character "Dante," who "seems to accept Virgil's fate as a doctrinal matter, without explanation." White, *Living Speech*, 201).
33. White, *Living Speech*, 202 n33.
34. Guido da Montefeltro was a thirteenth-century Italian mercenary whom Dante located in the Inferno because he advised Pope Boniface VIII to betray a promise of amnesty to certain enemies of Boniface. The Pope promised to absolve Guido of his treacherous counsel but Hell successfully laid claim to his soul because an

unrepented sin cannot be absolved and Guido's "repentance" and his agreement to give the wicked advice coincided in time: as a demon explained, "'it is not possible to repent and will [the same wrong deed] at the same time.'" White points out that "what really rankles Guido," when he discusses his damnation with the character "Dante," "is not that he gave the false counsel for which he is punished but that he ... was outfoxed by Boniface." (White, *Living Speech*, 162.) But White continues that the "real reason Guido is in the Inferno is the way he imagined the whole world, including the moral and religious law of God [which he saw] as a system of deterrence and incentives, essentially manipulative and inviting a manipulative reading on his part." (White, *Living Speech*, 162.) Unlike Dante, to Guido the most impeccably orthodox theological language was dead speech.

35. White, *Living Speech*, 201, 202 n33.

[6]

The Impossible Prayers of James Boyd White

Jack L. Sammons

Introduction

One way of reading James Boyd White's work is as a lifelong search for a religious voice that he could use with his students and the largely unknown and predominantly secular audience for his academic work. One is reminded in this of Bonhoeffer's references to the need for a non-religious language in which to proclaim the gospel "so to utter the word of God that the world will be changed and renewed by it."[1] Jim found a religious voice, I believe, and I will try to describe it here through considering his approach to literary texts from the perspective of this search. The voice he found, however, is not, as the Bonhoeffer quote might suggest—Bonhoeffer does not mean it this way—one that translates the word of God for a secular world. What he found instead was a religious voice through which he could prepare his students and readers for hearing that word, letting God's word, as it were, speak for itself. There is more to this than preparation, however. For Jim's unique religious voice has permitted him to offer to his secular audiences an alternative to their lives they may not have been able to consider otherwise, and in this to view those lives quite differently. In other words, he does what Stan Hauerwas says the church must always do[2]: tell the world that it is the world.

I am not suggesting through this description of Jim's work that he set out with this issue in mind, that it motivated his work, that he had a hidden religious agenda, or that his was a straight path towards discovery. Instead, I think the issue of speaking in a religious voice simply kept arising for him, and that we can understand each of his academic works as addressing some aspect of it, although I cannot do the analysis this claim requires here. I am saying, however, that the sermons Jim now writes, almost exclusively, do not just share a personal impulse with his academic work, nor are they just harmonious with it (although that they are), but that these sermons are a fulfillment of his life's work, and as such offer an important perspective on it.

In doing this, I will not explicate things Jim has said about this issue of a religious voice in a secular world. In fact, he has said very little directly.[3] Instead, I will try as best I can to set forth the theological implications of his performances of a very particular way of reading literary texts.

This is my destination. Frankly, it involves a journey beyond my capabilities. My hope, however, is that the path will be interesting enough to encourage others better suited for it to undertake the trip.

But Jim, as many of you may be thinking, has been resolute in keeping the religious voice he uses in his sermons—a voice only a few know—out of his academic work. In fact, he has been criticized for doing exactly this.[4] Because this is true, I think I should assist readers for whom this introduction may seem odd to get onboard before the train departs. To do this, we will start with an analysis of one of Jim's published sermons. This should permit me to set forth the issue of finding a religious voice for a secular audience in stark relief.

A Sermon on Love and Justice

In his sermon[5] on the parable of "the laborers in the vineyard" from the Gospel of Matthew, Jim wonders how paying the laborers taken in at the last moment of the day the same as those who worked all day can be offered by Jesus as an image of the Kingdom. In response to grumbling about this generous payment, the landowner says, "Friend, I am doing you no wrong; did you not agree with me for the usual daily wages? Take what belongs to you and go; I choose to give to this last the same as I give to you. Am I not allowed to do what I choose with what belongs to me"?[6] And the parable ends with Jesus saying, "So the last will be first, and the first will be last."[7]

This parable, Jim says, tells those gathered to hear his sermon that God's economy is not like ours—not one of proportions and entitlements—but is as "unjust" in our terms as forgiveness is.[8] It asks that we "give up the idea of justice for ourselves and with it the claims [justice] enables us to make upon others."[9] But how can we make sense of this? Wouldn't this give up the core of our social identity? One way out of this puzzle, he says, is to consider that the Master in the parable represents God "and that what he is giving the laborers is not money, but [undeserved] love."[10] In such an economy, unlike our own, there is no scarcity. When Jesus says that the first shall be last and the last first, He is telling us that in the Kingdom, "there is no competition, no striving to dominate, no exaction for wrongs, no struggle for scarce benefits."[11] In addition—and here is the crucial challenge to our thinking—all things are "subject to [this] larger economy of love."[12] When we connect our world to the world of the parable—and this is what the parable requires of us as readers—we can then imagine for ourselves a way of acting out of love, and doing so with things that are indeed scarce in our world, including life itself.[13]

This sermon's essence is as prayer, specifically one at the heart of Christian thought: Christ's prayer at Gethsemane, ending with "not my will, but yours be done."[14] For God, the sermon tells us, has willed that we live in the abundance of His gift of creation. This, it says, is offered as the truth of who we are, a truth to be tested against the experience of our lives. This message, however, is not a proposition. Instead, the parable works as a performance, as parables always do, by putting the reader's world into question when she imagines herself within the world of the story—"connecting to the Gospel," as the title of Jim's collection of sermons says—and the sermon displays this way of reading.

Through reading this way, something can be revealed and the reader transformed from his or her ordinary perceptions of justice by it. In a sense, the only way out of the parable is through a transforming revelation offering the potential of a new identity. In this the meaning of the parable—a meaning that can only be experienced—arises "in front of the text" between the text and the reader. And it is always there, always fresh, always generative, and always then to be preached anew. The parable's meaning is, in fact, as inexhaustible as God's gift of creation for this plentitude of meaning is part of that gift.

When the sermon tells us that the Master is a reference to God, Jim is reminding his parishioners that this is a parable offered by the One who preached in parables. In other words, you cannot read the parable in isolation from the rest of the text, which in its entirety is about the naming of this God. Transforming revelations then must be understood as revelations about this naming of God to be true to the text. In fact, it is through an understanding of her relationship to this textual naming of God, the sermon says, that the reader comes to know who she is and who she can become.

The world of this parable then is larger than its story suggests, larger even then the hermeneutic process I have just described. The transformation of love and justice it offers is more than a transformation of "worlds" for it cannot be completed in terms of any grand narrative or against any particular horizon. This expansion beyond grand narratives or particular horizons, then, is what the text demands. It must in fact if it is to lead the reader to that which it offers for her testing. So there is a sense in which this parable cannot be well read in the way I have just described; it requires something more: a reading of the text "as sermon" as Jim has done—a communal continuation of a process already at work in the text—and to this sermonic way of reading we will return later.

The God named in the rest of the text, however, cannot be named. It is polyphonic (and polymodal, to continue the musical terms that work best) and the variety of words we use to describe it reflects this polyphony as clearly as anything could, for there is no word or concept that could escape the multiplicities of the text's literary form—it is a library as Ricoeur says—and still be true to its naming of an unnamable God.

With this observation, let me turn to Paul Ricoeur to say that this naming of that which cannot be named also does not occur in the text. It too has meaning only in front of the text.[15] From the dramatic Walter Brueggemann, who wrote the introduction to Jim's book of sermons, we can add: "Thus even with reference to God, the imaginative, generative power of rhetoric offers to the hearer of this text a God not otherwise known or available or even—dare one say—not otherwise 'there.'"[16] This is not to say that the God of Jim's sermon is a rhetorical construct, but that God is a reality outside of the text "endlessly in the process of being rhetorically constructed."[17] Thus, with this text, as Jim reads it, there is no back-of-the-book answer. If asked what it really means, what is the name of God, or what is the unity of the text, one would need to refer back to the whole text—including all its internal tensions and inconsistencies—as one might do with the meaning of a poem that is there only in its performance. And, in fact, what I have described as Jim's way of reading the Gospel is best described as poetic—a "dwell[ing] in possibili[ties]" as Emily Dickinson puts this[18]—and yet it is one, as the sermon clearly shows, with great ethical, moral, and political consequences. As Jim's sermonic reading says, the parable addresses the issue of love and justice by offering to each reader the experience of a world alternative to her own, and, more than this, an alternative to "world" in which love and justice are one.

The Problem

Now imagine that your life's work is to teach and write about this issue of love and justice—the central emergent theme of Jim's work.[19] Imagine as well that the way in which you do this is as "living speech," always seeking to speak from your own heart, often autobiographically. Finally, imagine that your readers are inclined to say that your work has a certain, appealing, sermonic quality to it. It seems, that is, addressed in a surprising way to the unique person each reader is. Now, if this sermon represents what you have come to think about love and justice over time, how could you possibly say or write about this to your secular audience? How could you speak in the religious voice your own message now requires: not to the choir, but to the culture, and do so in its language?

The problems of doing this are familiar. These include, of course, the problems of translation, as Jim might put it, but they are not entirely this. The meaning of love and justice in the sermon, as we have seen, is embedded in the fullness of the sacred text within a church that speaks in such a different register with such a specialized vocabulary that we typically describe the church as having its own language. To try to speak of the Master as God in the language of the dominant culture would surely be to distort and to corrupt what is meant, for it would turn the meaning of the crucial term over to that culture and away from the text. It could not help but do this, for the language of the dominant culture always find a way to fit words like the religious words of the sermon within its own "enframing" of our lives, to use Heidegger's term[20] to which we will return; an enframing the culture mostly conceal from us. In other words, the dominance of the culture is such, the hierarchy of the status quo so imposing, that it takes over these words as it does everything else, turning them to its purposes, most often without our ever noticing. Thus, to speak of this Master as God within this culture would not be to offer an alternative to the culture at all. Instead, it would be to render God a vague spirituality at most or a question of belief rather than of trust; resembling the God of the Gospel, the Master of the sermon, not at all.

As I said, these problems are familiar. One problem, however, hinted at in the term "enframing," is not as well known. It is to this problem that I will turn my attention here because it is the problem Jim's work addresses most directly (and in doing so addresses the others as well.)

Following Heidegger, but with a theological turn Heidegger refused, it seems to me that the mode of thought religion requires—a mode of thought which should become clearer as we go along—has gone missing from the culture. What I mean is that as a culture we no longer know how to think religiously. This is more than a problem of language, although that it is; it is a problem of our inability to have the experiences that we call religious, and, therefore, to make sense of the expression of such experiences in any language.

If this is true, seeking a religious voice for a secular audience would seem an impossible task. Perhaps then the message of the prayer that is Jim's sermon simply cannot be offered to Jim's other audiences. And perhaps this is where we should leave it. Learn to live with this tension, as Jim says in *"This Book of Starres."*[21] Yet to learn to live with a tension is not to ignore it, and if your business is this matter of love and justice you cannot leave the problems of impossible prayers. The issue will press upon you over time, as I believe it has upon Jim.

There are those within the church—people I greatly admire—who would also suggest abandoning this effort as impossible.[22] These theologians are not suggesting abandoning the culture, the sectarian option as it is called. They think, instead, that the best way for the church to be an alternative to the culture is to first be the church: to learn to speak Christian, as Hauerwas puts it.[23] There is great truth in this, but "learning to speak Christian" requires a broader culture, not just a church, in which Christian can be spoken. We often speak, as I did before, of the church having its own language, but the language of the church is not autonomous. Even the specialized vocabulary of its unique register is always understood against a backdrop of the language of the dominant culture in which it is embedded. Just as dissonance in music is dissonance because it is always heard against an aural assumption of consonance, words like the Kingdom of God, the Lamb of God, the Good Shepherd, and even the Incarnation, mean what they do, in part, because they are always heard, even within the church, against what they are not. The words that are (endlessly) absent, as Derrida might put this,[24] are just as important to their meaning as the words that are present.

This is no small matter (and will become important here later on). It says that to be an alternative to a culture is, in no small part, to be defined by that culture. Yet if our culture, as I have said, is no longer capable of religious thinking, the church can only be an alternative to it, (and its words can only have the sort of meaning they do in the sermon, even within the church) if there remains somewhere within the culture the sort of religious experience upon which religious thinking depends.

(Practically speaking, not to search for these experiences would be the theological equivalency of the Shakers' abandonment of procreation.)

But now it is time to leave the sermon and its theology and to turn to Jim's secular work. I want to read these now, however, from the perspective of the sermon and this search for a religious voice. Bonhoeffer thought that "to utter the word of God so that the world will be changed and renewed by it"[25] was not a simple matter of translation from the language of the church to the language of the dominant secular culture. If, as I have suggested, the mode of thinking religion requires has gone missing from the culture, seeking to find a nonreligious language in which to proclaim the Gospel would surely be futile: the equivalent of listening to Wittgenstein's lion who learned to speak. What was needed, Bonhoeffer said, was not translation. It was instead the example of Christ's healings: "… these are events in which people are concretely drawn into a share in the vulnerability of God, into a new kind of life and a new identity. They do not receive an additional item called faith; their ordinary existence is not reorganized … : it is transfigured as a whole."[26] And, in this example, we can see a turn away from language towards experience or event, a turn towards something beyond language as Jim puts it.[27] It is to this turn that we will now turn our attention.

A Way of Reading as Art

As I read him, Jim's work starts with a personal concern for law students entering the practice of law. His primary motivating question is: how can my students find personal meaning in the life of a lawyer? To answer this question well, however, requires an examination of the broader question of our relationship to all traditions that threaten to dominate our lives. This is, Jim says, a question for law students about appropriating the language (and languages) of the legal tradition because each tradition is carried within its language: Can these students make this language their own in some meaningful sense?[28] This is also the question all of us must always try to answer for we are always in some fashion appropriating the traditions in which we live. Not to do this, Jim argues, would be to abandon our lives to tradition such that our lives could no longer be called our own. Resistance to this is always required, for we are all, in Nicholas Lash's felicitous phrase "spontaneously idolatrous,"[29] or, as Heidegger puts this, "das Mann" is not just something to be avoided, it is also who we are.[30] (Later on, Jim will borrow Simone Weil's term, "Empire of Force," to capture a violent and oppressive form of this natural idolatry he has always opposed.)

Law students, however, cannot make the language of the legal tradition their own, nor can we make any tradition our own, from the perspective of selves standing outside these traditions. And if the perspective must be from within, are we not then bound by the language of the tradition such that we lose our freedom to be who we are? For Jim, as for Ricoeur,[31] Gadamer,[32] and others the answer is no because traditions are not reified objects there to be examined at a distance by a subject. They are instead living "selves": open, alive, and "their meaning, value, and significance are completed only in their interpretation into [other] selves' own unfolding narrative identities."[33] Being within these living traditions is not a limitation on our freedom to be who we are, but the way in which we do this. We come to know who we are, we come to know what our traditions are, and we constitute and reconstitute both ourselves and our traditions only through an ongoing, intentional, and creative engagement, one through which as we appropriate our traditions we also appropriate ourselves.[34] And so Jim's law students, to own their own lives as lawyers, *must* struggle to work this out within the tradition that is the practice of law.

The question remains, however, how can they or how can we appropriate the language of a tradition from within it. For Jim, we can by reading literary texts: those that carry the tradition's language, and the culture within which it is embedded, within them. Through these texts we can "interrupt the relation of belonging [to a tradition] in order to signify it,"[35] Ricoeur says, for these texts provide a "distanciation,"[36] from both the tradition and ourselves such that meaning can be found in both. In more formal terms, because in literary fiction (and the law is such a fiction) "we start with an image without an original, then we may discover a second kind of ontology which is not the ontology of the original but the ontology displayed by the image itself because it has no original."[37] For texts to have this emancipatory function, however (and this, it seems to me, is not adequately displayed in Ricoeur, Gadamer, or Heidegger) they must be read in a particular way: metaphorically it is a patient farming in the text's soil to bring forth its bounty. It is this way of reading that Jim has spent his life performing for us.

Jim's way of reading—much of what follows will be familiar to his readers—starts in a respectful humility towards the text—a beginning step away from subjectivity so that it might be recovered in a far more modest role. Central to this (and central to Jim's lexicon[38]) is an act of imagination. Through creative imagination we look not at the author or at what the author has done, but *with* the author: standing where the author stands in order to be grasped by that which, uncovered in her art, grasped the author in its particularity.[39] In this, we do not enter the text, but its imagined world, a world which can call our own into question.

In the dynamic interplay of this clash of worlds, a "cultural dislocation" as he calls it,[40] words central to the tradition, like "love" and "justice," are suddenly opened to an infinity of meanings,[41] thus making clear our responsibility to discover their meaning *for us*, and, in doing so, to give life to both ourselves and to the traditions of which we are a part. In this, readers humble enough to be willing to risk their self-understanding can be transformed, and uncover through these experiences a different potential identity with ethical, moral, and political consequences, which offers a better way of life. It is a narrative identity, but one constantly "mak[ing] and unmak[ing] itself."[42] This process, Jim says, is a primary, perhaps universal, human project, one in which who we are always remains a work-in-progress.[43] For Jim in fact, this is a project that defines and constitutes our humanity.[44]

These transformations can be as common as a pun—two worlds of one expression colliding in a strange fashion (Velcro! What a rip off!)—as rare as Milton, or (and with different "texts") as surprising as Schoenberg's music or the paintings of Cézanne. But even when they are surprising, the identity we find in these is something always already there to be uncovered through the experience the text provides. And yet it is also not there: something potential, something still to come. It is both a past (we can never fully attend) and a projection (we can never fully realize or even know). In fact, it is this orientation of a past toward a possibility that makes these transformations, and the identity they offer, meaningful for us. We can then describe Jim's way of reading, as he might, as this ongoing creation of meaning.

Notice that in this way of reading—especially in looking with the author at that which grasped her—the reader is asked to adopt the same attitude toward the literary text that the sculptor has toward marble, the guitar maker toward wood, or the composer toward music. She is asked, that is, to open herself to it so that she might hear it speaking to her in compelling ways. The meaning she experiences through this, as we have noted, is not then a meaning that comes only from her. She knows it is not as these artists know that their creations are not entirely their own. But neither is it a meaning that can come only from the texts. In fact, the question to which the words of text responds is not the same question as the one it opens up to the reader. In this sense, its meaning for her is always "in front of the text" (as meaning was in the parable) and beyond its author: a meaning received and constituted simultaneously by the reader; a meaning both discovered and created in the act of reading; something thought in the middle voice; and something that, once thought, seems in retrospect to have been inevitable, as is true of all good art.[45] For what I have just described as Jim's way of reading—starting in respectful humility, driven by creative imagination, listening attentively to the voice of the materials of the literary art, grasped by something uncovered there, and so forth, is a description of a way of reading that is itself an art.

But What Is Art?

It would be possible to say here that by showing us this art Jim has offered to the culture the possibility of a religious experience, one that could permit religious thinking to return to it. It is possible, that is, to associate our experience of art with a transcendence, and possible then to call this experience religious. This is an experience, one might add, not far removed from the sort of religious voice grounded in experience Bonhoeffer described, and from it we could discover that the religious voice left within our culture is the artist's voice. It would be possible to say these things; it would be possible to leave it at this, but it would be far from convincing.

Art for our culture is not art as Jim has presented it. Art for our culture is aesthetic: either subjective expression or objective emotion (subjectivity's mirror image) and, in either case, something to be used. We often describe the beauty of art as transcendent, but, however pleasurable and important we may feel this beauty to be, it not something central to our lives; rather it is an escape: done as if on holiday. Associating our experience of art's beauty with a transcendence, and if with a transcendence then with religious experience, would be to turn our experience of art over to the culture in the way Jim's work resists. It would be merely "sentimental" to put it Jim's terms. To do this in fact would only return us to the problem of religious thought gone missing with which we started. For in the language of the dominant culture that which is transcendent is but a mystery to us, and, as a mystery it is nothing: ultimately meaningless and of no consequence because it cannot be thought.

And yet what the culture calls "mystery" is not "nothing," even for the culture, for this "nothing" delimits and thereby constitutes the culture's legitimate fields of thought. Despite its rhetorical importance to the culture, however, the culture constantly conceals mystery from us. In Heidegger's description, this is the result of a technological enframing of our world which refuses in its manic subjectivism to accept any limits on our own control.[46] It is such an enframing, he says, that conceals art's uncovering of our finitude from us, and by concealing it reduces art to the aesthetic.[47]

The art Jim offers through his way of reading is not this; it is not something peripheral. It is instead, as we have seen, something defining and central to who we are; something which turns upon mystery, as he acknowledges.[48] For Jim's art is not primarily about beauty, nor is it primarily about transcendence, it is instead about truth. "Art is truth setting itself to work," says Heidegger,[49] and Jim's art of reading displays this work of truth to us. In order to see that it does, however, we need to reconsider what he means by mystery.

As we have seen, the meaning that can arise from the clash of worlds in front of the text that is Jim's way of reading is not something chosen based on other values.[50] It cannot be this, we said, if it is to have its desired emancipatory effect. In other words, to appropriate a text (and a language and a tradition) is not and cannot be to impose one's own capacity for understanding upon it. In fact, considering this a matter of choice would leave the reader bound either to self or to tradition as the sources of the driving values. In simple Augustinian terms, words, like 'love' and 'justice' can never mean what we would like them to mean for these words do not belong to us.

Our inability to provide their meaning, however, also shows us that we are also incapable of providing our own identity, so tied are we to these words. Thus, the identities uncovered in the transformative experiences Jim leads us to, however much of a struggle may precede them, come upon us not as choices, not as decisions, not as something consciously thought, but more as intuitions prompted by imagination, the call of conscience as others describe it, the inner voice most my own because it is not my own, or perhaps as the perception of 'inevitability' so common to art as I noted earlier. These revelations seem to grasp each of us uniquely.

Now this may seem strange, but it is not. It is like the experience of "being moved by the spirit" of the Quaker meetings Jim describes,[51] the speaking of the muse of the good artist, the characters of fiction who write themselves, the "it was meant to be" of ordinary speech, or any of the other the numerous expressions we use to try to capture this common perception.

Thus, uncovering an identity in this revelatory way is not strange, yet there remains, nevertheless, great mystery in it. And it is here that we fully encounter that which is so difficult for the culture to acknowledge. In Jim's way of reading, we experience this mystery not as a "thing"—which would reduce it linguistically to the culture's control—but as a "nothing," other to us and yet real, very much within our world. Neither mind nor matter, one step beyond our understanding, one step beyond our control this is—"music starts where the person ends," as Vladimir Martynov puts this.[52] Yet we attend to this mystery in our reading, and do so in large measure, as we do "love" and "justice," because it is not within our control, because, that is, it displays our finitude.

In Jim's way of reading, then, we experience mystery as real and important, asking not, as the culture would ask, what is it, but asking instead how is it with mystery, and who are we in relationship to it? The identities we can uncover in reading this way, we can now see, are grounded in the very finitude our culture insists on denying. In coming to know who we are in relationship to mystery in this way, we always remain, as Augustine taught, mysterious to ourselves, always a question as he put it, or, as we might say now, always self-poetic, forever open to our own ongoing self-interpretation as odd as this seems. To say this in much more familiar terms, through Jim's art we find ourselves only by losing those selves (in mystery) first. And the mystery we experience in Jim's way of reading is nothing less than the mystery of being human.

Experiences like these cannot be isolated. They press upon us, asking that we consider what the world is like if in it we can experience mystery as central to who we are. When we ask this, we come to understand our world as having multiple modes of reality,[53] as itself always open to interpretation, never definite, never defined, never fully within our control, a world that is itself an ongoing process of actuality and potentiality in which there is meaning. In other words, the ground of being the self seeks in creatively uncovering its own identity through Jim's art of reading is also at once actual and potential, forever in the making, and meaningful for us because it is. Of course, and as Ricoeur puts this, "the introduction of the notion of an ontological ground of being against which human possibility comes to light ... represents a philosophical approximation of the idea of God,"[54] but this is not the point here, not yet. Instead, the point is that if human existence is meaningful because it is forever open to interpretation in this way, we *must* claim on this account that this openness is also the way the world is.

Notice now, however, that at this point Jim art of reading (through its own repetition through a variety of literary texts in part) tends to lead his readers away from the imaginative transformations opened by readings to the ontological character of the identities uncovered. Such identities, we can now see, are never fully sufficient. Behind any identity is a creative artistic capacity that is not itself part of any grand narrative or any particular horizon or any "world"; not itself an identity of transformation, but somehow prior to all these. Our creative capacity, then, on our own accounts as Jim's readers, always radically precedes any identity we might uncover. This means for us that not just our identity, but the "ordinary creation of meaning in the world," the meaning of our seeking meaning if you will, also rests upon mystery: the mystery of something which finally must just be affirmed as "lying at the radical origin of humanity itself."[55]

This creative capacity is the assumption at work in all of Jim's work. In it, we seem to have been, and we experience ourselves as being, created as creators of meaning. We seem to have been "called" to this task, called to creative meaning, and this call, "which ... comes from me and yet from beyond and over me"[56] is prior to any conception we could have of who we are; beyond any world we might creatively imagine. On his own account then, all that Jim writes, as well as all the literary texts he writes about, appear as a response to this call. We seem to have been spoken to, in other words, and "to be human is in part to be constituted by what is spoken to [us]."[57]

Called to an ongoing creation of meaning, in Jim's literary world we live in a perpetual Genesis, a world gifted with an abundance of meaning we are "inexhaustibly given to think."[58] Our role in it, in the words of Jean Luc Marion, is to "play redundantly the unthinkable donation."[59] Now it is not just mystery that defines us, but the mystery of this very donation.

Such is the essence of what is uncovered for us in Jim's way of reading as a form of art central to who we are. It is a world far different from the one the culture holds out to us. In it, each transformation offers for consideration not just the possibility of an uncovered identity, but also the uncovering of ontological truths along the lines I have just described. This is truth as *aletheia*,[60] in Heidegger's term borrowed from the Greeks: not something "true" that could be stated in other ways or found to be correct in a correspondence to that which could be known in some other way, but as a happening of truth in art.

Of course, these experiences of truth in this literary art lend authority to the identities uncovered. Could we be wrong in our perceptions of these? Of course! Do we risk fantasy and sentimentality? Of course: nothing in this escapes the requirements of good judgment. Nevertheless, because we experience these transformations as authoritative we come to trust these identities sufficiently to risk our self-understanding on them; trust them enough to wager that the way of life they offer will become true for us when tested against the narratives of our lives. This is the wager—call it hope—implicit in all of Jim's work.

Back to Church

You can see in the language of authoritative mystery, of calling, of donation, and of hope that Jim's secular work has offered his readers, through an art of reading central to our lives, an experience phenomenologically indistinguishable from what we would call religious. It is an experience that returns us to Bonhoeffer's lament for experiences that are themselves a religious voice, and experiences that can return to the culture that upon which the church must depend for its own continued existence. One way of describing what Jim has done in his preserving, "witnessing to" really, the *aletheiac* truth of each text he admires, keeping alive its potential for meaning for us, is what Heidegger said needed to be done in our time: he has brought forth an "abode" within this world to which the gods, the ones which for Heidegger have fled, could return. For, as Heidegger put it, "Where would [a god] turn on his return if men had not first prepared an abode for him"?[61]

To put this more concretely, Jim's way of reading brings his readers to the place where, in front of the sacred text read in the sermon, they have the capacity to relate their worlds to the world of the parable. They can "connect to the Gospel," at least in beginning ways, because they can now experience the connection. The central challenge of Jim's sermon—the challenge of an abundance of love in which even our economic differences can be rendered harmonious—is no longer strange to these readers, or as foreign as it is to the culture, because they already know that this strangeness is but a product of our thinking we must always be in control, and this, they also know, is not true. Their own personal experiences of our finitude, through Jim's art of reading, has revealed to them that what we may now think we are capable of doing is not the same as what is capable of being done.

So Jim found a religious voice for his secular audience; he has offered impossible prayers not far removed from the prayer at Gethsemane there at the heart of the sermon. This may not be the voice we expected, and perhaps not what Jim expected, but it is where his search led him I believe.

This conclusion, however, is not enough for our purposes here. I said in the introduction that Jim's secular work finds its fulfillment in his sermons. One might object at this point that Jim's impossible prayers are prayers to a virtual god. While prayers to virtual gods are not virtual prayers, neither are they the prayer that the sermon is. The sermon is not about a virtual god; it is not about a defining mystery; and not really about the religious experiences of being called, or of an unthinkable donation of meaning, or of hope. It is instead about the God of Abraham. In connecting parishioners to the Gospel, the sermon seeks to help them understand themselves in their relationship to this one God: unnamable, but forever being named in scripture. What are we to make of this for understanding Jim's work? In what way is *this* a fulfillment of it?

There is much to be said here, and I have but a few remaining paragraphs to say it. We could explore how Jim reaches a point in his writing where mythic language is required, not to turn away from the world, but to turn more fully to it; we could talk about the requirements of transformations more radical and complete than those literary texts can offer, and yet but one step removed from Jim's work; we could describe a radical distanciation that sacred texts with their generative circularity (sacred only because they say they are) can provide—a more complete "cultural dislocation" within a gathered time, and requiring, in front of the "Word of God" a more threatening humility, a larger wager upon the meaning of our lives; we could notice how sacred texts radically open our lives to the presence and the absence of a Wholly Other not reducible to meaning because it is its source, which they, perhaps uniquely, can think without destroying; we could wonder in all this whether it is necessary or even possible to make sense of any claim of uniqueness for the particular text to which Jim turns, especially when it is so clearly unique in his life. What I want to say here, however, while it relates to these, is something quite simple: a return to noting, as we did with the sermon, that to be read well this sacred text requires a way of reading different from the sort of dynamic hermeneutic engagement of reader and text we have been considering.

Jim's writings, I have always thought, are written against an unnamed tragedy which left us mired in idolatries that keep us away from the expansive human project of creative meaning. We can only escape this mire, as I read him, by somehow being more than we now are. For him, I think, and perhaps because of this tragedy, theology has always had a stake in the way we read. The criterion he uses to evaluate ways of reading is: How do they respond to this tragedy? Do they, that is, through the transformation they can provide, move us towards the freedom, openness, and responsibility of a certain fullness of being, one we can never reach but towards which we can forever move, a 'maturity of mind' as he sometimes puts this,[62] which is also an "invitation to create a community."[63] From this perspective, it makes sense to ask of any way of reading—reading the law as rules to use his most common example or reading Herbert "objectively"—if it would deny this fullness to us, deny part of who we are in our becoming. It would be very hard indeed, given the religious experience opened in Jim's own work, to think of this fullness as not including a relationship to that which we experience as divine.

If this is true, however, then Jim's shift to sermonic readings of this sacred text, self-proclaimed as God's word, appears as a shift towards a way of reading better reflecting the fullness of being he has always sought. Sermonic readings, like Jim's, reduce that which is sacred in the text to profane speech so that the sacred can be re-appropriated in our lives. This reappropriation of the sacred, consistent with the communal nature of the fullness of being Jim seeks, is reading as and by a community—one extending over time and yet gathered together in each reading—formed in large measure by this way of reading. Of course, there is no doubt that this sacred text can be read idolatrously too, and, in fact, the extent of the demands it makes upon readers make this more of a temptation. Yet the reading of this text as sermon—reading it in the midst of the people of "the book"; reading it poetically, with music, surrounded by its physical symbols; reading it in a context that constantly reminds us that we are not only rational minds but live in multiple modes of reality; rereading it in the sermon as preparation for the Eucharist's interruption of daily lives, knowing, that is, that soon the congregation will reenact the central moment of its own creation by ingesting the Word made flesh; rereading it knowing that it, this sacred text, needs us, "the most fleeting of all,"[64] and so always rereading it with charity, humility, patience, and the fearful uncertainty of our own responsibility for its meaning—is a way of reading, a way of being "in front of the text" really, demanding all of who we are including all we could become.

Surely then this is the way of reading towards which all of Jim's work points. Through it, and to return to the sermon's message with which we began, perhaps love can be experienced as abundant, rather than as limited and preferential; and perhaps in the experience of love's abundance there are those who can imagine themselves to be—if only in a momentary coherence—a people capable of love's justice. May it be so.

Notes

1. D. Bonhoeffer, *Letters and Papers from Prison*, enlarged ed. (London: SCM, 1971), 300.

2. See, for example, S. Hauerwas, *In Good Company: The Church as Polis* (Notre Dame, IN: University of Notre Dame Press, 1997). See also S. Hauerwas, *Hannah's Child* (Grand Rapids, WI: B. Eerdman Publishing Co., 2010), 158.

3. The most direct discussions are in J. B. White, *"This Book of Starres": Learning to Read George Herbert* (Ann Arbor: University of Michigan Press, 1994), xix, 91–95; J. B. White, "How Should We Talk About Religion? Inwardness, Particularity, and Translation," *Ethical Perspectives* 7 (2000): 316; and J. B. White, ed. *How Should We Talk about Religion: Perspectives, Contexts, Particularities* (Notre Dame, IN: University of Notre Dame Press, 2006), 1–8.

4. See for example Z. R. Calo, "Law, Language, and Love—James Boyd White's

'Living Speech: Resisting the Empire of Force,'" *Journal of Law, Philosophy, and Culture* 5 (2010): 221, 227–8.

5. J. B. White, *Connecting to the Gospel: Texts, Sermons, and Commentaries* (Eugene, OR: Wipf & Stock Publishing, 2010), 82.
6. Matthew 20:13–15 (New Revised Standard Version).
7. Matthew 20:16 (New Revised Standard Version).
8. White, *Connecting to the Gospel*, 84.
9. White, *Connecting to the Gospel*, 85.
10. White, *Connecting to the Gospel*, 85.
11. White, *Connecting to the Gospel*, 87.
12. White, *Connecting to the Gospel*, 87.
13. White, *Connecting to the Gospel*, 87.
14. Luke 22:43 (New Revised Standard Version).
15. See P. Ricoeur, "Naming God," in *Figuring the Sacred: Religion, Narrative, and Imagination*, ed. Paul Ricoeur, trans. M. Wallace (Minneapolis: Fortress Press, 1995), 223–34.
16. W. Brueggemann, *Theology of the Old Testament* (Minneapolis: Fortress Press, 1997), 58
17. Brueggemann, *Theology of the Old Testament*, 65 n.11.
18. E. Dickinson, "I Dwell in Possibility," in *The Poems of Emily Dickinson*, ed. R. W. Franklin (Cambridge, MA: Harvard University Press, 1999).
19. J. Gaakeer, "Interview with James Boyd White," *Michigan Law Review* 105 (2007): 1403, 1418.
20. See generally, M. Heidegger, "The Turning," in *The Question Concerning Technology and Other Essays*, ed. M. Heidegger, trans. W. Lovitt (New York: Harper & Row, 1977), 36–43. For Heidegger, enframing is ambiguous: both a danger and an opportunity.
21. White, *"This Book of Starres,"* 129.
22. See, for example, G. Lindbeck, *The Nature of Doctrine: Religion and Theology in a Postliberal Age* (Philadelphia: Westminster Press, 1984).
23. S. Hauerwas, "Speaking Christian: A Commencement Address for Eastern Mennonites Seminary," in *Working with Words: On Learning to Speak Christian*, ed. S Hauerwas (Eugene, OR: Cascade Books, 2011), 84.
24. See generally, J. Derrida, *Speech and Phenomenon and Other Essays on Husserl's Theory of Signs*, trans. D. B. Allison (Evanston, IL: Northwestern University Press, 1973).
25. Bonhoeffer, *Letters and Papers from Prison*, 300.
26. R. D. Williams, "Postmodern Theology and the Judgment of the World," in *Postmodern Theology: Christian Faith in a Pluralist World*, ed. F. B. Burnham (Eugene, OR: Wipf and Stock Publishers, 2006), 108.
27. See, for example, J. B. White, *Living Speech: Resisting the Empire of Force* (Princeton, NJ: Princeton University Press, 2006) 213–24.
28. See, for example, J. B. White, "The Life of the Law as a Life of Writing," in J. B. White, *The Edge of Meaning* (Chicago: University of Chicago Press, 2001), 221–56, 221.

29. N. Lash, *The Beginning and The End of 'Religion'* (Cambridge: Cambridge University Press, 1996), 21.
30. M. Heidegger, *Being and Time*, trans. J. Macquarrie and E. Robinson (New York: Harper & Row, 1962), 126–27.
31. See generally, J. Wall, *Moral Creativity: Paul Ricoeur and the Poetics of Possibility* (Oxford: Oxford University Press, 2005), 37–52.
32. Hans-Georg Gadamer, *Truth and Method* (London: Bloomsbury Academic, 2004), 361.
33. Wall, *Moral Creativity*, 38.
34. In this, no tradition, including religious traditions, can be more primordial, shall we say, than any other. None can provide a hierarchy of universal meaning to which appeal could be made. To make such a claim would be to deny the role of the self (with its own multiplicities) as the creative source of a living tradition's meaning.
35. P. Ricoeur, "Phenomenology and Hermeneutics," in *Hermeneutics and the Human Sciences: Essays on Language, Action, and Interpretation*, ed. J. B. Thompson (Cambridge: Cambridge University Press, 1981), 117, cited in W. D. Hall, *Paul Ricoeur and the Poetic Imperative: The Creative Tension between Love and Justice* (Albany: State University of New York Press, 2007), 51.
36. P. Ricoeur, *Figuring the Sacred*, 628–33. See also Wall, *Moral Creativity*, 42–43.
37. P. Ricoeur, "Lectures on Imagination," (1975) (unpublished), cited in G. H. Taylor, "Ricoeur's Philosophy of Imagination," *Journal of French Philosophy* 16 (Spring–Fall 2006): 98.
38. Jim's lexicon is brilliantly explored in Richard Dawson, *Justice as Attunement: Transforming Constitutions in Law, Literature, Economics and the Rest of Life* (Abingdon, Routledge, 2013).
39. See J. B. White, "Why I Write," *Washington & Lee Law Review* 53 (1996): 1036.
40. J. B. White, *When Words Lose Their Meaning: Constitutions and Reconstitutions of Language, Character, and Community* (Chicago: University of Chicago Press, 1984), 277.
41. White, *When Words Lose Their Meaning*, 277.
42. P. Ricoeur, *Time and Narrative*, vol. 3, trans. K. Blarney and D. Pellauer (Chicago: University of Chicago Press, 1988), 249.
43. White, *When Words Lose Their Meaning*, 40; see also J. B. White, *Acts of Hope: Creating Authority in Literature, Law, and Politics* (Chicago: University of Chicago Press, 1994), ix.
44. J. B. White, *The Edge of Meaning* (Chicago: University of Chicago Press, 2001), xi–xii.
45. For a discussion of inevitability, see J. L. Sammons and L. Berger, "The Law's Mystery," *British Journal of American Legal Studies* 2 (2013).
46. See generally, M. Heidegger, *The Question Concerning Technology* (1977); R. Rojcewicz, *The Gods and Technology: A Reading of Heidegger* (Albany: State University of New York Press, 2006); and J. Young, *Heidegger's Philosophy of Art* (Cambridge: Cambridge University Press, 2001).
47. See generally, M. Heidegger, "The Origin of a Work of Art," in M.

Heidegger, *Poetry, Language, Thought*, trans. A. Hofstader (New York: Harper & Row, 2001), 38–55.

48. White, *The Edge of Meaning*, 2.
49. Heidegger, "The Origin of a Work of Art," 38.
50. See generally, White, "Why I Write,"
51. White, *Living Speech*, 207–16.
52. G. Dubinsky, "Liner Notes," in *Kronos Quartet, Music of Vladimir Martynov* (New York: Nonesuch Records, 2012) (quoting Vladimir Martynov).
53. To experience the law in multiple modes of reality, see J. Vining, *From Newton's Sleep* (Princeton, NJ: Princeton University Press, 1995).
54. W. D. Hall, *Paul Ricoeur and the Poetic Imperative: Creative Tension between Love and Justice* (Albany: State University of New York Press, 2007), 14.
55. Wall, *Moral Creativity*, 47.
56. Heidegger, *Being and Time*, 320.
57. D. E. Klemm and W. Schweiker, "Meaning in Texts and Action: Questioning Paul Ricoeur," in *Meaning in Texts and Actions: Questioning Paul Ricoeur*, ed. D. E. Klemm and W. Schweiker (Charlottesville: University of Virginia Press, 1993), 4. Cited in Hallm *Paul Ricoeur and the Poetic Imperative*, 10 n.13.
58. M. Heidegger, *Country Path Conversations*, trans. B. David (Bloomington: Indiana University Press, 2010), 156.
59. J. L. Marion, *God Without Being: Hors-Text*, trans. T. A. Carlson (Chicago: University of Chicago Press, 1995), 107.
60. Heidegger's most complete discussion of *aletheia* is in M. Heidegger, *Parmenides*, trans. A. Schuwer and R. Rojcewicz (Bloomington: Indiana University Press, 1992). See also Heidegger, "The Origin of a Work of Art," 49–51.
61. M. Heidegger, *Gesamtausgabe 5*, ed. F.-W von Herrmann (Frankfurt: Klostermann, 1977), 270, cited in H. Dreyfus and M. Wrathall, eds., *A Companion to Heidegger* (Malden, MA: Blackwell Publishing, 2005), 463. This has been translated as M. Heidegger, *Off The Beaten Track*, trans. J. Young and K. Haynes (Cambridge: Cambridge University Press, 2002).
62. White, *The Edge of Meaning*, 7.
63. White, *Acts of Hope*, xii.
64. R. M. Rilke, "The Ninth Elegy" (Duino Elegies), in *The Selected Poetry of Ranier Maria Rilke*, trans. S. Mitchell (New York: Random House, 1989) 199–203.

[7]

Silence and Justice

Richard Dawson

In 2007, the *Michigan Law Review* marked James Boyd White's retirement. In one contribution, Robin West commented on his latest book, *Living Speech*. After saying that she found "the attention he bestows in that book on *silence*" to be "surprising," she asked, "How can this man who taught us, for decades, to appreciate the connections between just living and just speech, who for so long taught that the ethical impulse is to be found in the linguistic act, turn four-square and embrace silence?"[1] Her question sounded off-key to me, for it seemed that a distinctive aspect of White's justice-centered work *is* a concern with the topic of silence. This essay tunes in to this aspect.

"A Pressure Toward the Inexpressible"

White's *The Legal Imagination* makes the claim that "the activities which make up the life of the lawyer and judge constitute an enterprise of the imagination."[2] Resisting the dominant image of law as a system of rules, White offers an image in which "the lawyer is at heart a writer."[3] Contributing to the rehabilitation of narrative, he offers a line of inquiry on "what the narrative offers the lawyer":

> The process of telling a story generates a pressure towards the inexpressible.... Whenever a story is told, there is the possibility that it will take on a life of its own, a life beyond the intentions—and perhaps beyond the under-

standing and control—of the writer, a life so compelling that the auditor, whatever his wishes, cannot shake it off. You can see how important this force of narrative would be for a lawyer, at least if he could master it and claim its power for his own; you can imagine the tremendous pressure of a masterfully told story in a trial or negotiation.[4]

Might White's story about the "power" of storytelling help "shake" some prejudices that reinforce the image of law as a system of rules? Might we do well to hope that in the process of composing a story about White's work we feel a "force" of a going-"beyond" expression, ultimately a valuable silence?

"We Come at the End to a Kind of Silence": Shakespeare's *King Richard II*

A pressure toward the inexpressible can begin with a certain kind of question. White hints at this in *The Legal Imagination* when directing his reader to a work that "tells the story of the making of a language of authority":

> As you can imagine, when such a language is being made, everything is rethought at once; to question an old authority, an old system of reference and appeal, is to throw everything open. The essence of a language of authority is that it shall not be questioned but accepted as necessary; and, as Shakespeare's *Richard II* demonstrates, when such a language is taken as open to question, it loses its peculiar force at once.[5]

When "a language ... loses it peculiar force," its user will find that her (or his) reality was not as real as she had imagined. She is offered the experience of becoming disoriented over what is real, an experience that may stimulate a plethora of questions, including some about the adequacy of the languages with which to talk about the real.

White offers a reading of *Richard II* in *Acts of Hope*.[6] As part of his introduction, White says: "the story it tells is the deposition of Richard by Henry Bolingbroke, later Henry IV."[7] While at a basic level one person hands over a crown to another person, a vital level is the meaning of the event: "the subject of the play is less the 'crown' abstractly regarded than the various languages by which the crown is given meaning of one kind or another, as these characters organize themselves in relation to it."[8] White shows us how Shakespeare sets one language ("the language of kingship") against another ("the language ... of feudal honor"), which in turn is set against another ("the language of ... inheritance"), and so on. When Henry has the crown, he finds that following the linguistic competition in which he participated, "the language of kingship" that his predecessor used has lost its force. White writes:

> Henry ... is not—and in some sense cannot be—king and cannot call upon the resources and language of that office. When at the chaotic ending of the play Henry learns that Richard has been murdered ... he has no way of talking about his situation at all, except to undertake a crusade to the Holy Land by way of expiation.[9]

Henry finds that his "word" is not the "sterling" that the king's once was, to use Richard's metaphors.[10] Henry learns that having the crown does not give him an essential kingliness. At a more general level, he has the opportunity to learn that language does not function like a "mirror,"[11] merely reflecting a preexisting reality.

In the concluding part of *Richard II*, an imprisoned Richard self-consciously exercises his analogical imagination with respect to his place in the world. White ends his reading of the play exercising his analogical imagination with respect to the place of the play in the world:

> Shakespeare's work ... has affinities with Chaucer's *Canterbury Tales*, ... comprehending at once ... the immense and the miniscule. This way of writing, by poetic comprehension, unites the concerns of beauty and truth alike, because beauty can be thought of, as Coleridge suggested, as the comprehension of contradictions within an order and because on these understandings the truth of any utterance lies not in itself but in its relation to another; and the concerns of justice too, for justice can be seen to be a way of giving each voice, each possibility for speech, its widest and fullest range.
>
> This kind of work has obvious similarities to law, for, like law, it is a way of seeing what can be said on both sides; but not only both sides of an existing question, the very statement of which defines the language that can be used to respond to it, but "both sides" in a deeper way: seeing how competing languages can be framed and put to work, entailing as they do competing ways of imagining and acting in the world....
>
> The effect of the whole is ... to leave us in a position of greater uncertainty than ever before about our languages, with an increasing sense that we can have nothing to say upon which we can lean without question. Its movement is one of intellectual and moral affliction, as we are brought to the limits of our imaginations and understandings; like the characters in the play we come at the end to a kind of silence, but a silence that is itself a way of facing our situation in the world.[12]

The image of the "position" that "Shakespeare brings us to share," an image that we may find difficult to shake off, is helpful for thinking about the "position" that White brings us to share in *Acts of Hope* and elsewhere. We may not be able to hear "justice"-talk relating to the ancient principle of "hear the other side" in quite the same way anymore, for we might be inclined to "question" what is meant by "side." There are many "sides" for talking about "sides." Should we not be trying to hear "voice" against voice against voice? How are we to hear "each possibility for speech?" Is not "a kind of silence" called for? How are we to talk adequately about silence?

After reading White on Shakespeare in *Acts of Hope*, we have a helpful analogical resource for reading *The Legal Imagination*, in which White exposes his reader to a multiplicity of languages. We hear of, for example, "a language of criticism," "a language of description," "the language of diplomacy," "of education," "of judgment," "of the law," "of love," "of lover"s cliché," "of race," "of the rule," "of systems analysis," among others. In a section titled "Your Language in a Universe of Languages,"[13] White expresses the "hope" that "the comparison of legal and nonlegal speech will establish for us some common understanding of what the law leaves out, a sense of possibilities that seem never to be considered."[14] White's central concern, it seems fitting to say, is with aspects of the silence of "legal speech"—that which it "leaves out." We will do well to avoid overlooking (or, better, under-hearing) this concern, not least to equip ourselves for coming to a new appreciation of the possibilities of the legal hearing.

Even though White gives much help, in the form of "notes and questions," for "working through a book which departs so markedly from the familiar,"[15] his reader may find it difficult to express herself as to what the course is "about." The following summary statement from White may be helpful:

> You might sum up the experience this course offers by saying that it is an experience in the collapse of language under strain .... You have experienced ... the perpetual breaking down of language in your hands as you try to use it. None of our languages seems to be able to ... bear the stresses of our demands for truth and order and justice. Such, it seems to me, are the conditions of our existence.[16]

The course offers to induce "the collapse of language under strain," an "experience" that is a pressure toward the inexpressible, a potentially productive "justice"-related silence, one that can help us attune to "the conditions of our existence."

"You are Answered by Silence": Economics, Law, and "Literary" Language

It may be helpful here to say that White attends to more than one form of silence. He says as much in *The Legal Imagination*, which he may have written partly out of a desire to resist a form of silence that he considers objectionable.

> Much of our enormous literature of politics and society seems to be written

> with an impossible confidence ... in a simple vocabulary, as though to those who listened and received its truths it would explain all.... If you ask, "What is my place in all this?" you are answered by silence; the question does not fit.[17]

How dare White ask that impertinent question of justice! With a desire to avoid having no "place" to stand in the world, we might do well to wary of people who imagine that their language is a transparent machine that can "explain all." Such people may be offering a dehumanizing "silence," possibly in the name of science, which they set in opposition to mere story.

I made the acquaintance of White's work when writing an economics doctoral dissertation centering on the way in the creation of a market for fish quotas in New Zealand had adverse impacts on various Maori peoples, who have a painful history with a destructive silence. I owe the acquaintance to the institutional economist Warren Samuels. In an article titled "The Legal-Economic Nexus," Samuels wrote:

> James Boyd White, commenting on the falseness of the distinction between the market and government, has stated that to 'talk about "government intervention"' implicitly assumes 'that there is a pre-governmental state of nature called the market into which the government intrudes. But this is obviously silly.'[18]

The two words "obviously silly" provoked laughter. While I had been aware that the commonly used phrase "government intervention" was infelicitous, White's words struck a chord. Here was a person wittily putting the old debate between "pro-" and "anti-interventionists" in a new light.

I acquired a copy of the lecture from which Samuels quoted, and I found myself reading with great interest. White's lecture talked about "economics and law" as "two cultures in tension".[19] At the outset of his lecture, White stresses some limits to the language that he will use in talking about economics:

> To say that I shall speak about 'economics' may be somewhat misleading, for I shall actually focus attention mainly on one branch of it, namely microeconomics of the neoclassical kind. This is the economics of the 'Law and Economics' school—the economics that is proposed as offering a solution to the problems of choice inherent both in the law and in public life more generally ... . To use 'economics' to refer to this branch of the field, as I do, may be a solecism, but for a lawyer in the 1980's it is an easy and perhaps forgivable one, since this is the terminology generally used by those who have been most energetic, and successful, in recommending this mode of thought to us.[20]

White here tells his reader that he is carrying out a reduction of some kind in his use of the word "economics," but doing so for a particular reason; namely, to talk on the terms of those with whom he is engaging. As we can learn by reading his footnotes, White has Chicago Law and Economics in mind, including leading exponent Richard Posner. If you open any of Posner's books, you will find that he fails to make the kind of qualification White does when talking about "economics." This silence will chill those who value other ways of doing and imagining economics. They have no place in Posner's world, in which Posner's "economics" is an imperialistic "the economics," the one that should naturally be placed on the top floor of the social sciences building, placed above law. A Shakespeare reader might say that "King" Richard Posner seeks to silence any competition for imagining the economy, and the law.

Identifying Posner's aversion to competition when it comes to alternative stories can serve as a base for attuning to White's way of imagining the law. Let us turn to *Heracles' Bow*, in which White tells a story about "competing stories" in the law:

> Legal stories are told ... in competition with each other, one the necessary understanding that each is incomplete. This means that there is in the law an openness to multiple stories, multiple languages. This openness is not accidental but structural, and it has significant political and ethical consequences as well as intellectual ones. It is in fact built into the idea of the hearing, the central form of legal life and discourse, for at the hearing two stories are told in competition with one another, and a choice between them—or of a third—is forced upon a decider. This array of competing stories drives the listener to the edge of language and of consciouness, to the moment of silence where transformation and invention can take place, and a new story, perhaps in a new language, can be told.[21]

What can economists, including those who narrowly define economics as the study of "choice," learn from "competition" in the law? We might wonder what might become of economics if economic stories were told with White's triadic image of legal stories in mind. What might become of *Homo economicus* if s/he could have shifts of "consciousness"? Might economists become productively distanced from the word "economic" and find themselves "at the edge of language," wondering what valuable meaning they can give to it? Feeling a pressure towards the inexpressible (not just from one story but from at least three), might they become interested in paying attention to political economies of "silence"? What kind of silence might facilitate "transformation and invention" in the direction of justice?

A striking silence in White's work, at least after reading Posner, is his use of the language of concepts—"the concept of efficiency," "the concept of a market," "of utility," and so on. For White, one "pressure" of this language "is to direct attention away from language to something else: to the realm of ideas, to what is in the mind, or to some field of intellectual reality, and in each instance to something that is assumed to exist in a real apart from language."[22] White promotes a different kind of language. He tentatively gives it a name during his critique of economic imperialism:

> The ... attitude to have towards language, including one's own—I call it a literary view, though many physicists and biologists would recognize it too—is that all languages are limited; that none says the whole truth; that full translation from one to the other is always in a deep sense impossible. This means that the most profound obligation of each of us in using his or her language is to try to recognize what it leaves out, to point to the silence that surrounds it—to acknowledge the terrible incompleteness of all speech, and thus to leave oneself open to hearing other truths, in other languages. At its best the law does this, or strives to do so, for it is a constant linguistic competition. How to characterize the facts and the law, how to conceive of and feel about the case, and what, therefore, to do about it, are the central questions of a legal hearing.... The law ... should listen to economics, regarding it as one language, one set of metaphors, among many, and be willing to use it when appropriate and with appropriate qualifications.[23]

How should we speak about the concept of silence? Might the use of a "literary" language help us to hear the "silence" in our "speak" (and thus to formulate a better question than that one)? In moments of "silence" while "reading" White, we may come to "recognize" a justice-related "obligation"—to ourselves and to others—to which we had until then failed to give adequate attention, perhaps due to a lack of attentive silence. All of us, including economists, might do well to incorporate "the central questions of a legal hearing" into our own habitual modes of thought and expression. After reading White, we might wonder if any economists have attended to a process of "linguistic competition" over how best to talk about "competitive markets," especially the role of law in their constitution and reconstitution. If so, they might recognize that which White calls a "literary view" of language, and then come to imagine economics *as* a literary activity.

"He Retreats into Silence": Twain's *Huckleberry Finn*

Where might we begin in working out a literary economics, one that could help us resist leaving out, or silencing, the law in "law and economics"? If we were to propose a textbook in this direction titled *The Legal-Economic Imagination*, what readings might we include? Some passages from *Huckleberry Finn* could be ideal, especially those that reside in the opening chapter of White's course book.[24] We could draw from White's accompanying questions, which are concerned with the inexpressible. Before attending to a few of his questions, let us tune in to the novel.

Huckleberry Finn begins with Huck up against both "sivilizing" pressures from his foster mother and brutality from his father. Huck finds himself running with Jim, who is "owned" by Miss Watson (the sister of Huck's foster mother) and who is escaping from an imminent transfer of ownership. When Huck first meets Jim on Jackson's Island, he says he "was ever so glad to see Jim".[25] In an introduction to the novel, Toni Morrison attends to the significance of Jim in the novel:

> If the emotional environment into which Twain places his protagonist is dangerous, then the leading question the novel poses for me is, What does Huck need to live without terror, melancholy and suicidal thoughts? The answer, of course, is Jim. When Huck is among society—whether respectable or deviant, rich or poor—he is alert to and consumed by its deception, its illogic, its scariness. Yet he is depressed by himself and sees nature more often as fearful. But when he and Jim become the only "we," the anxiety is outside, not within.... The consolation, the healing properties Huck longs for, is made possible by Jim's active, highly vocal affection. It is in Jim's company that ... real talk—comic, pointed, sad—takes place. Talk so free of lies is produces an aura of restfulness and peace unavailable anywhere else in the novel.[26]

There is an important sense in which both Huck and Jim are outsiders, without a community in which there is communication—"real talk"—worthy of the name. This changes when they take to the river. The two of them establish a meaningful "we," with a kind of amity unavailable anywhere else. Twain's reader may or may not notice this reality, depending upon their "leading question". If we notice this reality, we may also notice a certain pressure towards the inexpressible. In this regard, we may come to appreciate Morrison's claim that "much of the novel's genius lies in its quiescence, the silences that pervade it."[27]

The novel's sixteenth chapter begins with Huck and Jim talking about nearing Cairo, Illinois, where Jim will be "free." Huck"s "deformed conscience"[28] (meaning the racist ideology in which Huck has been immersed) comes to life here, destabilizing the "we":

> Jim said it made him all over trembly and feverish to be so close to freedom. Well, I can tell you it made me all over trembly and feverish, too, to hear him, because I begun to get it through my head that he *was* most free – and who was to blame for it? Why, *me*.... Conscience says to me, "What had poor Miss Watson done to you, that you could see her nigger go off right under your eyes and never say one single word? ..."[29]

"Conscience" became disturbed at Jim's "freedom" talk. The Huck that sees Jim as Miss Watson's "nigger" is not the same Huck that has become a friend to Jim. With Huck we have not a unitary being but a plural "I." When thinking about Huck uttering "one single word" about Jim, an economist might have a productive difficulty in talking about what might be in his self-interest. The question is: Which Huck? Is there a self within Huck that is worthy of the name "self"? Is there a self within him that has an interest in maintaining the only community that he has?

With the language of race running through Huck, he paddles ashore with the intention to turn Jim in. Jim then speaks:

> 'Pooty soon I'll be a-shout'n for joy, en I'll say, its all on accounts o' Huck; I's a free man, en I couldn't ever ben free ef it hadn' ben for Huck; Huck done it. Jim won't ever forgit you, Huck; you's de bes' fren' Jim's ever had; en you's de *only* fren' ole Jim's got now.'
>
> I was paddling off, all in a sweat to tell on him; but when he says this, it seemed to take the tuck all out of me.[30]

This "friend" talk is a real jolt for the part of Huck that a few moments earlier had only seen "Miss Watson's nigger." What is going on within the "I" that lost its "tuck"?

Along comes a boat with two slave hunters. Huck cleverly tricks them to depart without checking the raft. Then we hear Huck:

> They went off, and I got aboard the raft, feeling bad and low, because I knowed very well I had done wrong, and I see it warn't no use for me to try to learn to do right; a body that don't get *started* right when he's little, ain't got no show – .... Then I thought a minute, and says to myself, hold on, – s'pose you'd a done right and give Jim up; would you felt better that what you do now? No, says I, I'd feel bad – I'd feel just the same way I do now. Well, then, says I, what's the use you learning to do right, when its troublesome to do right and ain't no trouble to do wrong, and the wages is just the same? I was stuck. I couldn't answer that. So I reckoned I wouldn't bother no more about it, but after this always do whichever come handiest at the time.[31]

We might say that Huck's efforts to deal with conflicting forces—the gift of a real friendship with Jim, and a "nigger"-hating "conscience"—has put him in the midst of confusion. In the position of being "stuck," his control of language and meaning is near the point of destruction. His rule, "do whichever come handiest at the time," may be a product of a will to economic efficiency and may sound morally unsound, but we may do well to resist making such a judgment.

"When Huck says that he will just do what comes handiest at the time, what does he mean by 'handy'"? So asks White at the beginning of a line of questioning,[32] which prods attention to the way in which "untangling" questions of "right and wrong" were "beyond his capacities."[33] After this, using imagery that resembles his summary statement on *The Legal Imagination* as a course ("the collapse of language under strain"), White says:

> What was called for in Huck's situation was nothing less than a new way of imagining human relationships and a new way of expressing one's imagination. Huck achieves the first – the experience of the boy and the slave on the raft is a genuine discovery – but he fails to do the second and retreats into silence: at the end of the book he 'lights out for the territories.' In this passage, Twain does achieve a new way of expressing a newly imagined relationship, but even he has difficulties.... Twain's crisis of imagination might become clearer if you pretend you are Twain, having written the passage you have just read. What will the rest of your novel be like: what will Huck and Jim do and say next, whom will they meet and on what terms? ... Can you imagine a friendship between these two people expressed in their actual lives in the world? ... You may be interested to know that Twain in fact stopped writing this book at this point for several years, apparently stuck, not knowing how to go on. Many critics think that the rest of the novel fails to live up to what was achieved here, that at this point the imagination collapses.... Are there matters as to which we are situated somewhat like Huck or Twain?[34]

That passage brings to mind this famous sentence in Aristotle's *Ethics*: "Friendship and justice seem to be exhibited in the same sphere of conduct and between the same persons."[35] (The original version of this sentence serves as an epigraph to White's *When Words Lose Their Meaning*.[36]) Twain's book offers a pressure toward "expressing a newly imagined relationship," the re-cognition of a common humanity, a justice as equality. (While Huck does not have the option of a crusade to the Holy Land, he can "light out for the Territory.") While Twain's Huck can do no better than saying that he "knowed [Jim] was white inside,"[37] we may come to re-know, with the help of Twain's cavorting with the white-black opposition, that an essential "whiteness," like an essential kingliness, is a product of the delusive imagination. White's questioning calls for a close reading of *Huckleberry Finn*, one that involves putting ourselves in Twain's place. In the process of trying to respond to the questions, I repeatedly had the experience that Twain "apparently" had; namely, that of "not knowing how to go on," being "stuck." Here "the imagination collapses," coming to a form of "silence." White's questions offer a journey to a place in which one can become aware of the pressure of the inexpressible, a pressure that suggests an intimate relation between "silence" and justice.

Some readers of *Huckleberry Finn* may not hear its potentially productive silences. In an essay in the first issue of the *Yale Journal of Law and the*

Humanities, Robin West offers a critical reading of the novel.[38] She infers that, unlike Toni Morrison's *Beloved*, it offers few insights for real questions of justice. With reference to Huck's decision to protect Jim from the slave hunters, West says:

> Huck, of course, ... does the right thing; and he does it against the weight of considerable community pressure and in the face of considerable danger. But at no point does Huck experience the conflict between the community's corrupt and racist moral code and his own sense of what he wants to do as a conflict between the positive code of the community and the demands of a truer, higher morality. At no point does he articulate a compelling case against the dehumanization of his friend, either to himself, to Jim, to the communities with which he interacts, or even to his confidant Tom. Never does he question the authority of the social code that dictates the abuses against which he rebels, nor does he reconceptualize what morality requires from the 'strands' of the community's splintered and disingenuous codes. Huck is not even a successful reformer. Huck stands by Jim not because he sees Jim's cause as just, feels for his dilemma, or shares his pain – in fact he doesn't. Rather, Huck stands by Jim because he feels himself bound by his promise to do so. Huck ultimately does the right thing for the wrong reason: he helps Jim out of fidelity to himself.[39]

In what sense and from which standpoint did Huck "ultimately" do "the right thing for the wrong reason"? West might have done well to elaborate on what she means by "fidelity to himself." The attention here could be on "himself." Huck "himself" is a complex collection of selves, which are continuously evolving through interaction between internal voices and between internal and external voices, not to mention striking silences. From whose standpoint is the "community's ... moral code ...corrupt"? West seems to be saying that "the demands of a truer, higher morality" are simply out there for us to plainly see and grasp. If so, has she has failed to engage with what she calls White's "sensitive reading and set of questions concerning *Huckleberry Finn*"?[40] A guiding question of White's here is this: How is Huck able to constructively respond to the racist language ("a destructive way of talking"[41]) that surrounds and pierces him? West might well want to ask a question like "How might Huck have been more successful?," but that is quite a different line of inquiry. Huck would indeed have done *extremely* well to ask "himself" some tricky questions that lead him to "experience the conflict between the community's corrupt and racist moral code and his own sense of what he wants to do as a conflict between the positive code of the community and the demands of a truer, higher morality." That, however, does raise the awkward matter of what "his own sense of what he wants to do" *is*. What do the words "his own" mean? Who is the "he" in "what he wants to do"? There seems to me to be a major identity crisis going on in

"Huck," and any pronoun that he or we might use to talk about what "he" is up to just seems to be a clumsy mess, beyond adequate expression. (After reading *Huckleberry Finn*, an economist may not be able to hear talk about the "concept of self-interest" in quite the same way again.) West needed to attend to and talk about the inexpressible in order to do justice not only to Huck but also to White's questioning.

In her essay, West makes the claim that "Huck ... personifies White's conception of the social critic".[42] Given her failure to attend closely to the experience of Huck, it seems to me that West is on shaky ground for aptly imagining such a critic. I am not sure at all who "the Whitean critic" is. This essay is part of what has become a long and rewarding struggle to make sense of who James Boyd White is—to make sense of what he is doing, of what he is saying, not saying, and cannot say. A careful reader of *The Legal Imagination* will appreciate that this struggle is not so much "about" White but about his reader: "In every paper he defines himself as a mind, and you might say that this act of self-expression is our real subject."[43] A White reader can expect the "self"-other opposition to collapse under strain, a collapse that is related to the topic of justice.

"How Can this Silence Possibly be Explained"?: Melville's *Billy Budd*

At various places in *The Legal Imagination*, White directs attention to the potential value of "authorial silence." I take this term from Wayne Booth's *Rhetoric of Fiction*, which gives particular attention to acts of communication by an author done with silence. Booth says: "By the kind of silence he maintains, ... the author can achieve effects which would be difficult or impossible if he allowed himself a reliable spokesman to speak directly and authoritatively to us."[44] (These effects include "the control of clarity and confusion," which can enable "a secret communion of the author and reader behind the narrator's back."[45]) Booth is touching on an issue about which it is most difficult to talk: the complex relationship between silence and speech. He claims that there is a sense in which certain kinds of "authorial silence" are forms of speech. In *The Legal Imagination*, White offers an explicit line of inquiry in this direction. One important landmark here is his engagement with *Billy Budd*. White invites his reader to read two passages from the novella and to attend to the control of "ambiguity," which can "enable Melville to make some ... kind of statement".[46] Following a passage in which the hero gets hanged, White writes:

> How is Billy Budd's death defined? What does Melville's ambiguity on this point enable him to say? ... Melville does not seem to make his position clear on this central question: how can this silence possibly be explained? Can one

regard Melville's refusal to take a position as central to his point? One could say that ... he forces the problem directly upon the reader.... Here is a world created like the one we live in: events are critically important, but no one can explain them with certainty. Language is made to break down and the burden is shifted to you.[47]

The writer uses a language and at the same time expresses a recognition of what it leaves out. Can you find a way to live and work within the language system of the law and be ironic or ambiguous about what you do? ... Is it possible to use legal language in a way that points to or recognizes what the law leaves out? You might say that that is exactly what Captain Vere finds he cannot do. Is this a paradigm for the whole of your experience of law?[48]

As you may know, Captain Vere dominates Billy's trial, for he sets about "electing individuals composing ... a drumhead court," "appearing as the sole witness in the case," and putting a stop to some important questions of justice "by a glance more effective than words."[49] He then takes it upon himself to direct the court's reasoning with a speech that is framed with a set of defective oppositions, including "warm hearts" versus "cool heads," the first of which he connects to "the feminine in man," a part that "must here be ruled out."[50] Vere, we might say, speaks with an impossible confidence in a simple vocabulary, as though to those who listened and received its truths it would explain all—he does not control a language in a "literary" way in order to express a recognition of what it leaves out. There is no person in this "legal" space with the willingness or ability to resist Vere and to start a real linguistic competition, to tell a compelling story, one that helps draw attention to the limits of Vere's language. This leaves nothing but Vere's pressure toward the fully expressible. Is this not the death of law worthy of the name? We might do well to wonder if Melville's authorial silence makes a place for his reader to take it upon herself to ask that fundamental question. I think that the silence does do this, and it does not surprise me at all that White both points to Vere's linguistic performance as a failure and suggests that doing what he "cannot do" lends itself as "a paradigm for the whole of your experience of law."[51] We can begin to do such "doing" by resisting the speech-silence opposition.

In an article in the first issue of the *Cardozo Studies in Law & Literature*, West contributed to a symposium on *Billy Budd*. Here she attends to "dimensions of Billy's femininity" that make the novel "of interest to feminist legal academics, lawyers, judges, and to feminism generally."[52] One dimension concerns "silence":

Billy's silence is feminine. Billy is both silent and silenced.... He is easily struck mute ... Billy's womanly silence renders his womanly virtue *totally* mysterious. Because Billy is silent, we cannot know the nature of his special virtue. Melville tells us several times that Billy is a 'peacemaker' ... But how, exactly, does Billy wage his peace? ...

The feminine ethic pushes women, as it pushes Billy, to see our idealized selves as peacemakers. But if we are to be more effective than was Billy in showing these men how to love one another – and if we are to avoid getting hanged in the process – then, unlike Billy, we must break our silence. We must participate in our community's moral, political, and legal conversations; we must acquire power, exercise it responsibly, and express, as well as exemplify, our virtue.[53]

Let us not stop to doubt whether women have been and continue to be "silenced" in oppressive and unjust ways. Nor let us stop to doubt whether a search for an essential feminineness, like kingliness and whiteness, is delusive. With a view to promoting "conversations" that connect West and White, we might do well to wonder how West might fittingly talk about the authorial silence of Melville, silence that may be central to nothing less than "a paradigm for the whole of your experience of law." (Does, for example, the suggestion that Melville's silence is "masculine" sound off-key?) We might also do well to wonder how West might have talked about the place of a "literary" silence in Billy's speech had he spoken. (Does "masculine together with feminine" sound off-key?) Such wondering might serve to unsettle our inherited language of gender, and perhaps do so in the spirit of Melville's novella. Here the masculine-feminine opposition breaks down and the responsibility of reconstituting it shifts to you. If West is able to reimagine the feminine-masculine relation, and perhaps even let it go sometimes in order to hear not a man or a woman before her but a *person*, she may be able to rehear the sounds of silence in White's work, and in her own.

"It Concludes in Silence": Herbert's *The Temple*

West's suggestion that we will do well "to be more effective than was Billy in showing these men how to love one another", readily connects to White's book on learning to read the poet Herbert, which has much to say and suggest about love. White outlines how Herbert "writes out of [a] ... sense ... that to speak is to sin, and in a radical way, for it is to assert ... the validity of our perceptions against the fact that we cannot accurately perceive or understand what is good and bad."[54] Let us pass over in silence a connection here to Huck. "One of the functions of Herbert's poetry," perhaps like Twain's novel, "is to make this sense conscious, and to counteract it."[55] This directly connects to silence, as White says during his commentary on Herbert's "Affliction":

This counteraction is paradoxically but necessarily in words—how else could it be done?—but often (in a sense always) it concludes in silence, a silence given meaning by the words that have come before.

'Affliction' has two such moments, of increasing intensity: when the speaker says: 'Now I am here,' acknowledging that his 'books'—his language—tell him nothing anymore, and aspiring to the utter silence of a tree; and at the close, when he affirms his humanity, against the tree, by claiming not a power to speak but a capacity to love—or, more bleakly, a need to love, which is in the nature of things mute: a feeling, a gesture, not sayable; at most a 'grone.'[56]

After reading that passage, we might be better equipped to hear the "mute" in Billy, perhaps sensing not a defect (as West does) but a gift beyond "language." Who might Captain Vere have become if he could have heard and responded to "a need to love"? What might have become of "the law"?

Let me return "home" to economics. Moving from the particular (Vere) to the more general: What might become of *Homo economicus* if she had the capacity to attune herself to a mute need to love? Might she be equipped to take seriously acts of justice? If so, what might become of the part of our world that we call, often with an austere economy of language, "the economy"?[57]

"Silence can be a Plan"

In Adrienne Rich's volume *The Dream of a Common Language*, there resides a poem titled "Cartographies of Silence."[58] Here is a fragment:

Silence can be a plan
rigorously executed

the blueprint to a life

It is a presence
it has a history   a form

Do not confuse it
with any kind of absence

It seems readily imaginable that White included the topic of silence in a blueprint to his *The Legal Imagination*, and to later work too. Not one to "confuse [silence] with any kind of absence," White has been centrally concerned with the art of managing "speech" acts of "silence." This is the art of speaking/silencing justly. If we can resist the common framing of the speech-silence relation as an opposition, we can be confident that we will be better equipped to hear White's performances. These can serve as a model for judging the performances of others, including our own.

Notes

1. R. West, "Speech, Silence, and Ethical Lives," *Michigan Law Review* 105 (2007): 1397, 1399.
2. J. B. White, *The Legal Imagination: Studies in the Nature of Legal Thought and Expression* (Boston: Little, Brown and Company, 1973), 758.
3. White, *The Legal Imagination*, 758.
4. White, *The Legal Imagination*, 863, 865.
5. White, *The Legal Imagination*, 817.
6. J. B. White, *Acts of Hope: Creating Authority in Literature, Law, and Politics* (Chicago: University of Chicago Press, 1994).
7. White, *Acts of Hope*, 47.
8. White, *Acts of Hope*, 49.
9. White, *Acts of Hope*, 73.
10. W. Shakespeare, *King Richard II*, ed. A. Gurr (Cambridge: Cambridge University Press, 1990), act 4, scene 1, line 263.
11. The mirror metaphor is Richard's, too. In the line immediately following the "sterling" metaphor, he says: "Let it command a mirror hither straight / That it may show me what a face I have / Since it is bankrupt of his majesty." Henry is unable to put the old "majesty" into his own face.
12. White, *Acts of Hope*, 78–79.
13. White, *The Legal Imagination*, 83.
14. White, *The Legal Imagination*, 83.
15. White, *The Legal Imagination*, xxiii.
16. White, *The Legal Imagination*, 760.
17. White, *The Legal Imagination*, 904.
18. W. J. Samuels, "The Legal-Economic Nexus" *George Washington Law Review* 1 57 (1989): 556, 1568.
19. J. B. White, "Economics and Law: Two Cultures in Tension," *Tennessee Law Review* 54 (1987): 161.
20. White, "Economics and Law," 162.
21. J. B. White, *Heracles' Bow: Essays on the Rhetoric and Poetics of the Law* (Madison: University of Wisconsin Press, 1985), 74.
22. J. B. White, *Justice as Translation: An Essay in Cultural and Legal Criticism* (Chicago: University of Chicago Press, 1990), 28.
23. White, "Economics and Law" 201-2.
24. White offers a fuller engagement with Twain's novel in his book *The Edge of Meaning* (Chicago: University of Chicago Press, 2001), 28–47.
25. M. Twain, *The Adventures of Huckleberry Finn* (London: Penguin, 1985 [1884]), 94.
26. T. Morrison, "Introduction," in *The Oxford Mark Twain: Adventures of Huckleberry Finn*, ed. S. F. Fishkin (Oxford: Oxford University Press, 1996), reprinted in S. K. George, *Ethics, Literature, and Theory: An Introductory Reader* (Lanham, MD: Rowman and Littlefield, 2005), 279, 282.

27. George, *Ethics, Literature, and Theory*, 281.
28. In 1895, Samuel Clemens (Twain) gave a lecture on ethics that drew from this chapter, one in which "a sound heart and a deformed conscience come into collision." Quoted in W. Blair, *Mark Twain & Huck Finn* (Berkeley: University of California Press, 1960), 143.
29. Twain, *Huckleberry Finn*, 145.
30. Twain, *Huckleberry Finn*, 146–47.
31. Twain, *Huckleberry Finn*, 149.
32. White, *The Legal Imagination*, 25.
33. White, *The Legal Imagination*, 26.
34. White, *The Legal Imagination*, 25.
35. Aristotle, *Ethics* (London: Penguin, 1976), 273; chapter 9, book 8, 1160a8.
36. J. B. White, *When Words Lose Their Meaning: Constitutions and Reconstitutions of Language, Character, and Community* (Chicago: University of Chicago Press, 1984).
37. Twain, *Huckleberry Finn*, 348.
38. R. West, "Communities, Texts, and Law: Reflections on the Law and Literature Movement," *Yale Journal of Law & the Humanities* 1 (1988): 129.
39. West, "Communities, Texts, and Law," 139.
40. West, "Communities, Texts, and Law," 139.
41. White, *The Legal Imagination*, 21
42. West, "Communities, Texts, and Law," 132.
43. White, *The Legal Imagination*, xxi.
44. W. C. Booth, *The Rhetoric of Fiction*, 2nd ed. (Chicago, University of Chicago Press, 1983), 273.
45. Booth, *The Rhetoric of Fiction*, 284, 300. An attuned Twain reader will notice that "in *Huckleberry Finn*, the narrator claims to be naturally wicked while the author silently praises his virtues behind his back" (159).
46. White, *The Legal Imagination*, 74.
47. White, *The Legal Imagination*, 75-76.
48. White, *The Legal Imagination*, 76.
49. H. Melville, *Billy Budd, Sailor: And Other Stories* (Harmondsworth: Penguin, 1970), 381–85.
50. Melville, *Billy Budd, Sailor*, 388.
51. White offers helpful insights on Vere in a review of Posner's *Law and Literature*. See J. B. White, "What Can a Lawyer Learn from Literature?" *Harvard Law Review* (1989): 2014, 2038–42.
52. R. West, "The Feminine Silence: A Response to Professor Koffler," *Cardozo Studies in Law & Literature* 1 (1989): 15, 16.
53. West, "The Feminine Silence," 17–20.
54. J. B. White, *"This Book of Starres": Learning to Read George Herbert* (Ann Arbor: University of Michigan Press, 1994), 29.
55. White, *"This Book of Starres,"* 29.

56. White, *"This Book of Starres,"* 29.
57. On an economy of love, see J. B. White, *Connecting to the Gospel: Texts, Sermons, Commentaries* (Eugene, OR: Wipf & Stock, 2010), chapter 11.
58. A. Rich, *The Dream of a Common Language: Poems 1974-1977* (New York: W. W. Norton, 1978), 16.

[8]

Meaning In the Natural World

Joseph Vining

J. B. White devoted much of his work to the rescue of meaning in language, art, and the human world. The first book he published after his seminal *Legal Imagination* was *When Words Lose Their Meaning*. *The Edge of Meaning* appeared as he was entering his fourth decade of teaching. Pick up the last of his books on law and life, *Living Speech*, and you find chapters headed "Living Speech and the Mind Behind It," "The Desire for Meaning," "Human Dignity and the Claim of Meaning," What he did—against the grain of twentieth-century thought—was inspired and inspiring, and is still.

Is there meaning in nature and natural objects that we do not put there? Are they a source of meaning for the modern mind, despite standard teaching that separates the human world from the natural world, or that incorporates the human into a natural world in which there is no meaning?

"The painting," White says in the first paragraph of *The Edge of Meaning*, "has much of its life and meaning in the world beyond words, in the world of color and form and texture, the world of sensation and vision. Something similar could be said about music as well—it is its own world, not reducible to language—and about the physical world of nature too: What in the end can one say about a foggy morning on a rocky coast; the bright blue flowers on the edge of a midwestern country road; the stone smoothed by the waters of a river into a shape with form and balance?"

Life and meaning may dwell in a world beyond words, in experience of visual art and music and also in experience of "physical nature." This essay picks up the last of these, physical nature, and pursues the thought through what I will call the problem of the objet trouvé.

The term "objet trouvé," the "found object," is from the modern history of self-conscious art, but what it describes can be seen to extend far beyond. An objet trouvé is distinguished in French from the "objet d'art" on one side and the artisanal and decorative "objet de vertu" on the other. Many of us have an objet trouvé tucked away somewhere. I go into a friend's office and see on his desk a stone, pink granite, etched with lines that remind me of a tree. I ask him why he likes it. "I don't know, I just do," he says. He had picked it up on the lakeshore and kept it ever since. On the corner of my desk is a stone that caught my eye on a beach by the Bay of Fundy, as that "stone smoothed by the waters of a river into a shape with form and balance" caught White's eye. Mine has an oval shape, when it is wet it is a handsome reddish brown, and there are concentric ellipses or ovals etched on it. When my eye happens to pick it out again on my desk I don't think just of the Bay of Fundy.

Objets trouvés are not all tucked away. You see them on fireplace mantels. You can hardly climb a flight of stairs in a California beach house without looking at a piece of driftwood set at the top. They mimic art, they come so close to art that the line between the found object picked up on the beach and art itself may quiver in our minds. Objets trouvés appear in museums. The "St Edmund" in Kettle's Yard Museum at Cambridge University is a piece of burnt willow picked up beside the River Cam.[1] The Richard Rosenblum Collection of Chinese Scholars' Rocks toured museums in the United States and Europe in the late 1990s. The descriptions of the rocks in the catalog published by the Harvard University Art Museums are not different from descriptions of works of art, thoughtfully and extensively examining every aspect and detail of the pieces.[2]

At home or in a museum these objects are called "found" rather than "presented" or "given" or "made," which would imply some one or more of us making, presenting, or giving. They are objects that are chosen and isolated out for special attention from the innumerable objects our attention flickers over in the course of a lifetime.

Many may also have on a stand a chambered nautilus cut in half. This I think is not the same. Art may mimic the chambered nautilus—using for instance the golden section traced in its curves—but the objet trouvé mimics art. There is a pull and a tug in the objet trouvé the eye lights upon. A landscape etched on a rock that you reach down and pick up is an objet trouvé pointing to the painted landscape. The painted landscape will be hung over the mantel, and perhaps have a ceiling light directed on it. The etched rock will be on the mantel or a shelf, and the object of nature mimicking nothing will be on a separate shelf. A dog also in the room, I should say, will be on a mat on the floor and would not be mistaken for either a thing of nature or a thing of art.

What then is the problem of the objet trouvé? Briefly stated, it is that the pathetic fallacy may not entirely be a fallacy. The thing of nature is as different from the work of art as nature is from the human mind and heart—nature as we now understand and investigate it; yet in the end, the thing made by us and at least some things made by nature are difficult to distinguish from one another. Each time we pick up and keep a stone there is a prodding to wonder whether deep within we must be thinking of nature more as we think of ourselves.

The problem of the objet trouvé may also encompass much of what judges and lawyers do in law and academic law. While they do not work with objects as artists do, they certainly work with texts framed and put on pedestals, arguing about them and interpreting or translating them. Judges invoke them as reasons and justifications for their most awful actions—ripping a baby from a mother's arms and giving it to someone else, putting someone to death, impoverishing someone, destroying someone's lifework. For any such action they and we must say they have authority, and the authority for it is found ultimately in a reading of such texts. There is no clear line between objects that can be framed or put on pedestals, and texts. If you were walking along the beach and you watched a wave pass over pebbles and move them about and withdraw, and you saw left there the words "You are loved" traced out in pebbles, you might think of walling off that spot, cutting it out and lifting it gingerly into a box, and bringing it home to contemplate. Word shapes that appear in a piece of legislation and that are the outcome of the processes of legislation, and judicial or administrative opinions that are the outcome of bureaucratic processes, may not be very different. We return to such texts at the end.

In fact whenever anything, a text, a reified "idea," a method, an attitude, an arrangement, is viewed at the start not as an expression of mind but as the product of "sociocultural forces" and as no more that the product of such forces, it presents something of the problem of the objet trouvé. Across the humanities, including art history and intellectual history, students can face the question of what we might call the "substantive blankness" of their objects of study. But lawyers facing the same question must resolve it in some way, or try to put it out of mind, as others are not required to do.

How often have you like me lain on your back studying the patterns of the branches of a tree against the sky? Absorbed in these branches, following their tracings and shapes like lines in music, are you reading them, translating them, interpreting them as you might interpret another"s painting of them? You can read, translate for yourself, interpret a phrase of Mozart's that is wonderfully reproduced or mimicked by note sequences from the wind chimes on your porch on a summer afternoon; but do you read, translate for yourself, or interpret the note sequences that continue to emerge afterwards, the phrases of the wind chimes themselves?

On the question of trees, in his late-nineteenth century autobiography John Ruskin describes his coming at age twenty-three to his own answer, which was not "no," but "yes":

> I found myself lying on the bank of a cart-road in the sand, with no prospect whatever but that small aspen tree against the blue sky. Languidly, but not idly, I began to draw it; and as I drew, the languor passed away: the beautiful lines insisted on being traced, – without weariness. More and more beautiful they became, as each rose out of the rest, and took its place in the air. With wonder increasing every instant, I saw that they 'composed' themselves by finer laws than any known of men. At last the tree was there, and everything I had thought about trees, nowhere.[3]

What is taught implicitly or explicitly in most schools today, and becomes the first instinct of many sensitive and sensible people, is that the pattern of a tree's branches, or the driftwood on the stairs, the piece of burnt willow called the St Edmund, my Bay of Fundy stone, the Chinese scholar's rock, White's stone smoothed into a shape with form and balance, cannot any of them be read closely. One aspect of it here cannot be looked at in relation to another there, this telling detail against that telling detail and all against the whole, the question *why* always hovering in the background, why is this done in just this way and why does just this way move me so? In the case of the wholly natural objet trouvé many might think today that there is no question *why* there is a graceful curve or a juxtaposition of detail. There is only the question *how*, how the curve or juxtaposition came to be. The question *how* is a question of process and of history, which does not reach the question *why* that we continue to push and push when we read a work of art or a text for its meaning, or read a person, or read our own lives. And if, when you lie staring up beneath a tree, you do bring your meaning to the shapes, the tracings, the marks, the contrasts of light and shade, and do not take meaning from them because you feel sure you know there was no meaning put in them in their making and so there is none there to be taken, then you are not interpreting them in saying what you may go on to say about them to someone or to yourself. You are using them as you might use any other device to say what you are otherwise moved to say.

But does any of us actually know that there was no meaning put in them to take? What we are trying to understand is part of the common experience of meaning in the various situations where we do have the experience. This common teaching depends upon a fundamental difference between meaning coming from within and meaning coming from without. So often the experience of meaning is experience of an intimation, which faint or strong cannot be defined enough to draw lines around it and speak of its being either inside or outside. If the meaning we experience in the presence of a natural object is something new, a discovery, or if it seems not new but richer or deeper than what we had before, why would we have to say that what revealed it to us was only a meaningless trigger, insignificant in itself? How could we be so sure that the meaning we sense, new or richer or deeper, was "already there" in us, created by us rather than "half-created," if it is so connected in time, place, sound, and sight to what we are arrested by and drawn to contemplate?

Return to the wind chimes on the porch imitating Mozart, and imagine listening to Arvo Pärt's contemporary *Te Deum* for chorus, orchestra, prepared piano, and wind harp. Pärt uses a wind harp, he says

> designed and built by a Norwegian master craftsman on principles similar to those of the Greek Aeolian harp. Its strings are set in motion by the breath of the wind.... it's as if the harp is waiting for the wind's caress. A wonderful tape was created that I have employed as a pedal point in the *Te Deum*; ...[4]

The winds heard through the harp are, in the *Te Deum*, an objet trouvé because the tape of the sounds they made is selected, a "wonderful tape". The tape was "created", but I doubt that Pärt thought of himself as creator. The ultimate source was "the wind"s caress", for which the harp was as if "waiting".

Pärt also says of the liturgical text of the *Te Deum*, "To me, it is like the panorama of a mountain range in its constant stillness. The Swiss painter Martin Ruff once told me that in clear weather he could distinguish more than twenty shades of blue; I immediately began to "hear" these "blue" mountains".[5] Pärt refers to the "spirit" of the listener to his music as a "prism" that can make the colors appear. Some see his music as a "form of prayer". Such discourse, using the words "prayer" and "spirit", is perhaps intentionally incompatible with acceptance of the understanding of the nature of the natural world now taught to us when we are young. The artist here has no knowledge, is sure that he does not know, that you do not take meaning from an objet trouvé because there was no meaning put into it in its making.

We may wonder whether the way we work to understand visual art or music or written texts, our approach to them or our "method" as professionals say, is different from our approach to an objet trouvé. Instinct might tell us a painting or a sculpture must have flaws, but that an objet trouvé cannot have flaws, or, perversely, is nothing but flaws. When we look long at the painting or sculpture, we attempt to understand and respond to each part of it, each detail meaningful and related in meaning to every other. The assumption behind looking long is that there is mind, conscious, semiconscious, and unconscious, behind the whole and all its parts offered to be visually read. But if a detail does not fit what we take from that mind's expression, no matter how hard we work to mold the "what" to connect the detail, we can treat it as a flaw and read it away. We can even think that the maker would have rued it and wanted it read away. The sculptor of the *Venus de Milo*, if with us today, might pause before replacing the sculpture's arms that its history took from it to give us the iconic form reproduced throughout the Western world.[6]

Can an unaltered stone focused upon by another and picked up and displayed and preserved—White's stone that had form and balance—be closely read in the same way, with details set aside as insignificant if they do not fit what one finally takes from it? There is mind, White's mind, in the selection of that natural object. There are parts or forms or aspects that struck his conscious or unconscious attention and led him to pick it out from all the other stones that he had seen on the way that brought him to it. You would not be foolish to seek to know what those aspects were, what White found alive to him, meaningful, beautiful. But even with the selector present, the best evidence of what they are is the thing itself, which is before you. One cannot help looking at it for oneself, and White would want you to. You would not be foolish in engaging in the same exercise that you would with a painting or sculpture or piece of writing before you, as if the stone were a painting, sculpture, or writing that its makers had made and remade many times before finally one day selecting what was being presented to them by themselves, as good enough despite its meaningless detail. Not foolish, that is, except for certain knowledge that every object presented by inanimate nature cannot have meaning.

We know, too, that after working with an objet trouvé other than our own, it does not shatter the world we experience together, and tell each other about, to accept that it can strike individuals in different ways or not at all. The same is true of an objet d'art.

The most common attention to an objet trouvé, I think, is love of a landscape, which is an object though it must remain where it is found. Love is not too strong a word for the connection. It can be seen across times, cultures, and positions in life. Neither the experience itself nor its inspiration to art, that in turn invites dwelling upon and discussion, can be dismissed by invoking the pathetic fallacy. There are the imperatives of one's own experience when one has it, and there is the witness of so many sane and reflective people. There is some current effort to dismiss it through the extension of evolutionary explanations to "evolutionary aesthetics," the "beauty" and "meaning" of a landscape resolved for example into a neural linkage between a particular retinal image and a prehistoric memory of prospective safety or good things to eat. This is speculative play, playing with the premises of a discipline based, interestingly, on the insights of one who in the end found landscape his only aesthetic experience.[7]

A linkage of a recognizable kind is succinctly put, perhaps too strongly for some, by the painter narrator of Reynolds Price's *The Tongues of Angels*:[8]

> What led me to the long horizontal west range was my growing sense that the line itself was a calligraphed sentence. Those hazy hard peaks on a harder blue sky. It was some coded combination of meanings that, if ever deciphered, would free mankind and forever reward us. I had few illusions of cracking the code. But as late as that summer, I did believe that if I could transfer the line to canvas and set all patient watchers to work on the tasks of translation, what grace might I not set loose in the world?

Landscape presses the problem of the objet trouvé one step further. A landscape does not come framed. The drawing does, the oil, the photograph, but not the landscape itself. The composition of the rock, the water, and the light in the leaves comes suddenly as a gift when we are moving, in space and, of course, through time.

We move up a valley, and look back. *There* is what grips us—but *here* it is that we are gripped. We move across a valley, emerge into an opening between two trees, and there it is, the composition. Five hundred yards before it would not have been the same, five hundred yards after it would not have been the same, and this gap in the forest is what allows us to see it.

The blue mountains that a composer hears or the line traced by peaks against a blue sky that a painter sees can be found by any one of us, but only if our paths are like theirs. To the eye of any one of us nature constantly changes as we move through it. Step to the left, step to the right, and it is different. Hence a dynamic element, a dimension of time, is added to the nature of the gift we wonder about when we are enthralled or see another sane and sensitive person enthralled by juxtapositions, lines, curves, foregrounds, lights.

Think of any example of landscape's pull on you or another. Here is a small example, an excerpt from an early attempt to capture it, *Grongar Hill*, interesting because of the steady popularity of these rhymed lines, in anthologies since 1727:

> Grongar Hill invites my song,
> Draw the landskip bright and strong;
>
> . . . .
>
> Now I gain the mountains's brow;
> What a landskip lies below!
>
> . . . .
>
> See on the mountain's southern side,
> Where the prospect opens wide,
> Where the evening gilds the tide;
> How close and small the hedges lie!
> What streaks of meadow cross the eye![9]

All this is perspective's gift.

The dangerous question is how much the gift of perspective is "merely a matter of chance." The question is of course companion to the question how much the form upon which the eye dwells from its vantage point is itself a matter of chance. How much (can the thought be even entertained?) is there a guiding of the personal and human journey to that point, a setting of that line of sight from that point to that set of forms seen so only from that point in wait for the eye to come to that point? You cannot entertain the thought that something dwells in or speaks from the composition and the form before the eye, and ignore the fact that the form appears as it does because of your place and perspective.

Return now to the "You are loved" in pebbles left on the beach by a wave and the problems presented by texts, including legal texts, which are not expressions of an individual or joint author. Can texts that are the result of legislative and bureaucratic processes be read closely? Are they like found objects, our objets trouvés, and subject to the same thought that they can be sources of meaning? Or are they like outputs of that category of computer program, not theory-based but heuristically put together by many programmers over many years, which a pioneer of computer programming, Joseph Weizenbaum, early and urgently warned about?

> [Some] programs rest on mathematical control theory and on firmly established physical theories.... [H]uman monitors can detect that their performance does not correspond to the dictates of their theory and can diagnose the reason.... But most existing programs, and especially the largest and most important ones, are not theory-based in this way.... [T]heir construction is based on rules of thumb, stratagems that appear to "work" under most foreseen circumstances, and on other ad-hoc mechanisms that are added to them from time to time.... [D]ecisions are made with the aid of, and sometimes entirely by computers whose programs no one any longer knows explicitly or understands. [A decision-maker] cannot help but base his judgments on "what the computer says," but no human is responsible at all for the computer's output. The enormous computer systems in the Pentagon and their counterparts elsewhere in our culture have, in a very real sense, no authors. Thus they do not admit of any questions of right or wrong, of justice, or of any theory with which one can agree or disagree.[10]

Should it ever happen, discovery of wave-traced word shapes on a beach might present the major question that human experience with objets trouvés presents. The anonymous output of such word shapes by systems in which human beings have had a hand cannot present those questions, I think, because of our responsibility for the nature of at least some things in the world. We all are ultimately responsible for these systems and for what they do, and for our subjection to them.

More importantly, outputs that are offered as texts to be read in law would be connected to action. To experience meaning in the presence of an objet trouvé moves us in the opposite direction, toward stasis, wonder, quiet listening, acceptance. Something becomes an objet trouvé all the more clearly when it is kept and protected from change—stone, landscape, or wind. It can be a candidate even for preservation over spans of time as some music and some art is preserved.

As for language itself, we return to the body of White's work. White shows language to us as a marvel like no other. For any of us during our lives, the meaning of language is personal. Meaning is not given to language by any system and there is no one in the world who can say what the meaning of a word must be, the marks and sounds called a word, or what must be the meaning of a phrase, sentence, paragraph, or book. Yet we are born into language. It is a given for each of us, to work with until we die. Each of us affects it to some degree, in its gradual change and possible progress, but we will have been affected by it much more. It is especially vulnerable to meaninglessness, meaninglessness and worse—the reverse of life and strength, which White presses us to see. Or it can be what White calls "living speech," which he has so beautifully demonstrated himself. But it is not part of the natural world around us. It is something else to be understood, with its own beauty and music.

What is the problem of the thing of nature brought into the world of art as if it were art? The problem is its unsettling whisper in our ear of what we may in fact believe, that it and that from which it comes, even the movement and shape of our own lives that brought us to it, are not chance or the results of a mindless system, but something breaking through the difference between nature and the human, which we can accept as a gift.

Notes

1. J. Ede, *A Way of Life: Kettle's Yard* (Cambridge: Cambridge University Press, 1984), 167. ("John Catto found this extraordinary bit of a burnt willow tree beside the Cam. He called it 'St Edmund.' Thanks to his perception and generosity in giving it to Kettle's Yard I am able to introduce this formidable presence into this book. I should think it is very seldom that so remarkable a 'natural object' has been preserved."); "New Light on Kettle's Yard," *Cambridge University Newsletter*, March/April 1995, 3 ("Nine of today's leading artists have been invited to make new work in the house in response to Kettle's Yard and its collection.... David Nash has made a sculpture inspired by a charred willow branch which Jim Ede adopted and christened 'St Edmund.'")
2. R D Mowry et al, *Worlds Within Worlds: The Richard Rosenblum Collection of Chinese Scholars" Rocks* (Cambridge, MA, Harvard University Art Museums, 1997).
3. J. Ruskin, *Praeterita: Outlines of Scenes and Thoughts Perhaps Worthy of Memory in My Past Life*, with an introduction by Kenneth Clark (London: Rupert Hart-Davis, 1949), 284–85.
4. University Musical Society, "The Estonian Philharmonic Chamber Choir *and the* Tallinn Chamber Orchestra Program," University of Michigan, November 5, 1995, 25; S. Greenbaum, "Arvo Pärt"s *Te Deum:* A Compositional Watershed," (PhD diss., University of Melbourne, 1999), 92-93, citing H. Robinson, "Arvo Pärt and Medieval Modernism," *Stagebill*, New York, Lincoln Center, 1995, 20C.
5. Robinson, "Arvo Pärt and Medieval Modernism."
6. A. Pasquier, *La Vénus de Milo et les Aphrodites du Louvre* (Paris: Editions de la Réunion des Musées Nationaux, 1985), 30-41 (drawings of possible placings of the lost arms).
7. C. Darwin, *Autobiography* (New York: Harcourt, Brace and Company, 1959 [1887]), 138, 139. ("I retain some taste for fine scenery, but it does not cause me the exquisite delight which it formerly did.... My mind seems to have become a kind of machine for grinding general laws out of large collections of facts, but why this should have caused the atrophy of that part of the brain alone, on which the higher tastes depend, I cannot conceive.")
8. R. Price, *The Tongues of Angels* (New York: Ballantine Books, 1991), 42.
9. *The Poetical Works of John Dyer* (Edinburgh: Apollo Press, 1779) (unabridged facsimile, Adamant Media Corporation, 2006), 13, 14, 17, lines 13-14, 41, 42, 114-18.

For a tribute to it, see W. Wordsworth, *To the Poet, John Dyer* in *The Collected Poems of William Wordsworth* (Ware, Hertfordshire: Wordsworth Editions Limited, 1994), 301: "Yet pure and powerful minds, hearts meek and still, / A grateful few, shall love thy modest Lay, ... / Long as the thrush shall pipe on Grongar Hill."

10. J. Weizenbaum, *Computer Power and Human Reason: From Judgment to Calculation* (New York: W. H. Freeman, 1976), 232, 236, 239. ("My own program, ELIZA, was of precisely this type" [232]). ELIZA was Weizenbaum's mock psychotherapist that listened and spoke. It was taken seriously by many both lay and professional, which so startled Weizenbaum that he stopped to write *Computer Power*.

[9]

Reading Materials

The Stuff that Legal Dreams are Made On
Gary Watt

"What in the end can one say about a foggy morning on a rocky coast; the bright blue flowers on the edge of a midwestern country road; the stone smoothed by the waters of a river into a shape with form and balance?"

This question, taken from the first page of James Boyd White's *The Edge of Meaning*, is the one I will respond to in this essay.[1] Obviously we must begin, where White begins, by acknowledging that words alone are not sufficient to express our experience of material stuff, whether that stuff is naturally occurring or fashioned by human hands; words are insufficient because material stuff "has much of its life and meaning in the world beyond words."[2] Nevertheless, there is something in White's expressed appreciation of "form and balance" that indicates the possibility of engaging with things in ways that might productively correspond with the ways in which we engage with words. I want to suggest that there is a materiality to the matter of words that is every bit as material as the stuff we hold in our hands and the stuff we hold within the scope of our physical view. This means that an appreciation of the forms of things can assist us to appreciate the forms of words and the forms of words can assist us in the appreciation of the form of things. Many practical benefits may follow if we our mindful of this mutual materiality. For instance, a more meaningful appreciation of the material world beyond words might open a way to improved environmental respect; and a more meaningful appreciation of the materiality of words might open a way to more just and finely honed judgment. Appreciation of the materiality of that which is humanly meaningful might also provide a solid basis for an appropriately harmonious, touching and responsive social constitution.

Modern legal language within European language groups derives by a disconcertingly direct line from Proto-Indo-European root language that was formed around 4500–4000 BC and was brought to Greece by the Greek speakers around 2300–1600 BC.[3] Between those periods, around 3000 BC, a piece of jade quarried in the Italian Alps was smoothed and polished into a sharp-edged hand axe, probably designed more for symbolic use to indicate status than as an everyday tool. The jade axe, which made its way to England and was eventually unearthed in Canterbury in the county of Kent, resides today in the collection of the British Museum. Neil McGregor, the director of the British Museum and author of *The History of the World in 100 Objects*, notes that the teardrop-shaped blade, roughly equivalent in size to a modern tablet mobile phone, was the cutting-edge technology of its day. He notes, elsewhere, that modern brain-scan technology has revealed that when a human hones a stone into a blade, the part of the brain that is stimulated is the part concerned with language and speech.[4] Does this mean that honing a stone is like honing a sentence? Yes, but it is more accurate to say that the process of forming a sentence resembles the process of forming a tangible tool—for the latter came first. If a sentence is indeed a just sentence in the sense of having a sound form and a good fit to the context and the occasion, we should credit its pleasing form to the same fundamental qualities that make for a pleasing material object. A just and fitting phrase appears well to human sense and handles well as a thing that can in practical terms serve a human need—whether that need is for symbolism or for purposes more pragmatic. There may be something in the sense that a statement is finely-formed, well-balanced and weighty that still owes something to a primal desire to take hold of it tangibly.[5] Even now when we are confronted by primal joy and primal grief, we relinquish modern means of language and find that meaningful expression can only be achieved by resort to earlier tongues of gesture, touch and tangible matter. Think how inadequate are words where meaning is most needed. In great grief, only a silent embrace and an eloquent look will suffice. In anguish, clothes are rent. In great joy, we are speechless. We might, in our exuberance have no response but to strip naked like Archimedes.

At the joyful dénouement of Shakespeare's *The Winter's Tale*, where King Leontes is reconciled to the faithful nobleman Camillo and his childhood friend, the King of Bohemia, the poet cannot describe the emotion except by giving an account of its ineffability. He reports that gesture and garment took the place of words. Note Shakespeare's typically graphic, even visceral, use of material metaphors:

FIRST GENTLEMAN
I make a broken delivery of the business; but the changes I perceived in the king and Camillo were very notes of admiration. They seemed almost, with staring on one another, to tear the cases of their eyes. There was speech in their dumbness, language in their very gesture. They looked as they had heard of a world ransomed, or one destroyed. A notable passion of wonder appeared in them...

SECOND GENTLEMAN
...Such a deal of wonder is broken out within this hour that ballad-makers cannot be able to express it.

. . . .

THIRD GENTLEMAN
...Did you see the meeting of the two kings?

SECOND GENTLEMAN
No.

THIRD GENTLEMAN
Then have you lost a sight, which was to be seen, cannot be spoken of. There might you have beheld one joy crown another, so and in such manner that it seemed sorrow wept to take leave of them, for their joy waded in tears. There was casting up of eyes, holding up of hands, with countenances of such distraction that they were to be known by garment, not by favour...I never heard of such another encounter, which lames report to follow it and undoes description to do it. (5.2.7-40, *The RSC Shakespeare*)

Let us suppose that words work because, through metaphor, they carry the image of an object into the mind's eye (or place the shape of an object in the mind's hand). Let us suppose also that objects are meaningful because they form a meaning in the mind that is something like a word. There is truth in Jacques Lacan's poststructuralist claim that words have a god-like dominion over things: that the symbol "is the murder of the Thing"[6] and that "it is the world of words that creates the world of things,"[7] but there is also truth in the opposite possibility that it is the world of things that creates the world of words. Indeed, the processes by which "we are able to transfer objects into the language of words" is, as one author puts it, "truly miraculous."[8]

What might a close correspondence between word and object reveal to us? One possibility is that it will reveal a new source of force. James Boyd White has written of the serious importance of being alert to, and resistant to, the "empire of force" that resides in unthinking and habitual resort to routine forms of words. What if material objects—and their counterparts in the mind and in the imagination—urge us to a certain instinctive response? Is there a risk that we might be enthralled to the force of material forms? Suppose, for example, that we see a tear in a piece of cloth. Is our instinct to "read" the matter pathologically and to respond with an instinctive urge to patch it up? If we have such an instinct, how much does it equate to a lawyer's instinct? Does such an instinct blind us to ways of reading matter in more nuanced and more positive terms? Consider how breaking and tearing held such positive connotations in the passage from Shakespeare just quoted. Consider how different would have been the love and fate of Pyramus and Thisby if they had read the crack in the wall more negatively and the tear in the veil more positively. Robert Frost's beautiful poem "Mending Wall" offers another insight into the constellation of human connection that opens up when stones tumble from a mundane boundary wall. The narrator of that poem cautions that something is lost when a wall is gained. For example, in the line "Before I built a wall I'd ask to know / What I was walling in or walling out."

I do not come to these matters with an empty hand. James Boyd White has provided practical guidance on the handling of difficult material, and not merely the material of words. A good starting point, for example, is his engagement with Frost's "Mending Wall."[9] Two notes of guidance that can be heard to chime throughout White's writings are "transformation" and "integration." We are encouraged to engage with material in a way that respects its original integrity, but also to transform it through fine arts of engagement into material that has a new integrity. Is this a call to patch over difficulties; a call to fill cracks with wax and paint over them—so as to achieve an integrity that is insincere in the original sense of that word? Of course, I do not think so; and of course, it is not. It is, on the contrary, a call to integrate the object to its context and to integrate the observer to both object and context in a way that is humanly meaningful. Let us hear what White himself has to say on the matter of matter. Starting with the composer's art of integration, *Justice as Translation* provides the following insights:

> Authority...lies in a kind of respectful interaction between mind and material, past and present, in which each has its proper contribution to make: not simply in the tradition, then, but in the tradition as it is reconstituted in the present text. The central excellence of the judicial mind is an excellence in the art of composition by which this is achieved.[10]

And a few pages later:

> Meaning and identity lie not in the object itself but in its relations with oth-

ers. The art of the lawyer, like that of the judge, is to put together the prior texts that are the material of law in new compositions, which, while respecting the nature of each item, so order them as to create a new arrangement with a meaning of its own. The art of law is the art of integration.[11]

One of the key challenges offered in *Justice as Translation* and also in *Heracles' Bow: Essays on the Rhetoric and Poetics of the Law*, is to distinguish the merely "material" from the materially "meaningful."[12] A bow, for example, is just a stick and a string. Only a community of human interest in the thing can make it meaningful. In *Heracles' Bow*, Professor White objects to the " ... reduction of the human to the material and the measurable—a reduction of the man to the bow."[13] Cautioning us not to regard the bow as brute material devoid of its social context,[14] he asks:

> Must we see the 'bow of Heracles' simply as an object, or can we see it as having a meaning that is essentially social and rhetorical: as standing for the autonomy and maturity of persons whose voluntary cooperation, upon equal terms, is always to be sought; a symbol of the attainment of full personality, For which community is always necessary?[15]

There is appreciation here for the human capacity to make the object more meaningful in the form of a metaphor than it is in its mere physical form. As he states later in the same book, "language" is "the living material from which meaning is made in our individual and collective lives."[16]

How are we to reconcile this claim for the positive potential of linguistic expression with the seemingly commonplace acceptance that language fails us where we need it most? One way is to develop an appreciation of the material quality of language, including the concrete quality of metaphors, and thereby to render language more touching. What if speech could be formed into an embrace? What if a judicial sentence could be honed and shaped into a touching and pleasing object that feels well in human estimation and fits well in its social context? The writing of James Boyd White urges the hope that we can redeem language from its limited routines in part by reconnecting it to its materiality; to that part of its primal heart that makes it most meaningful.

Crucially, though, the process of meaningful engagement with materiality is not backwards looking, but prospective. This is important in the context of law, for the law transforms the primal material of human life into a new legal matter. Attention to materiality becomes, accordingly, attention to the art of transformation or translation. *Justice as Translation* contains the following rich passage:

> ... it is in the ordinary lawyer's life that the client comes in the door, full of rage or a sense of injury, or greed or fear, and the lawyer goes to work, con-

verting these primitive feelings into the material for argument and thought of a quite different kind.[17]

In a similar vein, we read in *From Expectation to Experience* that "the law is transformative. It acts upon certain material—the problem or dispute or trouble brought by the client to the lawyer."[18] And in *Living Speech: Resisting the Empire of Force*, Professor White writes that "the lawyer or judge is perpetually refashioning the material of the law …",[19] and that:

> We live our lives on the faith…that law can convert the raw material of human experience—the pain, the fury, the loss—into the material of meaning, and in such a way as to permit or invite or enable meaningful action in response.[20]

And, later:

> The law is in this way a cultural process, working on the raw material of life—the injury to the body or the psyche, the failed business, the broken marriage, the vulgar words in the courthouse—to convert it into something else, something of its own …[21]

This brings us very close to the idea of law as an art of handling and honing material. An art, which corresponds to the art of writing as it is described in *Living Speech*:

> Writing is a material art that creates a new and immaterial dimension of experience, a field of life, running across time and space, resisting the natural process of decay.[22]

This "material art" by which law translates life into new matter is akin to the "material art" of writing. It is an art that has metaphor at its heart. *Translatio* is, after all, the Latin translation of the Greek term μεταφορά ("metaphor").[23] In his journal entry for May 10, 1853, Henry David Thoreau wrote about the abundant expressive and metaphorical capacity of the material world:

> He is the richest who has most use for nature as raw material of tropes and symbols with which to describe his life. If these gates of golden willows affect me, they correspond to the beauty and promise of some experience on which I am entering. If I am overflowing with life, am rich in experience for which I lack expression, then nature will be my language full of poetry—all nature will *fable*, and every natural phenomenon be a myth. The man of science, who is not seeking for expression but for a fact to be expressed merely, studies nature as a dead language. I pray for such inward experience as will make nature significant.

In *Walden*, Thoreau describes an effort which, in Professor White's description, was an effort to "reach a point beyond words":[24]

> I did not read books the first summer; I hoed beans. Nay, I often did better than this. There were times when I could not afford to sacrifice the bloom of the present moment to any work, whether of the head or hands... I grew in those seasons like corn in the night, and they were far better than any work of the hands would have been.[25]

According to James Boyd White:

> This is an image of life without language; yet it is presented in language, and it implies, what virtually every sentence shows, that for Thoreau language in the usual senses is full of metaphor, or more than that, is metaphor itself. The springs of life lie outside the circles of our languages.[26]

When we look elsewhere in the writings of James Boyd White, we find that the art of language that he describes as a "material art" of translation is an art that corresponds with other, more materially immediate, arts of crafting; such as painting and sculpture. Thus in *Acts of Hope: Creating Authority in Literature, Law, and Politics*, we read that:

> It is after all the nature of cultural processes, including law, to transform the material with which they work. A block becomes a statue, a palette of colors a painting, and, in the law, the trial of a bootlegger the occasion for a great constitutional case.[27]

This brings us back to the stone with which we began—the one that was "smoothed by the waters of a river into a shape with form and balance." All stones have a certain appeal to the human mind, but the standing stone has a special appeal. The sculptor Sir Anthony Caro sees "sculpture, the setting up of a stone, as a basic human activity. You are investing that stone with some sort of emotive power, some sort of presence."[28] The appeal is perhaps especially strong for lawyers and others who are concerned to establish the solidity of a cultural tradition. It is not by accident that the earliest laws were set up on standing stones or steles and etched into stone tablets. The fact that stones endure is not the only, or indeed the main, feature that makes them pleasing to human sense. If solidity were our only concern, we might as well admire a mountain. More important than solidity is stability. What makes a stone so significant to social sense is the fact that it can be artificially set up and made to stand, and may be thereby transformed—metaphorically (that is, literally)—from mere matter into meaningful material. It is a mistake, though, to suppose that a stone must be symmetrical if it is to stand with pleasing stability. When Professor White admired the stone that was "smoothed by the waters of a river into a shape with form and balance," he must have been admiring a form that had balance despite—or by virtue of—a degree of asymmetry. An architect friend of mine once advised me that the key to a harmonious structure is to seek balance without symmetry. What is true of architectural fascia is true of human faces. Higher levels of facial symmetry have been associated with higher levels of facial attractiveness, but it is also true that no naturally occurring face, no matter how attractive, is perfectly symmetrical. The same is true, even if it is less apparent, in the case of stones crafted by the natural flow of waters. It seems that we admire symmetrical forms provided that symmetry is not taken to unnatural excess.

Insight into the aesthetics of tangible materiality might produce insight into the pleasing shape of a social constitution. For example, though we admire equality as we admire symmetry, are we not opposed to a strict rule of equality—the equality of the scales—when it is taken to exact and unnatural extremes? "Indigenous" or "First Nations" art is profoundly responsive to the material form of a just constitutional disposition. Such art has shown itself, in many of its varieties, to be especially adept when it comes to expressing political justice in the form of fashioned materials without the medium of words. The anthropologist Gary Witherspoon has learned a great deal in this regard from Navajo culture. In his book, *Language and Art in the Navajo Universe,* he contrasts "static symmetry" with "dynamic symmetry":

> Static symmetry is absolute balance without any oppositions, contrasts, or disequilibrium. Dynamic symmetry expresses motion and energy created by oppositions, contrasts and disequilibrium.[29]

As an example he cites a painting in which colors are alternated in opposing figures.[30] This is reminiscent of observations made by the English artist John Ruskin in his book *The Stones of Venice*. Ruskin observed a profound dynamic at play in the work of the medieval colorists. He described it as:

> the union of one colour with another by reciprocal interference: that is to say, if a mass of red is to be set beside a mass of blue, a piece of the red will be carried into the blue, and a piece of the blue carried into the red; sometimes in nearly equal portions, as in a shield divided into four quarters, of which the uppermost on one side will be of the same colour as the lowermost on the other; sometimes in smaller fragments, but, in the periods above named, always definitely and grandly, though in a thousand various ways. And I call it a magnificent principle, for it is an eternal and universal one, not in art only, but in human life. It is the great principle of Brotherhood, not by equality, nor by likeness, but by giving and receiving; the souls that are unlike, and the nations that are unlike, and the natures that are unlike, being bound into one noble whole by each receiving something from, and of, the others' gifts and the others' glory.[31]

Ruskin describes a constitutional disposition that is pleasing and harmonious in its diversity because it presents something more than strict equality. It is also something more than static, because it entails a dynamic of giving and receiving. These are qualities to be admired in a great deal of First Nations' art. I recently had the privilege of visiting the Canadian west coast of British Columbia. From a European perspective it is a fascinating and challenging place—the last shore of the West, where the diaspora of Proto-Indo-European language and thought finally crashes against the great ocean. First Nations' art thrives here. Indeed, on arrival at Vancouver International Airport I was greeted by the wonderful sculpture *The Spirit of Haida Gwaii*, by Bill Reid, a master carver of the indigenous Haida people. It is a piece that is perfectly harmonious and moving because it is perfectly asymmetrical and dynamic. James Tully's book *Strange Multiplicity: Constitutionalism in an Age of Diversity* offers an extended engagement with the constitutional idea that is carried in Bill Reid's remarkable sculpture of a crowded canoe.[32] Tully acknowledges great virtue in the dynamic symmetry of the piece, which he expresses in terms of the fact that it is inherently moving and is not symmetrical or otherwise uniform:

> The *Spirit of Haida Gwaii* is designed to awaken and stimulate ... dialogical capacity for diversity awareness. As you walk around the canoe you soon realize that it is impossible to take it in from one comprehensive viewpoint ... Since recognition is never definitive, the particular constitutional arrangement of the members of the canoe is presumably not meant to be fixed once and for all.... the constitutional arrangement of the canoe is far from uniform. The members make up an association more akin to the irregular arrangement of an ancient, custom-based constitution than to a modern, uniform constitutional association.[33]

I was privileged to encounter another monumental example of First Nations' art on my recent visit to Vancouver. In the Vancouver Art Gallery, Haida artist James (Jim) Hart and his team were completing *The Dance Screen (The Scream Too)*. The solid screen is almost twice as high as a tall man and is wider than it is tall. Its thickness undulates around about a foot or so of rich red cedar. The undulations correspond to the beautifully worked forms and patterns that curve and contour over the entire face of the piece. And it *is* a face of sorts. A central stylized visage gapes its mouth into a door through which a child, or even with some endeavor a grown man, could dance. My initial encounter with this work was overwhelming, awe-inspiring. Only on later reflection did I appreciate that part of its challenge resides in the fact that it is contained within a European architectural space of classical columns, porticoes and a dome, a building which—enticingly—had once been the main courthouse of Vancouver. Another dimension of the challenge is the fact that it has a notional name—a title. It is supremely difficult to liberate stuff from the confines of its spatial context and from linguistic capture through conceptual naming, even for a culture like the Haida culture, which may be said to refer to, and to respect, image more than letter. The parenthetical subtitle *(The Scream Too)* is, perhaps, a way of opening the title up to infinite associations. The piece resembles a primal scream of nature and calls to mind a long tradition of First Nations' art, but for this observer it also calls to mind another tradition of art, that includes the studies by the Norwegian artist Edvard Munch, which he named *Der Schrei der Natur* (The scream of nature). Should we reject the norm of naming? Is it forceful? Is it imperious? I think it will be sufficient to have regard to it and to resist it where necessary. We cannot escape the conclusion that context and category is the social stuff that turns material stuff into what we recognize as art.

The Dance Screen (The Scream Too) has a speechless appeal in its very shape—it has a form and balance which one might fancy was made by water if one hadn't with one's own eyes seen Jim Hart and his son and their colleagues patiently scalloping the cedar with wood-turning tools and tenderly shaving it into a sea of wooden waves. The work will not be finally fulfilled until, like *The Spirit of Haida Gwaii*, members of the public are free to feel it, and hopefully to dance through it. One feels in the meantime an almost irresistible compulsion to touch the perfectly smoothed and crafted contours of the sculpture. The piece deserves endless engagement and it will no doubt receive it. There are, however, just a few of its features that I want to focus on here. The first is the potency of the portal. The second is the harmonious asymmetry of the screen. The third is its immense capacity to move despite the seemingly static nature of the structure.

The mouth of the screen invites us to enter, to dance. An aperture very often invites inquiry and communication, especially where it is in the nature of a door; a break in a hedgerow; a gap in a wall. We respond to such things because an obstacle—the wall, the hedge—has opened up to the possibility of human expression and progress. Aperture—a word that is cognate with the Proto-Indo-European for "off with the covers"—may be especially suggestive and stimulating to legal thought. I have argued elsewhere that law and dress (whether in the form of cloth coverings or other adornments) occupy the same social space and perform the same normative role,[34] and, compatible with that, others have observed that one of the dominant metaphors for law is that of the barrier or bulwark.[35] There is something about thresholds, and porous thresholds in particular, which excites the very soul of law. I must acknowledge, of course, that the connection to law is of my imagining and nothing that is demanded by the dance screen itself.

Turning to the aspect of asymmetry, it may be observed that, at first sight, the vast wall of carved wood seems to have formal symmetry about the plane of the central mouth. In fact, closer attention reveals that the symmetry of the piece is not strict. There are subtle and significant contrasting details across the central plane, including a raven on one side and a beaver opposite.

Neither is the piece as static as a narrowly scientific assessment might suggest. Even at an empirical level the piece is still moving. At the time of my visit it was still being carved out of huge hefts of honey-coloured wood; and now that the carving is finished, time itself will take up its tools. The tone of the wood will change with passing days and years. And different lights change things. As Bertrand Russell cautioned us to see, a varnished wooden table that is brown from a certain point of view is shining white from another angle, and its smoothness has the rough peaks and troughs of mountains when regarded microscopically.[36] What are the qualities of the table? What, therefore, is its identity? It is intriguing to think that every new viewer will cast a slightly different shadow on *The Dance Screen (The Scream Too)* and will cast a slightly different glance upon it. No matter how utterly still we might suppose the thing to be, it insists upon slipping out of all containment. In *From Expectation to Experience*, James Boyd White counsels us regarding the complexity of contemplating objects in relation to their context:

> JUST WHEN YOU begin to feel that you have some imaginative grasp of the meaning of the work or artifact in its original context, you are likely to discover that you cannot restate that meaning in any language available to you without great loss. This is partly because the meaning you perceive is specific to the cultural expectations against which it works as I have been saying, and partly for another reason, namely that this experience is shaped by the particular form of the object and by the nature of the materials as well.
>
> You could think of it this way. Why did the cathedral maker or musical composer not simply say what he meant in words? That would certainly be easier and quicker than doing all this work with stone and musical instruments. The answer is that he couldn't.[37]

Imagination is the source of our capacity for transformation and integration of the sort that James Boyd White advocates. Imagination, suitably exercised and embraced, allows one to attune oneself to the manifold connections between an object and its context, it allows one to appreciate the natures and potentials of those connections and it even allows one to propose and explore new possibilities for connection. Hope for transformation—for real translation—depends as much upon respect for the present connections as upon revelation of the new. Appreciation for connection must also be something more than a merely empirical awareness of the connection between components. There are better *Lessons on Objects* to be learned than those we find in Dr. Elizabeth Mayo's eponymous work of 1839, in which a "A Key" is described as to its parts: "The ring; barrel; wards; grooves; edges; surfaces; corners" and as to its qualities: "it is hard steel, or iron, bright, cold; opaque; smooth, stiff liable to rust; part of the barrel is hollow; the barrel is cylindrical; the ring is curved."[38] There is nothing in this early Victorian object lesson that communicates the potent symbolism of the key; its inherent promise to open doors to earthly and heavenly power and still less (though it would be unfair to expect it in a school manual) of the dynamic which drove the girl in the fairy-tale to chop off her little finger for use as a key.[39] We are told how a key feels, but not how it *makes* us feel.

When we reach for it, we can sometimes touch transformational meanings in the most meager matter. There is hardly any manufactured stuff more basic than bread. It is made of basic stuff and the compound cannot be unmade into its constituent parts. And yet even basic bread has the potential to acquire immense cultural meaning in context. As White puts it: bread is not only bread; "it is the material of sacrament."[40] That observation comes in *When Words Lose Their Meaning* in the course of contemplations on Jonathan Swift's *A Tale of A Tub*.[41] On the same page, White warns that:

> ... to strip an event or an object of all context and circumstance in the interest of 'plain truth' is to strip it of all meaning; to deny the value of the imagination is to destroy the capacity for sympathy and break down the system of our shared meanings—the 'fictions'—that constitute our culture.[42]

The cultural context of an otherwise ordinary object can produce an invaluable story. It yields a fictive value. It might even yield a financial value. A box of cigars owned by Winston Churchill will have immensely more value by all measures than an otherwise identical box owned by pretty much any other owner. When thinking of things in financial terms we must, of course, beware the error of materialism. That error is well known and reasonably obvious. Less well known, and harder to resist, is the intrinsic force that material stuff works upon the human mind. We instinctively reach to touch the smooth surface, to kick the pebble, to test the wet paint. Stuff touches us and has a moving effect upon us. Our drive to engage with stuff is often deeper than our obedience to the law of letters. The sign warns us not to touch the wet paint, but we do it anyway. We are subject to the object. There is a persuasive power to stuff, which we might call *real* rhetoric. Indeed, we might as well say that stuff speaks directly to our senses—in a voice that is variably striking, soft and sweet. In 1935, the gestalt psychologist Kurt Koffka wrote that "to primitive man each thing says what it is and what he ought to do with it ... a fruit says 'Eat me'; water says 'Drink me'; thunder says 'Fear me.'"[43] We may consider that we are no longer primitive, but is not the case, at the visceral level of appetite and gut feeling, that objects continue to speak to us in a primal language of deep urgings? Dramatists have always appreciated that stage properties or "props"—the bloody handkerchief; the golden crown; the ring; the skull—can hold and move an audience as profoundly as the words and gestures of human actors. Modern states the world over have tended to understate (and have largely failed to understand) the fact that the political domain is a scene made spectacular and compelling by means of its material stage and the material stuff through which it is performed. Shakespeare's forest-dwelling Jaques in *As You Like It* was right when he declared that "All the world's a stage" and "all the men and women merely players" upon it (2.7.142–43), but it is also true to say that the physical scene itself—the costume, the props, the stage—are also at play in an active way. Real rhetoric persuades us just as surely as sweet speech does. Stuff appeals to us, even in its natural, unworked state (one need only think of the primitive appeal of feathers, shells and nuggets of gold). Again, Shakespeare's Jaques sees the truth of the matter:

> And this our life exempt from public haunt
> Finds tongues in trees, books in the running brooks,
> Sermons in stones and good in everything. (2.1.15–17)

Some centuries later, Victor Hugo expressed a similar sentiment in his *Contemplations*:

> *...les choses et l'être ont un grand dialogue.*
> *Tout parle; l'air qui passe et l'alcyon qui vogue,*
> *Le brin d'herbe, la fleur, le germe, l'élément.*
> *T'imaginais-tu donc l'univers autrement?*[44]

The appeal of stuff in its natural state is undeniable, but the persuasive power of objects is perhaps more concentrated and direct where objects are, or are perceived to be, artificial or artistic; that is to say, where objects appear to have been made or influenced by the actions of men and women. Artificial, or "worked," objects invite us to interpret them as modes of direct or indirect human communication, and especially of authorship and authority; as Caroline A Jones writes "it is the point of artworks to be evocative objects, soliciting us to be their subjects."[45] Mute material moves us and moulds our lives as much as any stirring speech; and because it does so silently, it does so subtly, even secretly. Daniel Miller has observed the "unexpected capacity of objects to fade out of focus and remain peripheral to our vision and yet determinant of our behaviour and identity."[46] Given that the power and influence of objects is sometimes hard to discern, we should expect that poets and other imaginative artists will be well-placed to help us in the task of elucidation. Wallace Stevens, a poet I came to through James Boyd White, is a writer who clearly appreciated the potent way in which a commonplace object, when placed in relation to human perception, can command and over-rule its context. This is clearly shown in the following lines taken from his 1918 poem "Anecdote of the Jar":

> I placed a jar in Tennessee,
> And round it was, upon a hill.
> It made the slovenly wilderness
> Surround that hill.
>
> The wilderness rose up to it,
> And sprawled around, no longer wild.
>
> . . . .
>
> It took dominion every where ...

We are obedient, often blithely obedient, to the power of stuff. Suppose that Jack kicks a ball. We tend to say that the object (the ball) has been kicked by the subject (Jack). We naturally think of Jack as the subject of the story, and so he is. However, we also assume that Jack, because he is the human subject of the scene, is the active and powerful party and that the ball, as object, is inanimate and powerless. This is a mistake. If we examine the matter closely we find that the very language of object and subject contains a clue to an opposite truth in which Jack is revealed to be under the power of the ball. We readily accept that the verb "to object" connotes a strong action of opposition, but the same is also true of the noun. The noun "ob-ject" implies that the thing itself has power and is active. The noun "object" and the verb "to object" both originate in the Latin "to throw" (*jacere*). Etymologically speaking, an ob-ject is a thing thrown against us—from the Latin *ob-* (against) and *jactus* (thrown). It turns out that Jack, in our example, is not the powerful party. On the contrary, he is subject to the object. Again, the etymology assists us. Jack is sub-ject, because he is thrown (*jactus* again) under (*sub*) the power of the thing. Jack acts against the ball because the ball has already been thrown against his senses and his attention. We can see, in short, that when Jack kicks a ball, it is because the ball struck him first. There is a sense of this in Sigmund Freud's belief that when the "shadow of the object fell upon the ego," "the latter could henceforth be judged by a special agency, as though it were an object."[47] I am not asking us to believe that the ball is inherently animate; it will suffice to accept that before Jack made a conscious move to kick the ball, his own subconscious had animated the ball towards him. To put it another way, his subconscious self threw the object against his consciousness. Starting with this simple example, we can begin to challenge our natural assumption that the ball is under Jack's conscious power and begin to appreciate the opposite possibility that Jack is subconsciously under the power of the thing. Aristotle, that most keen observer of natural phenomena, said, in similar vein, that when an animal moves towards food, the active party is the food. The food moves the animal, not the other way round. He adds:

> it must necessarily be the case-that many motions are produced in the body by its environment, and some of these set in motion the intellect or the appetite, and this again then sets the whole animal in motion: this is what happens when animals are asleep: though there is then no perceptive motion in them, there is some motion that causes them to wake up again.[48]

There is hope for new and more meaningful human engagement with the material universe; hope for an appreciation that defies any unidirectional dominion of subject and object. Part of that hope is to develop a feel for tangible aspects of translation. We might transform mere rhetoric into material rhetoric; into a rhetoric that is real.

It is not controversial to suggest that one of the most stirring speeches ever heard, was Dr. Martin Luther King Jr.'s address to participants in the March on Washington for Jobs and Freedom, which he delivered from the steps of the Lincoln Memorial in Washington DC on August 28, 1963. Everybody knows that the address culminated with a description of a dream, but what is rarely recalled is that it began with material of a tangible rather than transcendental nature. Dr. King had a truly Shakespearean grasp of the persuasive power of props, even props formed to be held in the mind. He prefaced his address by saying "we've come here today to *dramatize* a shameful condition" (emphasis added), immediately before he delivered the following powerful passage of speech:

> In a sense we've come to our nation's capital to cash a check. When the architects of our republic wrote the magnificent words of the Constitution and the Declaration of Independence, they were signing a promissory note to which every American was to fall heir. This note was a promise that all men, yes, black men as well as white men, would be guaranteed the "unalienable Rights" of 'Life, Liberty and the pursuit of Happiness." It is obvious today that America has defaulted on this promissory note, insofar as her citizens of color are concerned. Instead of honoring this sacred obligation, America has

given the Negro people a bad check, a check which has come back marked "insufficient funds."

But we refuse to believe that the bank of justice is bankrupt. We refuse to believe that there are insufficient funds in the great vaults of opportunity of this nation. And so, we've come to cash this check, a check that will give us upon demand the riches of freedom and the security of justice.

It is not by accident that Dr. King took the stage upon the steps of the Lincoln Memorial, overlooked by the statute of Abraham Lincoln on his stone throne of justice and power; it is not by accident that he talks of drama and of architects, and of banks and checks and funds. He understood that in order to help people to reach the transcendental place of dreams, one has to place their feet upon the foundation of material reality. A mind must be touched, and coaxed into thinking as a touching thing, if it is to reach out and take hold of its dreams. Dr. King understood, as Shakespeare's Prospero understood, that it is "stuff" that "dreams are made on."[49]

And so we come, at last, in its fortieth anniversary year, to *The Legal Imagination*. In that uncontainable work, James Boyd White asks, in the latter pages of the book, "Suppose someone said: 'The law is all in there,' and pointed to the library. Is there a sense in which that statement is true?"[50] Now, as I come to the end of this short essay, I want to offer an answer to that question. The answer, I think, is "yes." Not because the law is only in passages of statutes and reports and textbooks and other such legal material, but because the questioner is indicating a passage that leads through an obstacle and takes us to meaningful engagement with material of all kinds.

Notes

1. J. B. White, *The Edge of Meaning* (Chicago: University of Chicago Press, 2001), 1.
2. White, *The Edge of Meaning*, 1.
3. G. Watt, "Rule of the Root: Proto-Indo-European Domination of Legal Language," in *Current Legal Issues: Law and Language*, ed. F. Smith and A. Lewis (Oxford: Oxford University Press, 2013), 571–89.
4. N. McGregor, *A History of the World in 100 Objects* (London: Penguin, Allen Lane, 2010), 17.
5. "It has of course been pointed out over and over again that all our words for mental processes—'grasp,' 'conceive,' 'understand,' etc. can be traced back historically to an earlier stage when they also signified a material process." O. Barfield, *Speaker's Meaning* (Oxford: Barfield Press, 2011 [1967]) 32.
6. J. Lacan, "Function and the Field of the Word and Language in Psychoanalysis," in *Écrits: A Selection*, trans. Alan Sheridan (London, Routledge, 2001), 77.

7. Lacan, "Function and the Field of the Word and Language in Psychoanalysis," 49.
8. F. M. Gatz, "The Object of Aesthetics," *Journal of Aesthetics and Art Criticism* 1, no. 2-3 (1941): 3-26, 10.
9. White, *The Edge of Meaning*, 200-201.
10. J. B. White, *Justice as Translation: An Essay in Cultural and Legal Criticism* (Chicago: University of Chicago Press, 1990), 172.
11. White, *Justice as Translation*, 214.
12. J. B. White, *Heracles' Bow, Essays on the Rhetoric and Poetics of the Law* (Madison: University of Wisconsin Press, 1985), 43n, 47-48.
13. White, *Heracles' Bow*, 42.
14. White, *Heracles' Bow*, 44n.
15. White, *Heracles' Bow*, 26.
16. White, *Heracles' Bow*, 126.
17. White, *The Edge of Meaning*, 139.
18. J. B. White, *From Expectation to Experience: Essays on Law & Legal Education* (Ann Arbor: University of Michigan Press, 1999), 182.
19. J. B. White, *Living Speech: Resisting the Empire of Force* (Princeton, NJ: Princeton University Press, 2006), 125.
20. White, *Living Speech*, 139-140.
21. White, *Living Speech*, 180.
22. White, *Living Speech*, 124.
23. As Quintilian acknowledged in his *Institutio Oratoria* III, 301-3.
24. White, *The Edge of Meaning*, 17.
25. H. D. Thoreau, *Walden; or, Life in the Woods* (Boston: Ticknor and Fields, 1854), 111.
26. White, *The Edge of Meaning*, 18.
27. J. B. White, *Acts of Hope: Creating Authority in Literature, Law, and Politics* (Chicago: University of Chicago Press, 1994), 180-81.
28. Quoted in McGregor, *A History of the World in 100 Objects*, 451.
29. G. Witherspoon, *Language and Art in the Navajo Universe* (Ann Arbor: University of Michigan Press, 1977), 172. See, further, G. Witherspoon and G. Peterson, *Dynamic Symmetry and Holistic Asymmetry in Navajo and Western Art and Cosmology* (New York: Peter Lang, 1995).
30. G. Witherspoon, *Language and Art in the Navajo Universe*, 172.
31. J. Ruskin, *The Stones of Venice* (London: The Folio Society, 2001), 282-83. (*The Stones of Venice* was first published in three volumes between 1851 and 1853).
32. J. Tully, *Strange Multiplicity: Constitutionalism in an Age of Diversity* (Cambridge: Cambridge University Press, 1995). I first came to Tully's book through Richard Dawson's *Justice as Attunement: Transforming Constitutions in Law, Literature, Economics and the Rest of Life* (Abingdon: Routledge, 2013).
33. Tully, *Strange Multiplicity*, 26
34. G. Watt, *Dress, Law and Naked Truth: A Cultural Study of Fashion and Form* (London: Bloomsbury Academic, 2013).

35. M. S. Ball, *Lying Down Together: Law Metaphor and Theology* (Madison: University of Wisconsin Press, 1985), 36.
36. B. Russell, "Appearance and Reality," in *The Problems of Philosophy* (Oxford: Oxford University Press, 1959), 11.
37. J. B. White, *From Expectation to Experience: Essays on Law & Legal Education* (Ann Arbor: University of Michigan Press, 1999), 97.
38. E. Mayo, *Lessons on Objects: Their Origin, Nature, and Uses for The Use of Schools and Families* (London: Haswell, Barington & Haswell, 1839), 49.
39. J. Grimm and W. Grimm, *Die sieben Raben* ("The Seven Ravens") *Kinder und Hausmärchen* (1812), 25.
40. J. B. White, *When Words Lose Their Meaning: Constitutions and Reconstitutions of Language, Character, and Community* (Chicago: University of Chicago Press, 1984), 134.
41. J. Swift, *A Tale of A Tub* (London: John Nutt, 1704).
42. White, *When Words Lose Their Meaning*, 134.
43. K. Koffka, *Principles of Gestalt Psychology* (New York: Harcourt-Brace, 1935), 7.
44. "things and being maintain a grand dialogue. /Everything speaks: the passing air and the fleeting kingfisher, / The blade of grass, the flower, the seed, the element. / Can you imagine the universe otherwise than this?" [my translation]. From "Ce que dit la bouche d'ombre" ("What the mouth of the shadow speaks"), in *Les Contemplations*, II.6.xxvi (1843–1856), by Victor Hugo. (The French text is from the edition Paris: Flammarion, 1995.)
45. C. A. Jones, "The Painting in the Attic," in *Evocative Objects*, ed. Sherry Turkle (Cambridge, MA: MIT Press, 2007), 233–42, 242.
46. D. Miller, ed., *Materiality* (Durham, NC: Duke University Press, 2005), 5.
47. S. Freud, "Mourning and Melancholia," in *The Standard Edition of the Complete Psychological Works of Sigmund Freud, Volume XIV (1914-1916): On the History of the Psycho-Analytic Movement, Papers on Metapsychology and Other Works* (1915), 237–58, 249.
48. Aristotle, *Physics* Book VIII, part 2, R P Hardie and R K Gaye (trans) "Physica" in W D Ross (ed) *The Works of Aristotle* Vol 2 (Oxford, Clarendon Press, 1930). See, also, Book VII part 1.
49. Shakespeare, *The Tempest*, act 4, scene 1, lines 169–70.
50. J. B. White, *The Legal Imagination: Studies in the Nature of Legal Thought and Expression* (Boston: Little, Brown and Company, 1973), 937.

[10]

Reimagining "The True North Strong and Free"

Reflections on Going to the Movies with James Boyd White
Rebecca Johnson

There is something magical about clear summer nights, the stars scattered across the ceiling of the world, their pinpoints of light an invitation to tilt your head back, possibly to catch sight of a comet. You seek out the North Star, trace the lines of the big dipper, find Orion and Ursa Major, drawing up the stories that go with the images written in the sky. Even as you tell yourself that the images are projections of a human imagination, they seem to have solidity to them, an existence independent of your gaze. And indeed, having grown up with the stories, it is hard to see the night sky without seeing the images there inscribed. And you are surely implicated in the seeing, drawn into particular relationship with both stars, and stories. And you wonder: what constellations of meaning might become visible by both seeing and finding connections between other points of light?

Over the past several years, scanning the night sky, I have frequently found myself reflecting on James Boyd White's *The Legal Imagination*. Sitting in his classroom in 1994, the heavy yellow book open on the desk in front of me, I was sometimes bemused by the invitation to consider distinctly odd ("seemingly non-legal") texts, to consider familiar texts in distinctly odd ways, or to be pressed to create lines of connection between texts (and ideas) not generally set alongside each other. The textbook was itself a scatter of points of light. We were invited to sort through the materials spread out there, select the texts/questions that caught our attention, and create lines of meaning or webs of connection between the texts and ourselves.

In this essay, I share some reflections about the process of using the writings of James Boyd White as a primary resource in the project of sketching out some new constellations of meaning, in which two legal orders might be drawn into more sustained and productive engagement with each other. In this context, my attention is on the night sky north of the 60th parallel, and the ongoing challenges of Indigenous/settler relations in Canada. My focus is a seminar course called "Northern Jurisprudence: Inuit Law and Film", a course deeply influenced by White's approach to law. I will share some thoughts both about the design of this class, its methodology, and lessons learned. Let me begin first with some background, including a few of the lines of connection that link James Boyd White to a Canadian law school seminar on Inuit law and film.

Forty Years of Reimagining: A First Line of Connection

The year 2013 marked the fortieth anniversary of two important moments. One was the 1973 publication of James Boyd's White's book *The Legal Imagination*. Another was the Canadian Supreme Court's 1973 decision in *Calder v British Columbia*.[1] In this groundbreaking case, (brought by Frank Calder, a hereditary chief of the House of Wisinxbiltkw from the Killerwhale Tribe and first status Indian to be elected to any legislature in Canada), the Court acknowledged for the first time that Aboriginal title to land existed prior to the colonization, and that it was not derived from statutory law. The *Calder* case had made its way through the court system as part of a moment of important Indigenous activism in Canada, responding to the release of the infamous White Paper of 1969. To situate the terrain, in 1969, Canadian Prime Minister Pierre Elliot Trudeau and his then Minister of Indian Affairs, Jean Chretien, had released a policy document responding to the government's own studies, which had acknowledged that Aboriginal people were the most disadvantaged and marginalized people in the country. The White Paper proposed that the government rectify the problem (referred to as early as 1928 as "The Indian Problem") and achieve equality between all Canadians by abolishing the Indian Act, eliminating Indian status, converting all reserve land to private property, and gradually terminating existing treaties. This vision of a reimagined relationship had been met with shock by Indigenous communities, and had generated a new period of Indigenous activism that culminated in the Calder case.

In the forty years since *Calder*, Canadian political and legal scenes have been witness to moments of significant reimagining. Sustained Indigenous political engagement and activism has led to Royal Commissions, legislative reforms, judicial decisions, treaty negotiations, land claims settlements, and even, in 1999, the splitting of the Northwest Territories to give birth to Nunavut, a new arctic territory as large as Western Europe, with a population of 30,000 people, 85 percent of whom are Inuit.

But one can as easily note that this reimagining has often seemed to stop at the level of the symbolic, leaving deeply problematic conditions of life in place. Indigenous communities do not share equally in the nation's wealth. There are persistent patterns of disadvantage and exclusion along many indicators of well-being, including access to such things as health, education, finance, and even clean water. Though the last of the residential schools closed in the 1990s, Indigenous children continue to be apprehended by social services in ways that produce the same outcome: the intergenerational severing of relations within Indigenous communities. And indeed, with respect to past and current grapplings with colonial history, recent years have seen a fair amount of cycling between governmental practices of acknowledgement and denial. So, on the one hand, in 2008, Prime Minister Steven Harper formally apologized to Indigenous Peoples for the devastation brought about through the Residential School system and its forcible removal of Indigenous children from their homes and communities; a Truth and Reconciliation Commission was established to deal with the legacy of this unresolved trauma.[2] And yet, only a year later, speaking at a G20 meeting, the very same Prime Minister publically declared that Canada has no history of colonialism.[3] It is hardly surprising that 2013 was also marked by the rise of the Idle No More movement,[4] with round dances, flashmobs, hunger strikes, and increasing activism.

For even in the context of what are real changes on the symbolic terrain, it is clear that much remains unchanged. Reimagining the shape of Canadian/Indigenous relations remains difficult, largely, one might argue, because of the reluctance/failure of the Canadian system to acknowledge that Indigenous peoples were (and are) self-governing with their own legal orders. Much of early Canadian history documents government efforts to prohibit Indigenous legal practices and institutions.[5] Indeed, until 1951, Indigenous people were prohibited from hiring a lawyer (or from raising funds with the intention of hiring a lawyer). It was as late as 1961 that Alfred Scow became the first Aboriginal person to graduate from the University of British Columbia Law School. At the time *The Legal Imagination* was published, it was a challenge to find

Indigenous students in the classroom, let alone "specialized" courses on Aboriginal law.

Over the past forty years, active work by Indigenous communities has produced a generation of Indigenous lawyers, academics, and judges with a comprehensive and nuanced view of Canadian law as seen from within. The Canadian legal community has seen some change as a result. There are now a significant number of Indigenous scholars and activists across the country, fluent both in Canadian legal traditions and in their own Indigenous traditions. More law schools offer multiple courses in Indigenous law, such as Indigenous Lands and Governance, Treaty Making, Indigenous Feminist Thought, and the Kawaskimhon (Aboriginal Rights) Moot. There is the Indigenous Legal Research Unit at the University of Victoria Law School; at the University of British Columbia Law School, Treaty Making is now a mandatory first-year course for all students. It is also increasingly common to find questions of Indigenous law that have been "mainstreamed" into courses like Constitutional Law, Criminal Law, and Property Law. There are more places where one can "specialize," such as the new Faculty of Law at Lakehead University, which has an explicit mandate to focus on Aboriginal issues.[6] There is also the Akitsiraq Law School in Nunavut (where professors from the South fly up to the North, so that the legal education can be delivered in Iqaluit, rather than drawing students from the North down to the South).[7] There have also been efforts to challenge territorial and jurisdictional bias in questions about law, as Indigenous scholars, activists and elders have taken charge of both the content and the form of education.[8]

At this point in Canadian history, one might note that projects of exchange have been ongoing, but that the direction of exchange has been largely one-directional. That is, over the past forty years, Indigenous scholars have become increasingly fluent in "Canadian Law," but there has been significantly less movement in the other direction: many lawyers, judges, and decision-makers within the Canadian legal system have minimal experience with Indigenous legal orders. Given significant changes in our engagement with Indigenous legal orders, it is increasingly important that the "traditional" Canadian legal system develops fluency in Indigenous laws. But this requires significant revisioning.

One project currently underway involves the development of a new degree program (inspired in some measure by the McGill transsystemic legal education model).[9] The project, envisioned and nurtured by people across the country, and currently situated at the University of Victoria, seeks to train/produce students who are not only qualified to practice Canadian law as conventionally understood, but who also have a much more robust capacity to engage with Indigenous legal orders on their own terms. The goal is a combined JD/JID (Juris Indigenarum Doctorate). This four-year program would take Indigenous law seriously, teaching all "core" courses in a transsystemic way. So, for example, constitutional law might be taught using Anishinabek and Canadian law alongside each other to explore how the two systems have dealt with questions about the foundation and constitution of their respective societies. Family law might be taught using Dene principles. One might use Cree law alongside Canadian law to learn how the two societies have developed practices for dealing with inter-and intra-group harms (a combination of "Tort and Criminal law" problems). The program, which would be open to Indigenous and non-Indigenous students alike, would involve the learning of an Indigenous language (most likely Salish, given the location of the university on Salish territory), and two field school terms embedded in and doing work with particular Indigenous communities. Throughout, there would be a weaving in of multiple forms of pedagogy, drawn from both settler and Indigenous ways of learning. For example, Kwakiutl scholar Maxine V. Matilpi's work on button blankets as Indigenous pedagogy emphasizes the production of knowledge in the context of work;[10] Lil'wet scholar Lorna William's work on collaborative learning focuses attention on learning through doing, and on the creative powers in a nonhierarchical (and noncolonial) model of education.[11]

As the project has been in development, I have been struck by the sense of hope coming from both the Indigenous scholars, and non-Indigenous scholars who have committed themselves to engage in this project. But I have also noted (in myself as well as in others) a reluctance to step into the project. In conversations about the new project, while many people are comfortable with the notion that Indigenous peoples may be able to teach about Indigenous legal orders, there is discomfort around settler involvement. In writing about her experience working for the Truth and Reconciliation Commission, Paulette Regan notes this phenomenon.[12] In acknowledging the harms of the colonial past, there is a sense of fear that any active form of engagement by settlers (even well-intentioned) holds the potential to produce further colonial harms—as if the result will invariably involve settlers "playing Indian" (appropriation) or a project of tutelage (claiming expertise or the right to speak for Indigenous communities).

While this risk is of course present, Val Napoleon argues that there is also a risk in disengagement. She argues that it is time for settler academics to offer not simply "support" but also "engagement." This means accepting that Indigenous law, like Canadian law, can (and indeed must) be capable of both being learned and being taught.[13] Val's challenge was for me to think more imaginatively about the resources that common-law scholars have already developed through transsystemic work. Her challenge was for settler scholars to be open to the new, but also draw from the best of the tools they have already developed. What might it take, she asked me, to take my existing law and film course, and adapt it for the combined JD/JID course? Could I imagine teaching that course in a transsystemic way?

Turning this question around in my head, I found myself returning to *The Legal Imagination*, and to the intellectual and pedagogical influence of Professor White's (Jim's) work in the design of the law and film class. I was reminded that, in his body of scholarship, Jim has long been offering a set of tools for exactly this kind of work. I also found that his work provided additional support for the project. In what follows, I sketch out some of those tools in the context of the class I began with, and then share some thoughts about the experience of using the tools in the context of this project.

Re-examining the Night Sky with Jim: Learning Law Through Film

> it is more valuable to think of law as ... a set of ways of making sense of things and acting in the world.... This is, after all, how we learn law, not as a set of rules nor as the art of unmasking, as Swift might put it, but by participation in a culture, learning its language and how to live within it; and this is how we practice law too.
> –JAMES BOYD WHITE, *JUSTICE AS TRANSLATION* (XIII)

Over the past decade, Jim's pedagogy has played a formative role in the design of my Legal Theory class, one known informally as "Law-and-Film." In its various iterations, the film course has drawn deeply on the pedagogies of *The Legal Imagination*.[14] It involves a similar gathering of divergent texts, and begins with White's premise that law is less a set of rules than an imaginative and intellectual activity, a way of imagining a shared history.[15] It takes as a given his insights about the importance of learning how to *live* within a language, a culture, a legal order. This invitation to inhabit a world *imagined* has been at the heart of the law and film course. In terms of concrete substance, I have long been drawing on his approach, finding it a rich way to interrogate more closely the premises at the centre of my own culture. Over the past ten years, I have been particularly interested in filmic texts that have focused on my own questions about the ways that gender, class, and race have been woven together in North American narratives about law and nation. In particular, I have focused on "The Western."[16] It was thus with a bit of irony that I began to see how, in my own work, my choice of cinematic text was failing to engage more directly with particularly Canadian patterns of colonization. Canadian narratives of arrival share much with their American counterparts but, as is often the case, local context shapes stories, both their substance and their method of telling.[17] As some say, if the U.S. West was won, the Canadian West was negotiated. At the level of the symbolic, the Canadian national narrative has been marked less by "the West" than by "the North." Our national anthem continually asserts that we are "the true North, strong and free." Museums and archives alike document (in terms descriptive, photographic, and cinematic) Canadian engagement (obsession?) with the North.

As I noted earlier, the past twenty-five years have witnessed what might be called a revolution of Inuit activism that has resulted in the creation of Canada's newest territory, Nunavut, a territory that captures much of the Northern territory and whose population is predominately Inuit, and where Inuktitut is one of the official languages. And yet, as Jackie Price notes, it is one thing for the Canadian State to acknowledge Inuit governance, but it is quite another to begin the more complicated conversation about just what that governance might "mean" for the Inuit or for the Canadian State.[18] An answer to that question requires a different level of engagement with Inuit law. This engagement is complicated on many levels, one of which involves the lack of settler fluency in Inuktitut. It is unsurprising that we continue to experience the kinds of challenges raised in White's book, *Justice as Translation*.

One of the real difficulties for settler society has been the limits of its own legal imagination, a tendency to understand its laws as universal and to project them onto others in a particular colonial fashion. How then might one work to make the Northern stars visible to Southern eyes? The challenge was to organize a class in legal theory to be taught in the South, to non-Inuktitut speakers, aiming to enable its participants to affectively inhabit the Inuit North and make it possible for them to begin imagining law otherwise. As with the film course taught in the usual way, the plan was to draw heavily on stories as tools for thinking, stories either about or by the Inuit. The goal was to have enough stories (and enough variety of stories and materials) that they could be read deeply, and be read against each other. Stories would be treated not as examples of "the truth", but as places where we could work at inhabiting a space, trying it on, and working as a group to explore what could be seen in those spaces of imagination and learning.

From a purely practical point of view, we were advantaged by the political and legal mobilizations around Nunavut, which have been accompanied by significant action in the "cultural" arena. There has been an explosion of cultural production with the founding of both an Inuit Broadcasting Corporation, which broadcasts in Inuktitut, and by the establishment of several film companies, the most well-known of which is Isuma Iglulik. With this recent and expanding body of cinematic texts there is space for a different encounter between Inuit and settler societies in the cultural arena. In the course we largely drew on stories that deal with intercultural encounters, contacts between Inuit and Qallunaat, which means, in Inuktitut, everyone who is not Inuit. This genre of stories, these intercultural encounters, invite particular kinds of experiences, ones where we actively try to imagine something from outside—searching both for what is similar and what is different.

Let me now turn to the details of this course, which takes its inspiration in part from the table of contents in *The Legal Imagination*. The goal is to think about situating different questions alongside each other. That means considering such things as: different understandings of law (language), the invisibilization of Inuit histories, the challenges encountered by text-based cultures trying to engage with oral histories, and the difference between external and internal perspectives on Inuit life. Here, *The Edge of Meaning*[19] also provides a model. In this book, struggling with questions about edges, White's discussion draws not only on more conventional narrative or analytical texts, but turns also to the visual (on Vermeer), the musical (in poetry), and silence. In opening space for considering multiple practices of shaping meaning, Jim's work invites viewers to look more deeply at the practices of Inuit tradition: storytelling, songs (*piisit*), drum-dancing, games.

At the outset, the title of the course (which included the phrase "Inuit law") required that we spend some time on the question of "law." In *The Edge of Meaning*, White includes a chapter titled "Reading Greek," which makes visible both the challenges and the possibilities inherent in efforts to inhabit even a single sentence in a different language. Given the participants' shared lack of fluency in Inuktitut, this was an issue to be explored in the class. Jim's essay "Teaching Law and Literature" (in *From Expectation to Experience*[20]) provided a model for thinking about the language challenge: there he describes his teaching of a seminar entitled "Learning Foreign Law," and speaks about the exercise of working backwards and forwards from one language to another. Taking this approach, we began with three Inuktitut translations of the English word "law": *maligait, piqujait* and *tirigusuusiit. Maligait, piqujait and tirigusuusiit*. These are words used to speak about that which has to be followed, done, or not done. The words themselves come from different cultural perspectives. *Maligait* is generally translated as "Canadian law," *piqujait* as "Inuit customary law," and *tirigusuusiit* as "taboos and superstitions." But, as Michele Therrien argues, these translations may be more helpful for mapping Canadian concepts to Inuit, than for elucidating Inuit concepts to Canadian English speakers.[21] As Michèle Therrien suggests, the back translation of the Inuit terms (what had to be followed, done or not done in Inuit culture) makes visible the complex relational dimensions of the concepts, and a way of understanding law less as a set of general prescriptions, than as a set of connections; connections that require attention not simply to the content delivered (do or do not do the following things) but also to the person who has made the request, and the relationship between the one asking and the one performing.[22] The terms emerge from a particular cultural perspective which requires an appreciation of the ways that different laws may apply to different people at different times and in different situations. It is perhaps the complexity of this form of relationality that led many early ethnographers to deny that the Inuit had any law at all. The challenge is, of course, to see how language helps us understand concepts of law which don't have a perfect overlap in the two languages/cultures. Jim's attention to language offers a tool that opens space for thinking about the ways that legal concepts (in this case, about what is to be followed, done, avoided) are embedded in their own social and cosmic relations, opening space for a richer discussion of Inuit legal ordering, and its embedding in language which captures in a different way the importance of correct relationships with not only people, but also with animals and the land.[23] Certainly, the centrality of relationship became one of the important themes in the course.

Let me now give a cursory sketch of the cinematic texts that we used in this class.[24] The course began with Robert Flaherty's 1922 film *Nanook of the North*. The first feature-length documentary, it is widely seen as the birth of modern ethnographic documentary. The film follows the experiences of its main character, Nanook, his wife Nyla, and their family. It contains extended scenes of building an igloo, hunting for walrus, and traveling by dogsled. There is also a much discussed scene where Nanook is introduced for the first time to a gramophone (and bites a record to make sense of it). There is a rich literature around this film, taking up questions about reality, authenticity, and staging.[25] For of course, the actor who played Nanook was really named Allakariallak, and the woman playing his wife Nyla, gave birth to Flaherty's son, a son who would be later relocated from his home in Nunavik (Northern Quebec) to a location 2,000 km/1,243miles north.[26] This film, problematic in many ways, was a touchstone through the course, enabling us to return to questions of representation, and of the relationship of the viewer to the viewed.

From here, we moved to *Kikkik*, a contemporary documentary about a high-profile murder trial occurring in the North in the 1950s. The *Kikkik* case is a particularly interesting one, since a person studying it can access the trial transcripts, a narrative account of the story in Farley Mowatt's book *The Desperate People*, a series of Inuit carvings representing the trial (by Inuit artist Peggy Ekagina, and part of the Sissons/Morrow collection formerly housed at the Yellowknife Courthouse), and two documentary films, made by Kikkik's own daughter (who had been a baby on her mother's back at the time of the killings). In short, this case enabled a rich discussion of the different genres in which stories of justice can be told.[27] This documentary focuses on the impact of Inuit relocations, the starvation that resulted, murder, and abandonment. This documentary shifts the focus from a North of hardy happy Inuit, to a North in which intercultural encounter is placed front and centre. Law is also at the center of this documentary, which asks us to consider the ways the judicial system dealt with the death of these three Inuit. The *Kikkik* case and documentary also enabled us to spend some time actively discussing the different genres one might use to tell legal tales.

From there, we made an affective shift, moving from "documentary" to "docu-comedy" with the film *Qallunaat: Why White People are Funny*. This film, a collaboration between filmmaker Mark Sandiford and Inuit writer and satirist Zebedee Nungak, is situated at the fictional QSI (Qallunaat Studies Institute), where Inuit researchers study the odd behaviours of the Qallunaat, the Inuit term for non-Inuit people. The focus here is on the Qallunaat's odd dating habits, lame attempts at arctic exploration, need for police, and obsessions with owning property.[28] The film features archival footage from a variety of National Film Board (NFB) documentaries, including clips from the 1960s when three twelve-year-old boys—the "experimental eskimos"—were sent from the North to live with white families in Ottawa, to be educated in Qallunaat schools.[29]

Our class discussion was enriched by a visit from two people who were featured in the film: Mick Mallon (who was the first principal at the school in Iqaluit, and is interviewed by Nungak in the film) and Alexina Kublu, who was the Language Commissioner for Nunavut.[30] We began looking more closely at the challenges of translation that had been raised in the previous films, drawing on the insights of both Mallon and Kublu.[31] There was, of course, a performative dimension to these visits that resonated nicely with Jim's work: Mallon brought in photos from the North, giving us the chance to talk about vision, to have some sense of the images we had been seeing in the cinematic context. Kublu generously used her own family to trace out for us the impact of both the "Eskimo Numbers," and "Project Surname" (which let us see the impact on a family in ways that would have been otherwise hard to capture).[32] This also helped us to see the ways naming is related to a very different cosmological understanding of the world. Kublu also brought a series of *ulu*'s (an all-purpose curve-bladed knife used in the North, a woman's knife). We were able to handle a variety of knives, as she told us stories of how the different knives (which are traditionally passed down from generation to generation) came to be hers. After the discussion of names, it was easier to situate the understanding that some of an ancestor's knowledge was contained within the ulu and so would be passed on. In these discussions, I found myself reflecting on Jim's insights about material culture, and thinking about the importance of understanding material objects for the project of intercultural understanding.[33]

This understanding then was carried forward into our viewing of the three films that make up the Isuma Igloolik Triology. The first of these (and the most well-known) is *Atanarjuat*. Winner of the Camera d'Or at the 2001 Cannes Film Festival, this particular film is based on a famous traditional Inuit story, or *Unikkaaqtuat*, understood in many quarters as a piece of "law." It is a complex text, one that embeds a series of legal principles having to do with that which must be done, that which should not be done, and the relationship between a people and the world in which they are embedded. It contains much about obligations people have to each other, about community, about harm, about things that upset balance and things that must be done to restore it. There is a rich literature around this particular film, including extensive discussions about the practises of consultation with many elders as the filmmakers drew on several versions of this story in producing a new adaptation of it for contemporary audiences. It is not too much of a stretch to think of this film as an explicitly legal text, a text which does not ask us to judge one particular person, but to see law operating at many levels over an extended period of time and to understand relationships between people and the environment in a certain way.

We have a very different kind of story unfold in *The Journals of Knud Rasmussen (TJKR)*. This film deals explicitly with the encounter between cultures. The film is historical in many senses, as it takes as its source material, the published journals of Knud Rasmussen from his travels across the North in the 1920s.[34] The film engages in a kind of double vision through its ability to take the words from those journals and recast them in a way that shifts their sense to capture an ostensibly Inuit point of view. What we have is a contemporary reengagement with texts gathered by an ethnographer who understood himself, in some ways, to be gathering fragments of a society in the midst of passing. One of the things that set his text apart from those of other ethnographers of his time was his connection to the very society he was visiting. Rasmussen's grandmother was Inuit from Greenland and so he could in fact communicate directly with the people he was visiting. Though he was an outsider in some ways, he was in other ways an insider. His fluency in Inuktitut enabled him to ask better questions, and to better record the answers he was given. At the heart of *TJKR* are questions about the implications of contact, particularly the encounter of Christianity with Inuit shamanism.[35] Genre becomes interesting again, since the film begins with the words written in the journals, but the telling of the story is from an internal perspective, from the viewpoint of its Inuit characters. There is a degree to which is like the *Wide Sargasso Sea* retelling of *Jane Eyre* (but taking an ethnographic text as the starting point).[36] Here, the cinematic nature of the text works powerfully to give us as viewers the experience of seeing the shaman's spirit helpers (the spirit helpers spoken of are visible throughout the text, though this is not clear to viewers until the end of the film). This is perhaps not a surprise to an Inuit audience, but is a bit of a shock to a non-Inuit audience. The film more powerfully enables us to occupy the world, and not simply listen to the descriptions. In this film, we also spend time exploring the place of songs (*pisiit*) in Inuit culture. Because there are levels and layers of song in this film (*pisiit*, operatic aria, hymn), there was also space for engaging in a more embodied way with the songs. In the context of the course, it helped that by the time we looked at this text, we had listened to several Inuit songs—without presuming that we knew the musical conventions, the sound was beginning to be familiar to our ears.

The question of encounter is also foregrounded in *Before Tomorrow* (2008). In this film, however, we are explicitly within the domain of fiction. The film was inspired by the novel *For Morgendagen*, by Danish novelist Jorn Riel.[37] The novel deals with the death of an entire community of Greenland Inuit in the early 1800s. The novel was adapted by Arnait Video Productions (the Women's Video Workshop of Igloolik) to be set in the Canadian North, which itself was historically marked by the decimation of Inuit communities through contact with southern diseases. This film focuses primarily on the relationship between a grandmother and grandson, the last two surviving members of the community, as they struggle alone through the winter. Both die at the end of the film, but this death is not the heart of the story. The story is largely one about the ways that community is made and knowledge is shared and passed along (not simply from grandmother to grandson, but also from her to the audience). The framing of the story invites us to take up questions of law, community, relationship, and (perhaps) jurisprudence, and to do so from an internal perspective. There is much that is not explained, but that is shown. The film embeds traditional stories (like "The Ptarmigan and the Snowbunting," and "The Raven and the Whale,") as tools of teaching, and invites us to engage with dreams and dreaming as sources of law. Certainly this film falls into the category of stories that one might refer to as truthful fictions. Absolutely fictional in its source, it nonetheless raises questions and reflects on a past, a tragic reality of Canadian history. There are many stories of this nature that one can imagine telling, particularly if one turns to questions of the Jewish Holocaust or any other number of genocidal moments in history (for example, *Maus*,[38] *Death and the Maiden*,[39] *Life is Beautiful* ["*La vita è bella*"][40]) *Before Tomorrow* in its Inuit story telling mode is in large measure different than other films in this genre. While one can still go to it with the question, who is responsible and what harms have they caused, this film stymies its viewers in attempting to pose, let along answer such a question. It offers a different set of tools for grappling with a traumatic event. This film presses our attention away from the question of judgement and instead moves toward the question of what it means to live in the face of tragedy and difficult conditions with a focus on survival and living, even in the face of those traumas.

We then turned to a French-Canadian film, *Ce qu'il faut pour vivre* (*The Necessities of Life*, 2008). Set in 1952, it features Tivii (played by Natar Ungalaaq, who we had seen in both *Atanarjuat* and *TJKR*), an Inuk man who contracts tuberculosis (TB), and is sent from the north to Montreal, to recover in a sanatorium there. Uprooted from family, unable to communicate, in a completely alien world, he becomes despondent and stops eating. A nurse finally transfers a young (bilingual) Inuk orphan named Kaki to the institution, creating a space for the two to heal together as Tivii plans to adopt the young Kaki and bring him home to the North. This Quebec film, directed by Benoit Pilon, and written by Bernard Emond, takes up the histories of TB and disease that emerged in the earlier films (the actor who played the role of Nanook died of tuberculosis, as did the character of Nuqallaq in *TJKR*, and the entire community in *Before Tomorrow*). The film does a masterful job of capturing Tivii's isolation, though it keeps a southern audience as its imagined viewer through what is translated and what we (the viewers) are presumed to know about the histories of deadly diseases brought from the South to the North.

We ended with *Map of the Human Heart* (1992), a more "Hollywood" film selection, by Australian director Vincent Ward. The Internet Movie

Database (IMDB) says that "fantastic improbabilities, happenstance and the undying bridge of love are part of this romantic fantasy about an Inuit who crosses years, oceans and the ravages of WWII to find his childhood love, a Metis girl, but finds that their cultures are the most difficult spaces to gap."[41] It was interesting ending where we began, with a film featuring Inuit characters, but told for a southern audience. Indeed, after seeing films featuring Inuit actors, the students were interested to see the Inuit character, played by Chinese-American actor Jason Scott Lee, and the Metis character, played by French actress Anne Parillaud.[42] The casting choices fostered important discussions about our assumptions around "authenticity" with respect to who belongs or doesn't belong to various communities, and about practices of representation.[43] It was also interesting to return to a film from the South at the end of a term having watched films operating at a quite different pace. As a class, there was much laughter over people's assertion that the story was moving "too fast" (given complaints earlier in the term that the Inuit films were moving "too slow").

Conclusion

These cinematic texts, some of which speak to a northern audience, are also invitations to southerners to inhabit a world *imagined otherwise*: to enter into the life rhythms of the North, feel and experience its seasons, its ways of practicing life, and its practices of community. They are invitations to look up to the night skies, and to see different stories written there: sister sun and brother moon; Narujuk and Qimmiit (a polar bear held at bay by a pack of dogs); the orphan boy or old man; to see a sky marking transformations between people and animals.[44] As a teacher/learner in the course (my learning curve was as steep as it could be) I have found myself thinking frequently about the question, "where is the law in all this"? Certainly, there are ethnographers who have made the argument that there is no law here, that it is just culture. I would push back. The experience of looking north through film, while thinking about law, was a powerful one.

Jim White's *The Legal Imagination* has been foundational in teaching this course, in thinking about the possibilities for transsystemmic education. In case it is not visible: there is a moment of terror in being a white woman from Canada's southernmost tip attempting to run a course about law in the top northeast of this country. Colonial histories run deep, and many (though by no means all) settler engagements with Indigenous law have occurred in the context of power imbalances that have raised questions of appropriation and cooptation. The challenge becomes how to acknowledge and recognize the harms of the past without being disempowered by guilt, or withdrawing from engagement for fear of failing to understand. In his work, Jim shows us the kinds of performances that are instructive, the stance one can take, the moments of openness, and the consistent willingness to engage with eyes wide open. His work urges (in appropriate measure) both caution and bravery. His titles capture the centre of it: *When Words Lose Their Meaning*, *Living Speech*; *Justice as Translation*; *Acts of Hope*. In his method and in his titles, he invites us to the world beyond the text, to practice all the verbs of possibility, all the verbs of imagination.

Notes

1. *Calder v British Columbia* (Attorney-General) [1973] SCR 313.
2. www.trc.ca. The apology can be viewed at www.cbc.ca/archives/categories/society/education/a-lost-heritage-canadas-residential-schools/a-long-awaited-apology.html.
3. D. Ljunggren "Every G20 nation wants to be Canada, insists PM," http://www.reuters.com/article/2009/09/26/columns-us-g20-canada-advantages-idUSTRE58P05Z20090926.
4. http://idlenomore.ca/.
5. See J. Borrows, *Canada's Indigenous Constitution* (Toronto: University of Toronto Press, 2010) and J. Borrows, *Recovering Canada: The Resurgence of Indigenous Law* (Toronto: University of Toronto Press, 2002).
6. http://law.lakeheadu.ca/deans-message/.
7. www.akitsiraq.ca.
8. For example, the Indigenous Governance program at the University of Victoria: http://web.uvic.ca/igov/ or the Dechinta Bush University in the North: http://dechinta.ca/.
9. www.mcgill.ca/centre-crepeau/transsystemic/articles.
10. www3.telus.net/mmatilpi/. See also M. Matilpi, "In Our Collectivity: Teaching, Learning, and Indigenous Voice" (2012) 35:1 Canadian Journal of Native Education 211.
11. www.ccl-cca.ca/ccl/Events/Minerva/PastLectures/PastLecturesWilliams.html.
12. P. Regan, *Unsettling the Settler Within: Indian Residential Schools, Truth Telling, and Reconciliation in Canada* (Vancouver: University of British Columbia Press, 2010).
13. V. Napoleon, "Thinking About Indigenous Legal Orders," in *Dialogues on Human Rights and Legal Pluralism*, ed. R. Provost and C. Sheppard (Dordrecht Heidelberg/New York and London: Springer, 2013), 229.
14. See Mark Weisberg's chapter in this volume for a more fulsome discussion of methodology.

15. J. B. White, *From Expectation to Experience: Essays on Law and Legal Education* (Ann Arbor: University of Michigan Press, 1999), ix.

16. For example, R. Johnson, "Law and the Leaky Woman: The Saloon, the Liquor Licence, and Narratives of Containment," Continuum: Journal of Media and Cultural Studies 19, no, 2 (2005): 181; and R. Johnson, "Living Deadwood: Imagination, Affect, and the Persistence of the Past," Suffolk University Law Review 62, no. 4 (2009): 809.

17. E. Morgan, "The Mild, Mild West: Living By a Code in Canadian Law and Film," Journal of Law, Culture & Humanities 2, no. 1 (2006): 115.

18. J. Price, "Tukisivallialiqtakka: The Things I Have Now Begun to Understand: Inuit Governance, Nunavut and the Kitchen Consultation Model" (PhD diss., University of Victoria, 2007).

19. J. B. White, *The Edge of Meaning* (Chicago: University of Chicago Press, 2001).

20. J B White (n 16).

21. L. Guemple, "Born-Again Pagans: The Inuit Cycle of Spirits," in *Amerindian Rebirth: Reincarnation Belief Among North American Indians and Inuit*, ed. A. Mills and R. Slobodin (Toronto: University of Toronto Press, 1994), 107–22.

22. M. Aupilaarjuk et al, *Perspectives on Traditional Law*, Vol 2, *Interviewing Inuit Elders*, ed. J. Oosten, F. Laugrand, and W. Rasing (Iqaluit: Nunavut Arctic College, 1999), 1–3.

23. Oosten, Laugrand, and Rasing, "Introduction," 2. Struck in the reading by the expressed desire of the elders to look for a new synthesis of Inuit and Western culture, the interviewing books fill an important function of making visible ways of being in the past, not articulated as a way of arguing for a nostalgic return, but to make visible its operation and successes, with the aim of helping in the project of synthesis for the present. (Ibid., 7)

24. The syllabus and reading list can be found at http://rebeccaj63.wordpress.com/inuit-law-and-film/.

25. This film was paired with two articles: S Arnold, ""The Men of the North" Redux: Nanook and Canadian National Unity" (2010) 40:4 American Review of Canadian Studies 452; J W Burton and C W Thompson, "Nanook and the Kirwinians: Deception, Authenticity, and the Birth of Modern Ethnographic Representation" (2002) 14:1 Film History 74.

26. This history is detailed in M. McGrath, *The Long Exile: A Tale of Inuit Betrayal and Survival in the High Arctic* (New York: Vintage Books, 2006).

27. R. Johnson, "Justice and the Colonial Collision: Reflections on Stories of Intercultural Encounter in Law, Literature, Sculpture and Film," No Foundations: An Interdisciplinary Journal of Law and Justice 9 (2012): 68.

28. This film is an Inuit analogue to the 1986 Australian satiric film *BabaKiueria* ("Barbeque Area").

29. In future iterations, I might make use of Barry Greenwald's film *The Experimental Eskimos* (2009), which follows the experience of the three boys (Peter Ittinuar, Zebedee Nungak, and Eric Tagoona), all of whom grew up to be political activists and leaders, instrumental in the creation of Nunavut, the world's largest self-governed Aboriginal territory. http://www.cbc.ca/passionateeye/episode/experimental-eskimos.html.

30. She has been the chair of the Akitsiraq Law School Society, and is a former

Senior Justice of the Peace for the Nunavut Justices of the Peace Program. She is a certified Inuktitut/English Interpreter, a member of the Canadian Interpreters and Translators Council, and recently retired Languages Commissioner for Nunavut.

31. www.nunavut.com/nunavut99/english/our.html.
32. On this history of first assigning numbers to all Inuit, and then assigning them family surnames, see V. Alia, *Names and Nunavut: Culture and Identity in the Inuit Homeland* (New York & Oxford: Berghahn Books, 2007).
33. See also Gary Watt's chapter in this collection.
34. K. Rasmussen, *Intellectual Culture of the Iglulik Eskimos*, vol. 7 (Copenhagen: Glydendalske Boghandel Nordisk Forlag, 1929).
35. Our understanding of the film was fleshed out through work done within the Inuit community on these questions. See B. S. d'Anglure, ed., *Interviewing Inuit Elders: Cosmology and Shamanism* (Iqaluit: Nunavut Arctic College, 2001).
36. Sara Daitch, in the class, referred to this genre as "the re-appropriation of ethnography" or ROE (not fish eggs) genre, whereby the culture who was the subject of the original ethnography use the appropriated cultural information written about them to re work the story as they understand it, from their perspective, for their own purposes.
37. For an interview with Jorn Riel about finding the bones of an old woman and young child in a deserted area of Greenland, http://www.isuma.tv/lo/en/arnaitvideo/interview-jorn-riel-author-morgendagen-tomorrow.
38. A. Spiegelman, *Maus: A Survivor's Tale* (New York: Pantheon Books, 1991).
39. Dir: Polanski, 1994.
40. Dir: Benigni, 1997.
41. Summary written by Keith Loh, on the IMDB site.
42. These choices were less disorienting than the choices in *Savage Innocent*, where the Inuit character is played by Anthony Quinn, or *Shadow of the Wolf*, where the Inuit roles are played by Latino actor Lou-Diamond Phillips, and Japanese icon Toshiro Mifune (who starred in Kurosawa's Rashomon).
43. We also considered the history of Nancy Columbia and Esther Eneautseak, Inuit women who played "Indians" in early film history. See K. Harper and R. Potter, "Early Arctic Films of Nancy Columbia and Esther Eneutseak" Nimrod 10 (2010): 1.
44. J. MacDonald, *The Arctic Sky: Inuit Astronomy, Star Lore, and Legend* (Iqaluit, Nunavut: Nunavut Research Institute, 2000).

[11]

Generating Law

Learning How to Take Care of What One Has Started
Thomas D. Eisele

The middle span of life is under the dominance of the universal human need and strength which I have come to subsume under the term *generativity*. I have said that in this stage a man and a woman must have defined for themselves what and whom they have come to care for, what they care to do well, and how they plan to take care of what they have started and created.
–ERIK ERIKSON[1]

Starting to Practice Law

After graduating from law school, I started practicing law with a Chicago law firm comprising more than eighty attorneys. The firm was collegial, not cutthroat. Most of the firm's partners and associates with whom I came in contact (with some of whom, I worked closely) actively sought to help me turn myself into a competent lawyer. This would seem to be a recipe for professional success, but for me it was not.

I found, instead, that I was struggling. I wanted to be a success—who does not? I tried very hard to be a competent professional. Yet I found my initial attempts at the work that I was asked to do, to be disconcertingly difficult and the results distressingly poor. Mostly, I did average legal work of marginal quality It was nothing to be proud of. Where was I going wrong, and why?

I could do the basics of legal research and writing: I located the cases, found the applicable statutes, made some progress with the rules and administrative regulations, and after a fashion I could put together a reasonable memorandum of law, or draft a passable complaint or answer. But little or none of my legal work breathed life. Much of it came from form books, or from the available models of previous work done by others in the law firm; and the instruments or documents that I accordingly drafted remained theirs, not mine. The instruments that I was drafting, and the memos that I was writing, and the advisory letters that I was trying to craft, were not so much mute as they were forgeries: to the extent that they spoke, it was not with my voice, but someone else's (usually, that of a ghost from the law firm's past). Or, worse yet, the legal instruments that I created enunciated their words in a nonhuman voice, some kind of mechanical vocalization which seemed to me to represent a deadened form of the law. Nothing vital came out of my legal work: not the law, not the problem at hand, not the document or instrument that I was crafting. And certainly nothing of myself—not my persona, not my mind—was expressed in my legal writings.

Then, out of the blue, a fresh copy of *The Legal Imagination*[2] came to me, and the book changed my relationship to the law. Jim White's book had been sent to me by a law review with which I had had no prior contact. The law review invited me to read and review White's book, an invitation that I accepted with alacrity.

Quizzical at the large volume bound in rich yellow covers, I began perusing it, first skeptically, then with increasing interest and excitement. Quickly, a new legal landscape unfolded, stretching before me. This land of the law was not a country of settled forms and ancient documents, to be replicated and reduced to repetitive iterations of the same old solutions to the same old problems. No, it was a more vivid geography confronting me. Here, problems of, say, how to approach a traffic accident, or what the meaning and significance of the death penalty might be in today's world, or how to sort out the claims between participants in a bar fight, or how to handle someone's dying (perhaps a person very close to me, perhaps even myself)—all of these questions (and many more) were posed to me, and left with me. How would I deal with them?

To help me think this responsibility through, there were poems, and historical accounts, and some literary criticism, and political tracts, and philosophical writings, and short stories, and humorous tales, and tragic odes, and more—put together attentively, in such a way so as to resonate within their juxtapositions. The writers of these texts had been confronted with problems typical of human experience in this confusing world of ours. Here were the texts that they managed to fashion in response to those problems, those mysteries, those opportunities, those trials. Now, what was I to make of these resources, these achievements, in view of the fact that there always exists the ever-attractive option that humans have to stand mute in the face of their experiences and frustrations, or to live in denial of them?

Two passages on death come to mind here. In Henry Adams's *Education*, he recalls his wrenching conversion from innocence to experience, when his sister died of tetanus. "The last lesson—the sum and term of education—began then."[3] Before this experience, Henry had only seen the "sugar-coating" that nature, that life, shows to youth. Now the horror of human mortality confronted him. And he rejects it. "Society, being immortal, could put on immortality at will. Adams, being mortal, felt only the mortality."[4] His sister died "after ten days of fiendish torture," torn by convulsions as her muscles grew rigid, yet her mind remained conscious of everything around her. For Henry Adams, there is no consolation. He is angry, bitter, at his sister's fate. "She faced death, as women mostly do, bravely and even gaily, racked slowly to unconsciousness, but yielding only to violence, as a soldier sabred in battle. For many thousands of years, on these hills and plains, Nature had gone on sabring men and women with the same air of sensual pleasure."[5]

Contrast with this passage, one from Macauley's *History of England*, where he recounts the execution of Monmouth, who had failed at trying to overthrow the Catholic king, James II. "The hour drew near; all hope was over; and Monmouth had passed from pusillanimous fear to the apathy of despair.... He alone was unmoved."[6] There is in Monmouth's response to his own death another form of human determination, related to Adams's rejection of our fate at the hands of nature, yet different. Monmouth becomes resigned to his own mortality. "I will make no speeches," Monmouth exclaimed; instead, he bade the executioner, "Do not hack me as you did my Lord Russell.... My servant will give you some more gold if you do the work well."[7] Monmouth's forlorn hope at this stage is not for survival, but for surcease.

In many of us, these conflicting emotions of bitter rejection and subdued resignation reside side by side. We reject our mortality just as much as we are resigned to it. In many of us, the task of anticipating our own deaths is unimaginable, yet unavoidable. Faced with such conflicting emotions and concerns, we in the land of the law have only the estate plan with which to work. Enter the testator's last will and testament. And enter the lawyer entrusted with the task of contending with our humanly mixed emotions. These are natural human emotions with which every lawyer who has ever drafted a will or a trust document, has had to contend—and to satisfy, if not to silence.

As it turned out, the readings in *The Legal Imagination* were not solutions to my problems of how to turn myself into a competent lawyer. Rather, the readings composing White's book simply made my problems more pointed, or more poignant. The readings that White had put together in a certain sequence showed me slices of human life, varieties of experience and expression, possible choices grounded within an inherited body of some profession's literature; but they did not guide me to a solution of the problems posed to me. They led me to experience the problems as my own, and they challenged me to find an adequate response, something commensurate with the weight and heft of the issues and concerns with which life presented each one of us. As an initiate of the profession, I had to come up with something adequate, even satisfying, something that a lawyer might responsibly say or professionally do in the face of such challenging matters. Simultaneously, I had to maintain my sense of myself as a person, as a human being, as well as my sense of myself as a competent professional. (Or else, if I did not maintain my self-conception under the pressures exerted within this crucible of experience, then I had to explain to myself this apparently irresistible impulse to change myself in the face of my duties, both professional and personal.)

White put the challenge his book posed to its reader in the following way: "The questions and assignments in this book ... are meant as occasions for the play of the individual mind and imagination, as ... an independent mind."[8] What did I make of these occasions?

Seeing Law as an Art or Craft

I do not believe that I had ever worked out for myself in law school, or in the beginnings of my legal practice, what I thought a lawyer was, or what a lawyer did. Perhaps I had not done so because the matter never seemed an open question (or was never put in question by anything I had encountered in law school). Instead, the matter seemed settled. Well, what *is* the role or task of the lawyer as a professional? I would say that one of the common attributes ascribed to the lawyer in our society envisions the lawyer as a kind of "hired gun." On this view, a lawyer is a paid advocate who has learned certain complex and arcane legal terms and rules, a professional who manipulates those terms and rules on behalf of his client in order to reach a result favorable to that client. This makes the lawyer's task a technical job, one encompassing the techniques and tools of the lawyer's craft. There is enough truth to this view of a lawyer that it can be very difficult to shake free of, or to modify and cabin within useful limits. Yet such a view places the lawyer in relation to the law such that he or she is only a technician, engaged in not much more than sophistic manipulation of legal words and rules. A lawyer gets paid to use his or her tools at the behest of his or her client, and the client's payment puts the lawyer in a kind of literary serfdom or servitude to the client.

If this portrait approximates the vision of lawyering that I brought to law school, I do not believe that I was ever helpfully cautioned against it (certainly never disabused of it) either during my career as a law student or during the opening years of my practice. In my experience, this picture of the legal profession, or something very close to it, was widely accepted. But White's book explicitly questioned this picture of what it is to be a legal professional, and his book even countered this perhaps naïve conception by reconceiving the matter, and by inviting me to imagine how I might proceed differently.

Today, almost forty years after the event, while there are aspects of my five-year practice of law that are hazy or about which I have little or no memory, I still can recall the revelatory impact I felt reading White's suggestion "that law is not a science—at least not the 'social science' some would call it—but an art. And this course is directed to you as an artist."[9] The lawyer an artist? Outrageous. Yet, strangely appealing, too. Such a conception took seriously the notion that we craft the law out of the materials we have at hand within the medium of (in my case) the Anglo-American common law tradition. Could that claim be true; could it be made plausible in the events and readings that would unfold in the pages to follow? White seemed to think so: "There is no body of rules expressing the art of the lawyer any more than that of the sculptor or painter. You are as free as they, and as responsible for what you do. It is true that one of the mediums of the lawyer's art is rules, and the lawyer must know rules, and the other materials of the law, as the sculptor must know clay and the painter paint and canvas."[10] On White's portrayal, the artistry of the lawyer is bound to specific resources in language and to specific ways of using language in formulating and expressing one's thoughts. (One instance is what we call "rules"; White frequently refers to these media generically as various "forms of expression" used by lawyers.) The lawyer is a writer who works in and through the medium of written and spoken words. He or she uses texts and documents and rules and arguments and speeches throughout his or her professional life. And White adds to this central claim, several accompanying images in the book: such as, the judge as a kind of poet and the judicial opinion as a kind of poem; legal writing as narrative, as telling stories; statutes as setting the terms of cooperation among various people, including the writer and the audience; the need to appeal to one's imagination in finding or thinking through a possible legal response to a concrete situation in the world. These themes coalesce or aggregate to paint a portrait of the lawyer as an artist working within a medium, a medium generally consisting of our language; but, more specifically, a medium comprising its own literature of the law.

There is another challenge in all of this talk of artistry and craft, and Jim White does not flinch from making that challenge explicit: "In asking you to define for the moment the lawyer as writer, to regard yourself in that way, I am asking you ... to trust and follow your own curiosity; to work out in your imagination various future possibilities for yourself."[11] This remark puts the responsibility for our professional development on our own shoulders, asking us to craft ourselves and our careers out of the seemingly inert materials that the law makes available to us as workers within the medium of the law. I am being asked how I as a lawyer might relate myself and my concerns to the law and, through the law, to others, including my clients. *The Legal Imagination* seemed to me to show its reader possibilities of action and relationships the likes of which had not (in my experience or knowledge) been imagined or portrayed in the legal literature prior to its publication. So, White's question remains pending: "What can I manage to make out of these opportunities"?

The responsibility to respond fruitfully to this query rests with each of us independent souls. "The activity which I mean to encourage in defining as I do the lawyer as writer is an enterprise of the independent intelligence and imagination."[12] We are pinned to this duty even in our own independence, since our independent status implies that we have an option, that we can decline the invitation extended us by White, if we so choose.

Generating Law Out of Legal Media and Genres

White's emphasis on our "independent" status can be misleading, if his remarks are taken to betoken license without limits. Instead, White goes to great lengths to remind us that, as with any artist, we are working within a given tradition and within a given medium. Both of these make possible our making sense, but both of these also condition (through limitation, by imposing limits upon us) what can be said and meant in any particular place at any specific time. "What you must ultimately learn is what to do with rules and judicial opinions and all the other forms of expression that are the working stuff of a lawyer's life, just as the sculptor must learn what to do with clay and marble. You may feel that you are constrained by your material, as indeed you are. But compare the pianist, who is told what notes to play, in what order, how long and how loud; yet art is surely possible there."[13] Any tradition, as any medium, empowers us and constrains us simultaneously. It is only because it does so that we can so much as utter a meaningful sound or make a meaningful mark. Any act of liberation still presumes or entails conditions for any further action—otherwise, it becomes wantonness; and wanton action leads to nihilism and nullity, not to freedom of expression that can be meaningful.

To show in detail how all of this takes place is beyond my capacity; there is a sense in which nothing can substitute for the experience of working one's way through *The Legal Imagination* and seeing how things fit together, gaining resonance and coherence as one goes. But I can instance one aspect of how these matters work, as an example perhaps that might stand as a representative for the rest of the experience to be had in reading and assimilating White's book.

In saying that we are to consider "the lawyer as a special sort of writer,"[14] White prepares us for his further characterization of the law as a kind of literature to which the lawyer contributes and which the lawyer helps to create. Some readers may take this to mean that law, given its basis in language, is susceptible to being given a literary flair. But I take it that White intends his claim to carry us deeper into the media of the law. For example, he wants us to think of judicial opinions as being as much constructed out of words (and passages of words) as are poems. This means that judicial opinions are literary *constructs*—they are built by an author, and they are meant to be the way they are because of the sequential construction given them by their author. And, too, White wants us to see statutes as one way of establishing the terms of cooperation between the statute's writers and the statute's readers (its audience), and to realize that statutes are one possible device for organizing our future experience (and, thus, our futures). All of this leads us to see the law as comprising a vast literature, composed of diverse forms or genres: here a sequence of appellate court opinions; there a series of trials and their transcripts; over there a number of separate statutes, or perhaps a commodious codification of various legal rules (something like the Uniform Commercial Code, deriving both from judicial opinions and from statutory enactments); and yet further along a set of administrative rules and regulations. All of these legal media and linguistic formulations are types of legal material, created by authoritative bodies of the state and its officers and agents. But, then, too, there are private sources of law as well, generated by the work of individual private attorneys laboring on behalf of their clients. So, we also have the opinion letter; the will; the trust deed or indenture; the commercial contract; the real estate sales contract; the warranty deed; the quit-claim deed; and so on. These are the instruments and documents that lawyers use to make their meaning settled and clear; and to effect the actions that their clients wish taken. These documents and instruments are the ways in which lawyers traditionally have found their voices, managing to say what they mean and mean what they say.

It remains equally true, of course, that a substantial portion of the vitality of such instruments and documents resides in the fact that their initial meaning is not—and cannot be—their eventual or final meaning. Any good contract foresees that an ongoing relationship between the parties to that contract (a lease of real estate, for example, where landlord and tenant are bound to one another for the course of the leasehold) invites, indeed requires, each party to return again and again to the terms of this contractual relationship, renewing or revising those terms and their envisioned relations to the extent that the parties have (and can exercise) the energy, the vision, and the power to enact such renewal and revision. The initial contract continues to live only in so far as it is reinvented and reinvigorated.

How, specifically, does any of this meaningful activity take place? It exists in the actual enactment of meaning within the instrumental or the documentary genres that the Anglo-American common law tradition makes available to us. Law is an activity of making meaning in concert with others through the use and recreation (re-creation) of the forms of law inherited from the traditional linguistic and legal media carried with us, generation after generation.[15]

What I discovered, as a young lawyer in Chicago during the 1970s, is that, if we view our legal forms and formulations as literary genres existing within the medium of the law as literature, then it is possible to find vitality within such confines. I do not say that this discovery is necessary or inevitable; only, that it is possible. It happened for me, back then, back there, during those times in those circumstances.

Viewing the law as literature, and taking the contracts that I was being asked to draft, or the wills and trusts that I was seeking to create, as genres within which I had the literary license (and constraint) to make my meaning manifest (and the meaning of my client), the documents lived—and I thrived—as never before in my short career as a lawyer. Perhaps more than anything else, I found that I had been treating the inherited forms of the law (the forms in the form books, the models in the law firm's archives) as though they answered from the beginning the legal problem confronting me. Or, perhaps it is more accurate to say that I had thought of the form as though it were predesigned and predetermined to solve problems that were already known and defined, already fixed and determinate. In such a state of mind, however, there is no actual work remaining for the lawyer to do, because both the problem, and the instrument (or the document) responding to the problem, are taken to be settled. On such a deadened understanding, the instruments or the documents did not require any work or contribution from me, their supposed drafter, because the instruments or documents already were known and finished, before I had even applied myself to the matter at hand. A finished piece of work prior to the application of the artist's hand is a dead artifact. How can *that* be humanly interesting, engaging, or enlivening work? Such a conception asks us as lawyers to do essentially nothing.

With the help of White's instruction, and my self-tutelage gained from working through the materials amassed in *The Legal Imagination*, I came to realize that there was no preset or prescribed solution to any legal problem—until I had fashioned it for myself, by myself, out of the materials the law made available to me. The problems posed to me by my clients' affairs and concerns were pressingly real and unresolved, unless I had the professional wherewithal with which to resolve those problems. So I needed to engage with the problems, and with the genres available to me, in a creative way—that is, in a way that created a solution for the problems posed. (I should note, to be sure, that my employing law firm remained a community of colleagues. While my work contributed my voice to the mix, my work in no way overrode or negated the fact that other voices, other selves, would be added to the product of our collective activities as lawyers in league with one another, exercising and expressing our collegial judgements.)

One might think, reading the foregoing, that this is a very modest adjustment in one's view of the law, somehow making old forms come alive out of some mysterious view of the law as a literary enterprise. I can only report what I know (which is limited, I acknowledge). What from one angle can appear to be a modest insight, a very slight alteration or variation of perception, still can mean a lot to the person absorbing that insight or perception. (An analogous situation or experience, perhaps, may be the way in which, in part II of the *Philosophical Investigations*,[16] Wittgenstein asks us to look at a primitive drawing, first as a duck, then as a rabbit; and the ensuing rapid vacillation between those two equally possible ways of reading this primitive figure can seem—can be—revelatory.) What I learned was that it was deadening for me to imagine that the settled forms of the law (settled though they be) already solved the problems of transacting business through a contract, say, or passing title to a house, or devising one's property at death. Instead, it was my business to unsettle the forms and then re-settle them. I came to realize that I could make these things happen for my clients—or fail to happen—only in so far as I designed the document that way, with specific words, and warranties, and promises, or limitations, and caveats, and the like. Nothing happened in the law for me or my clients until I made it happen. And I could make it happen only by using the right words in the correct document in the proper context or circumstances. What made my words the "right" ones, or the document I used the "correct" one, or the circumstances "proper" for my words and actions, was not something already determined prior to my actions in engaging with these materials and fashioning something adequate out of them. All of these deeply normative matters (of rightness, correctness, propriety) were to be divined by me in my individual and independent professional engagement with these matters and materials, always in view of the interests and concerns expressed by my client. The competent legal solution did not exist a priori in these forms or these genres or these formulations; it could be made manifest only out of what I managed to create through my mastery of these professional means and media.

This was my responsibility, and my professional doing—or undoing. I would have to try it and see where it led me, whether I prospered or failed as a professional.

Learning How to Take Care of What One Has Started

For me, this book was a postgraduate form of education. After law school, this was my introduction to lawyering as an art or craft. I learned the art of adding to the literature of the law in a form that would be simultaneously my own contribution, and yet also acceptable to the profession at large, recognizable by other legal professionals as being a part of the professional literature, an addition or contribution to the law as it exists at the time that one is trying to enter the profession and become a dues-paying member.

What makes such an education possible at this stage in one's life, when one has finished with law school and is trying to make one's way within the profession itself? Or perhaps I should ask, "What makes it necessary"? In my epigram to this essay, I reference a remark by Erik Erikson, which suggests that at a certain stage in life there is a universal human need for coming to some understanding of what one cares about most in life and how one intends to take care of that passion. Erikson calls this need, "generativity."

His is a term of art, so of course it collects meanings and associations in Erikson's work that are out of bounds in this essay. The term does suggest, however, that Erikson is pointing to our human need to generate descendants, people who (or things which) will succeed and survive us, who will carry on our identity and our persona into the unknowable future. Plato famously spoke of our writings as being attempts by human beings to achieve immortality, as our progeny (in a sense). Legal documents and legal instruments, too, reach into the future and outlive their drafter, their creator. Are they an attempt to grasp legal immortality? I wonder.

In this essay, I have been sketching in brief my own journey of generativity. In my case, "generativity" stands for the ability of a person to generate recognizably authentic legal instruments and documents, ones that speak to the difficulties and complexities of life in which the lawyer and his or her clients find themselves. In this regard, finding the ability to generate my own responses to matters presented to me, responses at once individual and also credited (if not always wholly accepted) by other legal professionals, was how I came to fulfill this universal human need in my own career as a lawyer.

This discovery for myself of a way in which to practice authentically a life in the profession of law within the American common law system had several important implications (or consequences). I might try to specify, in closing, what some of those implications and consequences were, in terms recalling Herbert Fingarette's observation on how a human being comes to take responsibility for something in his or her life: "In truth, acceptance, commitment, concern are aspects of what, from a different vantage point, may be seen as conduct which realizes in the concrete the possibilities defined by the socially given forms. It is, one discovers, a matter of emphasis and not of separate existence."[17]

Having gone through law school, I had inherited the "socially given forms" of the Anglo-American common law tradition. But I had not accepted them, I had not realized concretely their manifold possibilities, in my practice of law, until I had struggled with those forms for two years or more, and then had come into fruitful contact with *The Legal Imagination*, with its wonderful yet daunting challenges for its reader.

One consequence was that I came to understand that professional work is still my own work as a person—something that I possess and for which I am responsible—in a way more direct and immediate than I had previously thought. Taking it personally was my way of taking my work professionally. Yes, the law imposes constraints on me. Yes, there are limits to what I, or any lawyer, can do with the law. Yes, I am bound by the conventions, rules, principles, and precedents of our legal system. Yet the same is true of the artist. He too is constrained by his medium of words or paint or plaster or whatever. He too is limited as to what he can do or achieve with his materials. He too is bound by fidelity to the conventions, rules, principles, and precedents, histories, and traditions, of his art, his profession. Still, to say this—any or all of it—is not to excuse us from acting, from having to act effectively as a lawyer or an artist. Rather, it pins us down exactly to our responsibilities to act as a professional lawyer or professional artist does. These constraints, these limits, these bonds, define us exactly, us and our position, from which we must act. The challenge to action, the duty to act, is the same for lawyer and artist: what can he or she do from within *this* particular set of circumstances and with *these* materials?

Law as an art implies both that the practice of law bears a certain kind of relation to the media and materials in which it takes place, and that it itself constitutes a kind of human activity, a species of human action. As to these two points, I simply wish to say the following. The relation of the lawyer to his or her media and materials is a *reciprocal* one, by which I mean that legal materials serve and create (re-create) the lawyer just as he serves and creates (re-creates) them. What these materials are and can become (what they mean) is in part dependent upon what the lawyer makes of them, and makes them be and mean. And vice versa: what the lawyer is and can become (what he or she means) is in part dependent upon what these media and materials make of him or her, and make him or her be and mean. Each unsettles the other, and then seeks re-settlement; this is one aspect of what it means to become, to be, a member of a learned profession.

Before I had read Jim White's book, I had allowed myself to be dictated to by the legal forms I had used. In this respect, I placed myself outside the law. I was subject to its dictates, but I was not one of its initiates; I was not an insider with an insider's knowledge of how things worked within the profession. What seems wrong with the view of law as being a structure of inflexible techniques and tools and rules that one must learn, and then to which one must conform as one learns to manipulate them in argument, is that the law student or young lawyer, on this view, is external to the law.

What is wrong with this view of law is not that it subordinates us to the law in a certain sense—because I think that this implication or suggestion, rightly understood, is accurate. Correctly understood, we *are* servants of the law, perfect indentured servants working off the indenture we have freely imposed upon ourselves by becoming initiates of the profession. It *is* bigger than we are—yet it lives through us. We become a contributor by further fashioning and enriching the medium of the law, the institution of the law, of which we are a part.

This form of servitude is not enacted toward a client or the interests of a client, so much as it enacts a form of servitude to a tradition and an institution, a medium of thought and expression. This form of servitude is not the kind of servitude to a client that the "lawyer-as-hired-gun" vision of law implies for the law student or lawyer. Even in its depiction of "manipulation" of the law, one does not gain a sense from the latter of an artist immersing himself or herself in the medium of the law and working from within to fashion a solution to a given legal problem.

White's book portrays the practice of law differently. The voices in which lawyers may speak, and the forms of speech in which their vocables take shape and resonance, are multifarious. White's book seems to me to release to us the knowledge that, most often in a legal dispute, there is a range of acceptable results, a range of acceptable readings or interpretations, a range of acceptable strategies. Not just any expression, and not every instrument, will count as law; not just any remark, or any document, will serve a legal function. But more than one can count as legally recognizable, more than one can serve a legal function. The law does not force you as a student or a practitioner into a straitjacket, unless you yourself insist on trying on such a jacket for size and parading around in it.

This indicates a second strand of White's work that influenced me. His vision of law as an art throws you back on yourself, as the primary or initial (but not the sole or final) touchstone for the adequacy and persuasiveness of your legal judgments. You yourself are the generator and judge of your work as a lawyer. Rightly understood, this thought again increases one's responsibility. The more autonomy over one's work that is permitted, then the more one becomes answerable for everything he or she does.

White's vision of the law places the responsibility for each professional's growth and maturation squarely where it belongs, on his or her own head and shoulders. What can each of us manage to generate from such a position?

Notes

1. E. Erikson, Gandhi's Truth: On the Origins of Militant Nonviolence (New York: W. W. Norton, 1968), 395.
2. J. B. White, *The Legal Imagination: Studies in the Nature of Legal Thought and Expression* (Boston: Little, Brown & Company, 1973).
3. White, *The Legal Imagination*, 110.
4. White, *The Legal Imagination*, 111.
5. White, *The Legal Imagination*, 111.
6. White, *The Legal Imagination*, 111.

7. White, *The Legal Imagination*, 112.
8. White, *The Legal Imagination*, xxi.
9. White, *The Legal Imagination*, xxxiv–xxxv.
10. White, *The Legal Imagination*, xxxv.
11. White, *The Legal Imagination*, xxxv.
12. White, *The Legal Imagination*, xx.
13. White, *The Legal Imagination*, xxxv.
14. White, *The Legal Imagination*, 3.
15. See J. B. White, *When Words Lose Their Meaning: Constitutions and Reconstitutions of Language, Character, and Community* (Chicago: University of Chicago Press, 1984).
16. L. Wittgenstein, *Philosophical Investigations* (Oxford: Basil Blackwell, 1953), II, xi, 193–94.
17. H. Fingarette, *On Responsibility* (New York: Basic Books, 1967), 13.

[12]

A Gift in Yellow Clothing

Learning and Teaching with *The Legal Imagination*
Mark Weisberg

Can reading a book change your life? Maybe not, but working with one can help. Learning and teaching with *The Legal Imagination*, responding to its invitations and challenges, has done that for many of my students, and for me. Through writing and speaking, listening and responding, we've discovered our voices. We've become more confident. We're better writers, more present in, and more responsible for, what we say. We've learned to trust our own minds and to appreciate our colleagues' gifts. In this essay, I'll explore how that's happened and what it's meant.

The book arrived on my desk in late spring 1979. I'd seen it in a flyer from Little, Brown, and on a whim, ordered a complimentary copy. I had been teaching for ten years and was about to attend the first annual Canadian Law Teachers Clinic. Held at the Banff Centre in Banff, Alberta, the clinic consisted of thirty colleagues and several facilitators. We met for ten days, in small groups and in plenary sessions featuring demonstrations of several teaching methods.

The first session was to demonstrate the Socratic Method, my preferred teaching strategy. I came prepared, having read the case we'd be asked to discuss. In law school, I'd been mostly silent, fearful of participating, but at this session, I surprised myself by volunteering an answer to the instructor's first question. I was confident in my answer, but for several minutes of intense questioning, felt pressed by the instructor to retract my answer.[1] Eventually, he turned to others. At the end of the session, the instructor returned to the original question. My answer had been the correct one, but he never acknowledged that. I was angry. I felt

I had been manipulated and embarrassed—not for any educational purpose, but for the instructor's difficult position of having to deal with an early, correct answer to his central question.[2] More important to me, I realized I taught as he did. I had told myself that challenging students, as he had challenged me, pushing them with tough questions, not giving them time to breathe, would strengthen their thinking muscles and toughen them up. That hadn't been my experience just then. To the contrary, I was left angry, feeling unacknowledged, and powerless to do anything about it at those moments.[3] Was that how my students felt? If so, how was my teaching furthering their education? And if not, how to change?

Enter James Boyd White's *The Legal Imagination*. Returning from the clinic, I began reading the book. In university, I had studied the humanities, so the book's combination of fiction, history, poetry, and law appealed to me. The author's questions and comments were refreshingly different from those in most law school casebooks, and the writing assignments looked provocative and challenging. The book spoke directly to students, treating them as individuals, and it was jargon free. Intrigued, I asked to offer a course using the book, called after the title, and my dean and the curriculum committee agreed.

I taught Legal Imagination every year after that, until I retired in 2011. Through using that book and teaching that course, I discovered my vocation as a teacher. Correspondingly, many of my students rediscovered gifts they had forgotten they had and came to appreciate those of their colleagues.

What My Students Learned

In his preface and introduction to students,[4] Jim White explains what he hopes working with *The Legal Imagination* will enable. He hopes: (a) it will invite students to experience their work as the product of an independent mind, intelligence, expression, and character; (b) it will encourage them to "define [their] responsibilities"[5] as writers and as participants in a community; (c) it will invite them to "draw [on their] own experience of social and personal life";[6] (d) it will ask them to explore a central question: "How [can] an intelligent and educated person … possibly spend his life working with the law?";[7] and, to borrow from a subsequent article, (e) it will emphasize, not just the cognitive and logical dimensions of language and thought, but also the "emotive, associative, and imaginative."[8] I'll explore each of these dimensions in turn.

Develop an Independent Mind, Intelligence, and Expression (Voice)

You'd think college graduates would already possess these qualities, yet many students experience their legal education as demanding that they should conform to a formula and as requiring them to keep themselves out of what they write. And they imagine that's what awaits them in a life in the law.

The Legal Imagination invites the opposite. Most significant are the writing assignments. They begin asking writers to describe an experience: "Give a brief account of a conversation between a legal and a non-legal mind";[9] "Give an account of an occasion upon which the law controls the way a person speaks";[10] "Give an account of a judgment you once made of another person."[11]

To respond, writers must draw on their experiences and imaginations. That ensures unique content. No two stories will be identical. However, while it may invite vivid prose, unique content does not compel it. Early in the course, for most of my students, it didn't. Most first papers featured writers more keen to withdraw than to step forward, more reliant on conclusions than the evidence that led to those conclusions.

As the course continued, that changed. Three factors propelled that change: the students regularly received my responses to what they wrote, they read and responded to each other's work, and they listened to each other in the classroom.

Regular Feedback

Although the best method for improving writing is to write regularly, receiving constructive feedback also helps. Since students in the course commit to writing almost weekly, to help them progress I thought I should respond quickly to what they wrote. After two or three assignments, I also met individually with each student to discuss their work and encourage them.

Rather than criticize what people wrote, I tried to offer them my experience as their reader—what, in a wonderful essay, Peter Elbow calls a "movie of the reader's mind."[12] Like a mirror, that movie allows a writer to learn how a reader perceives what and how she wrote, and learning that, to ask herself whether that's what she had wanted her reader to experience. If it wasn't what she'd wanted—and often that occurred when a writer, fearful of revealing too much, hid behind labels or abstractions or cynicism—I hoped to encourage her to risk stepping forward and becoming more present to her subject and to her readers.

Less judgmental than criticism, which tends to focus on the writer, movies of a reader's mind invite writers to make their own judgments, and, as I discuss later, to own them.

Here are two examples, one responding to the first assignment, asking the writer to "give a brief account ... of a conversation between a legal and a nonlegal mind," and then, "based on [his] response to Part One," to explain "what distinguishes the legal mind, what set's it apart from others."[13] The other responds to the second assignment, which asks the writer to find a passage of good writing, explain why it's good, and then, looking at her own response, explain whether she thinks it's good writing as she has defined it.[14]

Natalie,[15]

Reading this paper, I experience two writers. One seems self-conscious and anxious, opening with a disclaimer, asserting that she's tentative about what she's written, pausing to apologize for setting a false tone, careful to respond to all the questions James White asks, ambivalent about her responses to them.

The other writer feels engaged, energized by her metaphor of learning languages as entering new worlds, being able to see and experience two ways at once. She's curious about those experiences, eager to break the narrow confines of a single, limited perspective, eager to embrace the possible.

I know which writer I prefer. If, as I suspect, you share my preference, as the term progresses, I'll be interested to learn what that writer discovers as she engages more fully the possibilities of the language and world she's begun to identify.

Devin,

You offer two radically differing responses to Scalia's dissent. They differ not only in perspective, but also on almost every writing dimension. The first, in Part Two, praises Scalia for being sarcastic. In it you assert that by being sarcastic, Scalia is more effective than he would be were he to write a more traditional dissent, but you don't explain how or why that's true. You assert that by using "incredibly" in one sentence, Scalia sounds more genuine, but you don't explain how or why. Similarly with your assertion that his style makes his argument effective. These feel like conclusions, but conclusions lacking an argument, as if you were telling me something and expecting me to trust your judgment.

In Part Three you respond in kind, risk matching Scalia word for word, phrase for phrase. Rather than generic, your language is detailed, evocative, unique. Only you could have written it.

Reading Part Three, I encounter a passage that offers me room to respond, even invites me to respond. I don't have to agree with you (or with Scalia), but I can't ignore you. And even if I think it's inappropriate or ineffective to respond as you and he have done, at least I know something about each writer.

In her introduction to Wild Mind, Natalie Goldberg reports what novelist Cecil Dawkins said to her after reading another of Goldberg's books on writing. "Why Naa-da-lee, this book should be very successful. When you're done with it, you know the author better. That's all a reader really wants ... to know the author." Isn't that what you want?[16]

Following several responses like these with individual tutorials allowed me to reinforce the positive dimensions of each person's work, to encourage them to continue risking being present to their subjects, and to note, as I describe shortly, how they and their classmates were responding to each other's work: with interest and without judgment. I wanted to support the book's message: you have permission. Go for it.

Peer Reading and Responding

Following Jim's suggestion, I reproduced several papers each week and distributed them at least a day before we met. That allowed people to experience each other's work and offered fuel for the upcoming class discussion.

Additionally, after the second assignment, I asked the students to hand their papers to someone else, and *respond* to the one they received. I chose "respond" rather than "criticize," explaining, as I did earlier, that the former focuses on the reader, the latter on the writer, the former withholds judgment, while the latter judges.

Asking writers to respond to each other rather than criticize is easy to suggest, not so easy to perform. As Peter Elbow notes, academic culture is primarily a doubting culture.[17] Legal education is a prime example. As teachers, "we pride ourselves on our ability to criticize an argument and want our students to develop that skill."[18]

In responding to a colleague's paper, many students couldn't escape that training in critique. However, after reflecting on that exercise and reading several papers each week, people's critical reflex abated. Rather than looking for flaws in arguments, students reported being interested in what they read, curious about the writer, and as one student wrote, "surprised by how honest so many of the essays were."

Reading and admiring their peers, noticing how those writers risked stepping forward and writing honestly, encouraged their readers to do the same. As their critical stance receded, they became much less guarded in what they wrote. Their prose came alive.

Classroom Conversations

Classroom discussions mirrored the writing assignments. At first, most students were cautious, reserved. They seemed to be looking over their shoulders at an imagined critic, who was busy vetting each comment.

As one obvious imagined source of criticism, I wanted to get myself out of the way. Jane Tompkins says it well.

A class doesn't get to know itself until it has been let go. People's personalities won't be visible, their feelings and opinions won't surface, unless the teacher gets out of the way on a regular basis. You have to be willing to give up your authority, and the sense of identity and prestige that come with it, for the students to be able feel their authority. To get out of the students' way, the teacher has to learn to get out of her own way. To not let her ego call the shots all the time. This is incredibly difficult. But I think it is a true path for a teacher.[19]

Adopting a strategy devised by my friend Don Finkel,[20] in my course syllabus, I told the students that I wouldn't be responsible for leading class discussions.

To reinforce that message, at the beginning of the first several classes, it was my habit to keep my head down, writing in a journal. After several minutes of confused silence, someone would begin speaking. At first tentative and cautious, students soon realized that they could shape the discussion and bring their insights and personal concerns to it, again without fear of judgment. The resulting conversations were engaged and lively, with most everyone participating. As one student put it, the classroom offered "an opportunity to know my peers in a different way.... We weren't sitting there trying not to look intimidated or trying to be intimidating".[21] Instead, many people reported themselves experiencing "the joy of authentic communication."[22]

I didn't stay silent throughout, and eventually felt comfortable inserting myself with a question or a comment. Doing so, I felt more a member of a community of inquiry than a decisive, authoritative voice, which would tend to shut others down. I don't mean that the obvious imbalance in role and power disappeared; what dissolved was fear: fear of looking foolish, of being mistaken, fear of being judged. That made all the difference.

Define Your Responsibilities as a Writer and as a Participant in Your Community

Being silent at the beginning of each class made palpable the question: what does it mean to be a participant in a community? For what am I responsible? To whom? Too often, I think, our classrooms obscure that question. A Socratic classroom tends to focus on only several students, leaving the rest relieved for being off the hook that day. Lectures tend to assign students their roles. Sit, listen, take notes. They offer learning opportunities, but they don't challenge students to understand and situate themselves as members of a community.

Each year I was impressed how students responded to this challenge. As the course began, one or two students understood themselves as responsible for initiating discussion, but as the class got to know each other, that responsibility became shared. Sharing that role, as well as sharing the burdens and benefits of participating honestly, suggests the class members felt responsible to each other.

Written work followed a similar path. Individual voices became more distinctive. Writing became richer and more detailed. This all suggested that people had begun to trust each other. Appreciating each other's writing, they wanted to respond in kind, almost as if one good turn deserved another. If my colleagues can write this way, I owe it to them and to myself to try to do it.

It's apparent that appreciating their classmates contributed significantly to the open and trusting community each class developed, and encouraged the honest and engaged writing the students produced.

In my last year teaching Legal Imagination, I added a practice that enhanced this developing trust. I borrowed it from my Yale colleague Jean Koh Peters. She calls it "A Thing of Beauty." At the beginning of each classroom day, one student would present something she'd experienced as beautiful and explain what it meant to her. It could be an object, such as a musical instrument, or a dress they'd received while working in Africa. It could be a film, a painting, even a handmade birdcage. My favorite was a musical composition for piano and flute that student had written (for her wedding, it turned out). She recorded herself on the piano, played the recording, accompanying herself live on the flute.

After the course ended, I asked the students to let me know how, if at all, the Thing of Beauty had contributed to their experience. Here are three representative responses.

> "I enjoyed the Thing of Beauty this semester. It allowed our class to peer into the legal imagination in a way that complemented our weekly writing assignments ... It helped to build instant trust among the students."

> "The Thing of Beauty allowed our class to speak to each other in a way that you don"t usually find in Law School. By choosing something that we thought was beautiful and explaining it to the class, we were encouraged to open our minds and our hearts to one another ... and in turn we established trust, honesty, respect and confidence. In short, we built a community."

> "The Thing of Beauty adds extra depth and context to the people in class and creates more of a bond between us. It reminds me that there are aspects of law school that aren't just about mass-producing lawyers by pumping us full of information and marking us against one another. It humanizes us and generates respect among peers."

I'd expected positive responses, but these were deeply encouraging. Along with beginning to trust themselves, students began to trust their peers. If I were to teach again, I'd include the Thing of Beauty in every class.

As the discussions and written work contributed to this increased trust and commitment, so did the writing assignments. By inviting writers to draw on their experiences of personal and social life, the assignments suggest that we cannot write or talk about law in a vacuum. Or practice it in a vacuum. To respond to that invitation requires a writer to integrate personal and professional, and a person who feels integrated is more likely to trust herself and to be willing to risk writing and responding authentically.

Draw on Your Experience of Social and Personal Life

To illustrate what happens when students draw on their experience of social and personal life, I'll let them speak for themselves. Here is one piece, written several years ago.[23] It's a hybrid, responding to Writing Assignment 6 and Writing Assignment 12. Assignment 6: "Give an account of an event in the life of another person ... in which you show him or her to be different from yourself. You are here asked to express your sense of what it would be like to be someone else, to engage in the literary creation or rendition of character ... You should attempt here to 'realize the complexity and profundit'" of another"s experience."[24] Assignment 12: "Give an account of a real or imaginary event in which you express how two or more people have organized their social relations. What expectations exist and how do they arise?"[25]

> The train station platform would never be described as attractive. Or respectable. Or even clean. The tiles which cover the walls are a curious bright orange colour, in rich contrast to the grey grit and grime of the train tracks, which has now spread to the platform. Outdated posters advertising computer training courses line the opposite walls. Outside, the streets are crowded with people drunk, or high, or both. Strip clubs, tattoo parlours and tobacconists take turns occupying the eclectic shop fronts. The gaudy flashing neon lights of the strip clubs are reminiscent of an amusement park. The cheap techno music blasting from inside the clubs sounds like the tunes from a merry-go-round, and the men who stand at the doors of the clubs encouraging one to come in are the like the side-show attendants at a carnival.
>
> It's a Wednesday night and my friend Fitz is waiting on the platform for his train. He has a sports bag over one shoulder and is leaning, distractedly, against the wall. He's been at football training at a nearby oval and is heading home. He's tired but relaxed. He's been here before, done this before. His eyelids keep closing. Each time they fall, his head sinks a little closer to his chest.
>
> Two policemen come down the escalators and look around the platform. Their blue uniforms are starched and ironed. They puff their chests out, like

birds performing a mating ritual, and they walk down the platform like cowboys, legs wide and toes pointing outwards, in a slow but steady pace. Fitz hears the sound of their boots, and looks up, half-expecting to sees spurs at their ankles and ten-gallon hats on their heads.

"Oh great," he sighs, "not again."

He can tell by the way the policemen are approaching that they"re not coming to ask for directions. They walk past the thirty-something woman in the pale blue dress sitting on the only bench on the platform. They"re looking right at him, smug, bored. He tries to avoid eye contact.

This is not the first time Fitz has been in a situation like this. Police seem to have a strange affinity for him. They like to stop him arbitrarily, question him about his whereabouts, search him, and threaten to take him down to the police station.

There's something you should know about Fitz. He's Samoan. And a promising football player. So he's big and sort of wild looking. His hair is an unruly mop which he tries optimistically to tame into braids. But his eyes sparkle like a lake which has been turned silver by the moonlight. And his cheeks burst with dimples when he smiles. He smiles a lot.

One of the cops, the younger looking one with the recently shined boots, speaks.

"Excuse me mate, what are you doing here?"

"I'm waiting for a train." Fitz tries not to sound sarcastic.

"Where are you going?"

"Home."

"Where have you been?"

Fitz can't help himself. "What business is that of yours?"

This time the older cop speaks. He can't be more than twenty-six, but he's got the voice and attitude of a wizened county sheriff.

"Just answer the question mate. No need to get smart."

Now Fitz is annoyed. He tries to muster his calmest tone. "I don't have to answer these questions"

"Alright then, if you wanna get smart with us, that's fine. We can always take you down to the station and continue this conversation there. How would you like that?"

Fitz backs down. He knows he's walking on ice here. Two young coppers like this. It's best not to talk back. And don't even bother trying to assert your legal rights. Fitz knows he's under no obligation to answer their interrogation. He studies law, part-time, at night school. Everyone has a right to remain silent during police questioning, or so he learned in criminal law. He can't be taken down to the station unless he's charged with a crime. Fitz knows this. But he also knows cops like these two. He's had these kind of encounters before, on other train platforms, street corners, in shopping malls and parking lots. He knows that the rules of criminal law don't always govern what these cops will do.

"Alright then, that's more like it."

The police pause and look at Fitz some more. The three men stand there not saying a word, trying to out stare each other. After a few moments, the younger cop speaks.

"Could we have a look in your bag there, please?"

"Why?"

"We have reason to suspect you may be carrying a knife"

Only a month ago, parliament had passed new laws prohibiting the carrying of any knives. Police now had the power to search anyone they suspected of carrying one. Of course, they had to have reasonable grounds for their suspicion, but Fitz knows, as anyone could tell you, that cops have an their own definition of what satisfies reasonable grounds. Often it's nothing more than a Samoan on a train platform in the wrong part of town on a Wednesday night. So Fitz swings the bag off his shoulder and unzips it for inspection.

The younger policeman takes the bag, places it on the gritty ground and crouches down to rummage through it. The older one remains standing. While the younger one searches, he stares at Fitz, never taking his eyes off his face. But Fitz isn't looking at him. He's watching the younger cop search his bag, with a weary, bemused look on his face. He knows they won't find anything. Fitz is a devout Christian, goes to church every Sunday, and is more often than not at the Saturday church barbeques. Thursday night is choir practice. The cops would be more likely to find a Bible in his bag than a knife.

The younger cop lifts Fitz's football shoes out of the bag and looks up. "Footy player, huh?"

"Yeah"

"What position d'ya play?"

"Half-back."

"Oh yeah, I used to be a winger. For Canterbury."

"Yeah?"

He puts the shoes back and stands up. Putting his hands on his waist, he looks across to the older cop.

"Nah, nothing."

They both look back at Fitz. The bored look has returned to their faces. The older one speaks.

"Alright then, you're lucky. You stay out of trouble though, okay?"

Fitz nods. The two cops turn around, recommence their swagger, and walk back past the woman in the pale blue dress sitting on the only bench on the platform.

The Legal Imagination is rich with stories. "The story," Jim has written, "is the most basic way we have of organizing our experience and claiming meaning for it."[26] Richly detailed, stories evoke; they persuade. Rather than tell, they show.

Fitz's story is all of that. It's not a lecture on racism and racial profiling; it *embodies* racism and racial profiling. It's a personal story, revealing something significant about our society. By showing what is: racism, it reveals what isn't: fairness and equality.[27]

The person who wrote that story also wrote this recently:

> It was the last semester of my law degree when I took the Legal Imagination course. I had years of university education behind me, but Legal Imagination made me question everything I'd learnt, but in a good way. For the first

time, instead of learning sections in a statute or principles from a judgment, I was encouraged to think about what I already knew, about the impact legal training and the legal profession could have on my character, and to critique the role and influence of the language I use. Imagine, after years of learning black letter law, being asked, as James White does in The Legal Imagination, "To what extent can you give yourself—can you demand and take—a life that does express your individuality and character?" and being urged, "not to give up but to make the most insistent demands for a life of self-expression that you can."

What followed from those questions leads me to the next section.

Explore How, as an Intelligent and Educated Person, You Can Lead a Meaningful, Fulfilling Life in the Law

Each year, in my first Legal Ethics class, I asked students to jot down what they were most looking forward to in a life in the law and what they were most fearful of. Consistently, they reported fearing they might not be able to lead a meaningful, fulfilling life as a lawyer. Strong pressure to conform, to ignore their consciences; no time for reflection, possibly even no time for a life beyond work. Not a reassuring list.

In Legal Imagination, the same theme dominated early discussions. The first assignment asks students to imagine they're writing to a friend who's thinking of going to law school and to tell her what to expect when she arrives. The next part invites them to reflect on what their letter suggests would distinguish a legal mind from any other.[28]

As the aforementioned response from my former student indicates, when they wrote and talked about their legal education and explored what it might mean to have a legal mind, the students also focused on their upcoming careers. Initially, their responses mirrored those in my Ethics class. However, as their writing improved, and they built a trusting, honest community, people began to imagine the possibility of leading a meaningful life in the law. They began to believe their individual voices might matter. I think that's a consequence of people's increased confidence, confidence in their abilities as writers and speakers, confidence that they could bring their whole selves to their work.

Through its structure, particularly the writing assignments, *The Legal Imagination* offered a method for gaining that confidence: describe a real or imagined experience; reflect on what it means to have had that experience; repeat. The additional practices I've described, most of which Jim's book encourages, also helped: collaborate rather than compete; appreciate each other's unique gifts; be present; work to create a community.

Embrace the Emotive, Associative, Imaginative in Your Writing and Thinking

When they write about learning, educators often describe it as involving three dimensions: knowledge, skills, and attitudes. The first two are always present in legal education and receive sustained attention. The third is also present, but rarely the subject of inquiry. Our interactions with each other model social relations. How we are treated and how we treat others can affect how we think of ourselves and possibly how we'll act later.

Attitudes formed an important, and often explicit, dimension of Legal Imagination. As I've mentioned, in his assignments, Jim often asks writers to reflect on what it means to have written as they did, what kind of character a writer has given herself. To focus on character, on what it means to have written or spoken, emphasizes that attitudes matter and are an important subject for legal education. Rather than assume that everyone will leave law school lawyerlike, this course asks what it means to be lawyerlike and invites everyone to explore that question in what and how they write and speak.

Along with that comes Jim's invitation to draw on or imagine personal experience as an avenue to good writing—and, by implication, good lawyering. Combined with a classroom environment that values personal experience, it becomes far more likely that students will embrace the emotive, associative, and imaginative.

What I Learned

> The first goal of education—if we think it has anything to do with values—is to bring students to a knowledge of the world within: its geography and anthropology, depths and heights, myths and primary texts ... Our second goal should be to help the student bring his subjective vision into community ... The classroom, then, must be a meeting place for both silent meditation and verbal witness, of interplay between interiority and community.[29]

To invite students to connect personal and professional, to ask them to explore the character they give themselves in their writing and speaking, and then to ask whether they can bring that to a life in the law, these are challenges *The Legal Imagination* presents, and challenges it invites teachers to support and enhance. What have I learned supporting them?

Six Practices

I can identify six related practices that have become articles of faith for me.

Embrace Non-Judgment

Law students come of age competing. They compete for university places, and in turn, for law school places, then for clerkships and for the "best" jobs, for partnership, and on for other rewards. As teachers, we contribute. We grade; we rank; we reward "excellence."

When we compete, we're typically critical, of ourselves and of others. We're guarded. We fear being mistaken, and consequently, often are reluctant to experiment, reluctant to differ from what (we think) others expect. Of course, that's not always true, but in a world where we're constantly judged, by others and by ourselves, I think those tendencies predominate. When they do, they tend to tether the imagination.

Together with reading Peter Elbow, teaching Legal Imagination helped me learn to embrace non-judgment. In an essay on teaching writing,[30] Elbow distinguishes between what he calls empirical feedback and normative evaluation:

> For learning, empirical feedback is a good thing and normative evaluation is a bad thing. Empirical feedback, in the case of writing, means learning what the words did to the reader. Normative evaluation means having the words judgmentally ranked according to some abstract standard. I have found that empirical feedback seems to encourage activity; to release energy. Presumably, when one gets accurate, honest, human feedback—with all the inevitable contradictions between responders—one learns not to be scared to put forth words. Normative evaluation seems to inhibit words.[31]

As I described earlier, when offering feedback on essays, I adopted Elbow's suggestion. To enhance this message, I also didn't grade individual papers, asking instead for a portfolio and self-evaluation at the end, followed by a final tutorial. Too often, we're tempted to look at our grade and ignore the more detailed written responses. Not grading directs people to those responses. After several papers, students stopped asking "how am I doing" and began more seriously to set and work toward their own standards.

I've learned to be patient, to wait for students to discover for themselves, and almost inevitably, they do. As Mary Rose O'Reilley writes, "Students do not really listen well to the answers to questions they have not learned to ask".[32]

Perform Your Message

We tell our children to do what we say, not what we do. True, we're acknowledging our weaknesses as parents, but we'd prefer to do better, to model the behaviors we support.

That's become a primary goal for me—frequently to ask myself whether my actions are consistent with my goals. With its structure, Legal Imagination encouraged me to work for that convergence. Over many years, my friend Don Finkel modeled it for me, several friends and writers reinforced it, and it's become a foundational belief in my work and life.

I've described several practices I hope do perform their message. I don't always succeed, but I keep trying.

Discern the Gift, Not the Gifted

> That's what teaching should be about but isn't: discerning the gift. Too often the central activity of our discipline is judging. The major thing we have learned to do in life is to assign grades.[33]

I've already written about this topic, here and elsewhere.[34] I repeat it, because it's been a central part of my experience teaching Legal Imagination. Like an inverse funnel, this course has allowed me to witness a diverse spectrum of individual gifts I never would have seen in a traditional exam-based, even paper-based law school course. And it's taught me that believing in those gifts and providing space and encouragement for them to appear, will help them emerge. Most important, encouraging and celebrating individual gifts will help many students appreciate their own and those of their peers. Feeling that, they will approach their futures more confident that they can lead a meaningful and fulfilling life in the law.

Give Permission

I've come to think of giving permission as my vocation. More accurately, I think of it as:

> encouraging my students to give themselves permission. Permission to bring yourself to your work, to step forward, to risk being present in what you write and what you say. Permission to care. Permission to take yourselves and your classmates seriously: as writers, as thinkers, as individuals responsible for the shape of the law. Permission to set your own goals and see what it might mean to work toward accomplishing them.[35]

Without the writing assignments in *The Legal Imagination* and the opportunities they created, I would not have found my way to this insight and would have had no way to practice it.

Get Out of the Way

Earlier in this essay, I offered an excerpt from Jane Tompkins's book reflecting on her life as a university teacher. She calls getting out of the way exceptionally difficult but a teacher's true path.[36] It's certainly been mine.

If Possible, Collaborate

During the last twenty years of my teaching life, I regularly co-taught with medical school colleagues a course for medical and law students. I've coauthored a book, the product of ten years of weekly telephone conversations and three shared retreats with a colleague at another institution. I've shared thoughts about teaching with a lifelong friend, also at another institution. I've visited his classroom. I've worked with colleagues at a faculty development office. These collaborations have enriched my teaching and learning immensely.

Unlike research, teaching typically is a solitary activity. We own our classrooms. Rarely do we invite colleagues to visit, and equally rarely do we visit their classrooms. We frequently share and discuss our research; rarely do we do so with our teaching. And ironically, unless you work in an education faculty, anything you might write about teaching won't be valued as highly as what you write about your discipline. If it's valued at all.

Collaborating with colleagues about teaching, observing and learning from them, has enriched everything I do. Those interactions prompted me to develop, and they offered me paths to that development. Without them, my teaching life would have been much diminished.

I think of Jim as I encounter him in *The Legal Imagination* as a collaborator. He speaks directly to me and to my students. He provokes me with his questions, intrigues me with his choice and placement of passages. He challenges everyone with his writing assignments. He has been a companion in my development as a teacher.

I wish every teacher similar companions.

Writing this essay, I've been fearful that it would become too much about me rather than about Jim's book and its influence. It is about me, perhaps too much, but I hope that shows how using the book has affected me, how working with it has prompted so much learning. I know that without *The Legal Imagination*, I would have struggled to find my vocation as a teacher and would not have experienced the joy of reading so many wonderful stories, watching so many students develop as writers and thinkers, and being a member of many learning communities. I am deeply grateful.

Notes

1. "If you want to get people to seem dumber than they are, try asking them a hard question and then saying, '"Now think carefully."' P. Elbow, "Teaching Two Kinds of Thinking by Teaching Writing," in *Embracing Contraries: Explorations in Learning and Thinking* (New York and Oxford: Oxford University Press, 1986), 55, 56.
2. For a vivid account of a law professor challenging and humiliating a student for no educational purpose, see, S. L. Carter, *The Emperor of Ocean Park* (New York: Knopf, 2002), 111–14.
3. Here's highly respected teacher and scholar Wayne Booth: "Still, I may as well confess that the most startling debasements of character I have ever observed ... have taken place during the three years of law school." W. C. Booth, "A Teacher's Journal, 1972–1988, in *The Vocation of a Teacher: Rhetorical Occasions* (Chicago" University of Chicago Press, 1988), 221, 264.
4. J. B. White, *The Legal Imagination* (Boston: Little, Brown, 1973), xix–xxiv, xxxi–xxxv.
5. White, *The Legal Imagination*, xxi.
6. White, *The Legal Imagination*, xx.
7. White, *The Legal Imagination*, xxxii.
8. J. B. White, "The Judicial Opinion and the Poem: Ways of Living, Ways of Life," *Michigan Law Review* 82 (1984): 1669, 1690, reprinted in J. B. White, *Heracles' Bow* (Madison: University of Wisconsin Press 1985).
9. White, *The Legal Imagination*, 45.
10. White, *The Legal Imagination*, 182.
11. White, *The Legal Imagination*, 315.
12. P. Elbow, "Methodological Doubting and Believing: Contraries in Inquiry," in *Embracing Contraries: Explorations in Learning and Teaching Thinking* (New York and Oxford: Oxford University Press, 1986), 254, 261.
13. White, *The Legal Imagination*, 45.
14. White, *The Legal Imagination*, 78.
15. To protect their privacy, I've changed the students' names.
16. Responding to my recent request to describe what participating in Legal Imagination had meant to them, one student wrote: "Through the individualized feedback I received on my writing, I learned that an unclear sentence sometimes corresponds to an uncertainty in my thinking. This encouraged me to acknowledge the uncertainties that come up when I am reading a text, and to make decisions about how to address those in my compositions. I became better at delineating my thoughts and expressing them clearly ..." This is one of several responses I have on file.
17. Elbow, "Methodological Doubting and Believing." My Yale colleague J. K. Peters and I have written extensively about this topic in our essay, "Experiments in Listening," *Journal of Legal Education* (2007): 427-47. I borrow from our argument in parts of this essay.
18. "Experiments in Listening," 432.

19. J. Tompkins, *A Life in School: What the Teacher Learned* (Reading, MA: Addison-Wesley, 1996), 147.
20. D. L. Finkel, *Teaching with Your Mouth Shut* (Portsmouth, NH: Heinemann Boyton/Cook, 1999), 111–22.
21. Comment from a former student, on file with the author. For an amusing and revealing account of an inauthentic classroom, see M. Beck, *Expecting Adam* (New York: Berkley Books, 1999), 76–78.
22. Beck, *Expecting Adam*, 76–78.
23. This essay was published in *Legal Studies Forum* (XXVII): 395–405.
24. White, *The Legal Imagination*, 315.
25. White, *The Legal Imagination*, 536.
26. J. B. White, *Heracles' Bow; Essays on the Rhetoric and Poetics of the Law* (Madison: University of Wisconsin Press, 1985), 169.
27. "Something tells you about nothing. It is the power of the juxtaposition of detail." N. Goldberg, *Wild Mind: Living the Writer's Life* (New York: Bantam, 1990), 205.
28. White, *The Legal Imagination*, 44–47.
29. M. R. O'Reilley, *The Peaceable Classroom* (Portsmouth, NH: Heinemann Boynton/Cook, 1993), 32.
30. P. Elbow, "Exploring My Teaching," in *Embracing Contraries: Explorations in Learning and Teaching Thinking* (New York and Oxford: Oxford University Press, 1986), 69–84.
31. Elbow, "Exploring My Teaching," 75.
32. O'Reilley, *The Peaceable Classroom*, 34. For an extensive discussion on what it means to listen, see M. Weisberg and J. K. Peters, "Experiments in Listening," *Journal of Legal Education* 57 (2007): 427–47, reprinted in J. K. Peters and M. Weisberg, *A Teacher's Reflection Book* (Durham: Carolina Academic Press, 2011), 63–93.
33. O'Reilley, *The Peaceable Classroom*, 90–91.
34. M. Weisberg, "Discerning the Gift," *Change*, May/June 1999, 28–37.
35. Peters and Weisberg, "Experiments in Listening," 142.
36. Tomkins, *A Life in School*.

Select Bibliography

Aristotle. *The Art of Rhetoric*. Edited by H. C. Lawson-Tancred. London: Penguin Books, 2004.
Aristotle. *The Nicomachean Ethics*. Translated by H. Rackham. Edited by J. Henderson. Cambridge, MA: Harvard University Press, 2003.
Bakhtin, M. *Problems of Dostoevsky's Poetics*. Minneapolis: University of Minnesota Press, 1984.
Ball, M. S. *Lying Down Together: Law Metaphor and Theology*. Madison, University of Wisconsin Press, 1985.
Bate, J., and Rasmussen, E., eds. *The RSC Shakespeare: Complete Works*. London: Macmillan, 2007.
Beck, M. *Expecting Adam*. New York: Berkley Books, 1999.
Billig, M. *Arguing and Thinking: A Rhetorical Approach to Social Psychology*. Cambridge: Cambridge University Press 1987.
Binder, G., and Weisberg, R. *Literary Criticisms of Law*. Princeton, NJ: Princeton University Press, 2000.
Booth, W. C. *The Rhetoric of Rhetoric*. Malden, MA: Blackwell Publishing, 2004.
Booth, W. C. *The Vocation of a Teacher: Rhetorical Occasions*. Chicago: University of Chicago Press, 1988.
Borrows, J. *Canada's Indigenous Constitution*. Toronto: University of Toronto Press, 2010.
Borrows, J. *Recovering Canada: The Resurgence of Indigenous Law*. Toronto: University of Toronto Press, 2002.
Boswell, J. *Life of Johnson*. 3rd edition. Oxford: Oxford University Press, 1970.
Burke, K. *A Grammar of Motives*. Berkeley: University of California Press, 1969.
Butler, P. *Let's Get Free, a Hip-Hop Theory of Justice*. New York: New Press, 2009.
Cardozo, B. N. *Law and Literature and Other Essays and Addresses*. New York: Harcourt, Brace & Company 1931.
Cardozo, B. N. *The Nature of the Judicial Process*. New Haven, CT: Yale University Press, 1921.
Carter, S. L. *The Emperor of Ocean Park*. New York: Knopf, 2002.
Castoriadis, C. *L'Institution Imaginaire de la Société*. Paris: Seuil, 1975.

Cicero, *Ad Herennium.* Translated by H. Caplan. Cambridge, MA: Harvard University Press, 1981.
Coleridge, S. T. *Biographia Literaria, or Biographical Sketches of my Literary Life and Opinions.* Edited by J. Engell and W. Jackson Bate. Princeton, NJ: Princeton University Press, 1983.
D'Anglure, B. S., ed. *Interviewing Inuit Elders: Cosmology and Shamanism.* Iqaluit: Nunavut Arctic College, 2001.
Darwin, C. *Autobiography.* New York: Harcourt, Brace & Company, 1959.
Dawson R. *Justice as Attunement: Transforming Constitutions in Law, Literature, Economics and the Rest of Life.* Abingdon: Routledge, 2013.
Dolin, K. *A Critical Introduction to Law and Literature.* Cambridge: Cambridge University Press, 2007.
Dworkin, G., R. G. Frey, and S. Bok, eds. *Euthanasia and Physician-Assisted Suicide: For and Against.* Cambridge and New York: Cambridge University Press, 1998.
Dworkin, R. *Life's Dominion: An Argument About Abortion and Euthanasia.* London: HarperCollins, 1993.
Dyer, J. *The Poetical Works of John Dyer.* Edinburgh: Apollo Press, 1779. Unabridged facsimile, Adamant Media Corporation, 2006.
Ede, J. *A Way of Life: Kettle's Yard.* Cambridge: Cambridge University Press, 1984.
Elbow, P. *Embracing Contraries: Explorations in Learning and Thinking.* New York and Oxford: Oxford University Press, 1986.
Erikson, E. *Gandhi's Truth: On the Origins of Militant Nonviolence.* New York: W. W. Norton, 1968.
Ferry, J-M. *L',Éthique Reconstructive.* Paris: Les Éditions du Cerf, 1996.
Fingarette, H. *On Responsibility.* New York: Basic Books, 1967.
Finkel, D. L. *Teaching with Your Mouth Shut.* Portsmouth, NH: Heinemann Boynton/Cook, 1999.
Gaakeer, J. *Hope Springs Eternal: An Introduction to the Work of James Boyd White.* Amsterdam: Amsterdam University Press, 1998.
Gadamer, H-G, *Truth and Method.* London: Bloomsbury Academic, 2004.
Geuss, R. *Philosophy and Real Politics.* (Princeton, NJ: Princeton University Press, 2008.
Glendon, M. A. *Rights Talk: The Impoverishment of Political Discourse.* New York: Free Press, 1991.
Gold, M. K. *Debates in the Digital Humanities.* Minneapolis: University Of Minnesota Press, 2012.
Goldberg, N. *Wild Mind: Living the Writer's Life.* New York: Bantam, 1990.
Gould, S. J. *The Hedgehog, the Fox, and the Magister's Pox, Mending the Gap between Science and the Humanities.* New York: Harmony Books, 2003.
Greenfield, S., G. Osborn, and P. Robson. *Film and the Law.* Oxford: Hart, 2010.
Grimm, J., and W. Grimm. *Die sieben Raben* ("The Seven Ravens") *Kinder und Hausmärchen.* Berlin: Realschulbuchhandlung, 1812.
Hall, W. D. *Paul Ricoeur and the Poetic Imperative: The Creative Tension between Love and Justice.* Albany: State University of New York Press, 2007.
Hampshire, S. *Justice is Conflict.* London: Duckworth, 1990.
Hanafin, P. et al., eds. *Law and Literature.* Oxford: Blackwell Publishing, 2004.

Hayles, N. K. *How We Think, Digital Media and Contemporary Technogenesis.* Chicago: University of Chicago Press, 2012.
Heidegger, M, *Being and Time (Sein und Zeit,* 1927) Translated by J. Macquarrie and
E. Robinson. New York: Harper & Row, 1962.
Heidegger, M, *Parmenides,* (Lectures 1942-43) Translated by A. Schuwer and R. Rojcewicz. Bloomington: Indiana University Press, 1992.
Heidegger, M. *The Question Concerning Technology and Other Essays.* Translated by W. Lovitt. New York: Harper & Row, 1977.
Hugo, V. *Les Contemplations* (1843- 1856). Paris: Flammarion, 1995.
Koffka, K. *Principles of Gestalt Psychology.* New York: Harcourt-Brace, 1935.
Kuhn, T. *La Structure des Révolutions Scientifiques.* Paris: Flammarion, 1972.
Lacan, J. *Écrits: A Selection.* Translated by Alan Sheridan, 1977. London: Routledge, 2001.
Latour, B. *We Have Never Been Modern.* Translated by C. Porter. Cambridge, MA: Harvard University Press, 1993.
Lessig, L. *Code Version 2.0.* New York: Basic Books, 2006.
Letsas, G. *A Theory of Interpretation of the European Convention of Human Rights.* Oxford: Oxford University Press, 2007.
Llewellyn, K. N., and E. Adamson Hoebel. *The Cheyenne Way* (1941). Norman: University of Oklahoma Press, 1987.
Luhmann, N. *Law as a Social System.* Oxford: Oxford University Press, 2004.
Lyotard, J. F. *Le Différend.* Paris: Les Éditions de Minuit, 1983.
MacDonald, J. *The Arctic Sky: Inuit Astronomy, Star Lore, and Legend.* Iqaluit, Nunavut: Nunavut Research Institute, 2000.
Manderson, D. *Kangaroo Courts and the Rule of Law: The Legacy of Modernism.* Abingdon: Routledge, 2012.
Mayo, E. *Lessons on Objects: Their Origin, Nature, and Uses for the Use of Schools and Families.* London: Haswell, Barington & Haswell, 1839.
McGrath, M. *The Long Exile: A Tale of Inuit Betrayal and Survival in the High Arctic.* New York: Vintage, 2006.
McGregor, N. *A History of the World in 100 Objects.* London: Penguin, Allen Lane, 2010.
Miller, D., ed. *Materiality.* (Durham, NC: Duke University Press, 2005.
Mills, A., and R. Slobodin, eds. *Amerindian Rebirth: Reincarnation Belief Among North American Indians and Inuit.* Toronto: University of Toronto Press, 1994.
Monateri, P-G, ed. *Methods of Comparative Law.* Cheltenham UK: Edward Elgar, 2012.
Mowry, R. D. et al. *Worlds Within Worlds: The Richard Rosenblum Collection of Chinese Scholars' Rocks.* Cambridge, MA: Harvard University Art Museums, 1997.
Multatuli. *Max Havelaar, or the Coffee Auction of a Dutch Trading Company.* Translated by R. Edwards. Introduction by R. P. Meijer. Harmondsworth: Penguin, 1987.
Nietzsche, F. *On Truth and Untruth.* Translated by T. Carman. New York: HarperCollins, 2010.
Nussbaum, M. C. *Love's Knowledge.* Oxford: Oxford University Press, 1990.

Nussbaum, M. C. *Poetic Justice: The Literary Imagination in Public Life.* Boston: Beacon Press, 1995.

O'Reilley, M. R. *The Peaceable Classroom.* Portsmouth, NH: Heinemann Boynton/Cook, 1993.

Oosten, J., F. Laugrand, and W. Rasing. *Perspectives on Traditional Law.* Iqaluit: Nunavut Arctic College, 1999.

Ost, F. *Raconter La Loi: Aux Sources de L'imaginaire Juridique.* Paris: Odile Jacob, 2004.

Ost, F. *Furetière: La Démocratisation de la Langue.* Paris: Michalon, 2008.

Ost, F. *Shakespeare, La Comédie De La Loi.* Paris: Editions Michalon, 2012.

Pasquier, A. *La Vénus de Milo et les Aphrodites du Louvre.* Paris: Editions de la Réunion des Musées Nationaux, 1985.

Perelman, C., and L. Olbrechts-Tyteca. *The New Rhetoric.* Notre Dame, IN: Notre Dame University Press 1969.

Peters, J. K., and M. Weisberg. *A Teacher's Reflection Book.* (Durham: Carolina Academic Press, 2011.

Plato. *Republic.* Translated by R. Baccou. Paris: Garnier-Flammarion, 1966.

Plato, *Gorgias.* Edited by W. Hamilton. Harmondsworth: Penguin, 1987.

Plato, *Laws.* Translated by A. Castel-Bouchouchi. Paris: Gallimard (Folio, Essais), 1997.

Posner, R. A. *Law and Literature: A Misunderstood Relation.* Cambridge, MA: Harvard University Press, 1988, 2nd ed. 1998, 3rd ed. 2009.

Powell, H. J. *The President as Commander in Chief.* Durham: Carolina Academic Press, 2013.

Prest, W. *William Blackstone: Law and Letters in the Eighteenth Century.* Oxford: Oxford University Press, 2008.

Price, J. "Tukisivallialiqtakka: The Things I Have Now Begun to Understand: Inuit Governance, Nunavut and the Kitchen Consultation Model." PhD dissertation, University of Victoria, 2007.

Price, R. *The Tongues of Angels.* New York: Ballantine Books, 1991.

Provost, R., and C. Sheppard, eds. *Dialogues on Human Rights and Legal Pluralism.* Dordrecht Heidelberg/New York and London: Springer, 2013.

Quintilian, *Institutio Oratoria.* Translated by H. E. Butler. Cambridge, MA: Harvard University Press, 1980.

Rasmussen, K. *Intellectual Culture of the Iglulik Eskimos*, volume VII. Copenhagen: Glydendalske Boghandel Nordisk Forlag, 1929.

Rawls, J. *Theory of Justice* (1971); *Théorie de la Justice.* Translated by C. Audard. Paris: Seuil, 1987.

Regan, P. *Unsettling the Settler Within: Indian Residential Schools, Truth Telling, and Reconciliation in Canada.* Vancouver: University of British Columbia Press, 2010.

Ricoeur, P. *Le Conflit des Interprétations. Essais D'Herméneutique.* Paris: Seuil, 1961.

Ricoeur, P. *Temps et Récit* vol. I. Paris: Seuil, 1983.

Ricoeur, P. *Figuring the Sacred: Religion, Narrative, and Imagination.* Edited by Mark Wallace. Translated by D. Pellauer. Minneapolis: Fortress Press, 1995

Rousseau, D, *Le Nouveau Constitutionnalisme : Mélanges en L'honneur de Gérard Cognac*. Paris: Economica, 2001.
Ruskin, J. *Praeterita: Outlines of Scenes and Thoughts Perhaps Worthy of Memory in My Past Life*. Introduction by Kenneth Clark. London: Rupert Hart-Davis, 1949.
Ruskin, J. *The Stones of Venice* (1851–1853). London: Folio Society, 2001.
Russell, B. *The Problems of Philosophy*. Oxford: Oxford University Press, 1959.
Salmon, C. *Storytelling. La Machine à Fabriquer des Histoires et à Formater les Esprits*. Paris: Editions la Découverte, 2007.
Sandel, M. *Democracy's Discontent: America in Search of a Public Philosophy*. (Cambridge, MA: Harvard University Press, 1996.
Sarat, A., M. Anderson, and C. O. Frank, eds. *Law and the Humanities: An Introduction*. Cambridge: Cambridge University Press, 2010.
Sarat, A., C. O. Frank, and M. Anderson, eds. *Teaching Law and Literature*. (New York: Modern Language Association of America, 2011.
Scott, W. *Guy Mannering*. London and New York: Dent and Dutton, 1954.
Searle, J. R. *Speech Acts: An Essay in the Philosophy of Language* (1969); *Les Actes de Langage: Essais de Philosophie du Langage*. Translated by H. Pauchard. Paris: Hermann, 1972.
Serres, M. *Ecrivains, Savants et Philosophes Font le Tour du Monde*. Paris: Les éditions du Pommier, 2009.
Sherwin, R. K. *Visualizing Law in the Age of the Digital Baroque: Arabesques and Entanglements*. New York: Routledge, 2011.
Shklar, J. *The Faces of Injustice*. New Haven, CT: Yale University Press, 1990.
Smith, F., and A. Lewis, eds. *Current Legal Issues: Law and Language*. Oxford: Oxford University Press, 2013.
Spiegelman, A. *Maus: A Survivor's Tale*. New York: Pantheon Books, 1991.
Swift, J. *A Tale of a Tub*. London: John Nutt, 1704.
Taylor, C. *Sources of the Self: The Making of Modern Identity*. Cambridge: Cambridge University Press, 1989.
Taylor, C. *The Ethics of Authenticity*. Cambridge, MA: Harvard University Press, 1991.
Thoreau, H. D. *Walden; or, Life in the Woods*. Boston: Ticknor and Fields, 1854.
Tompkins, J. *A Life in School: What the Teacher Learned*. Reading, MA: Addison-Wesley, 1996.
Tully, J. *Strange Multiplicity: Constitutionalism in an Age of Diversity*. Cambridge: Cambridge University Press, 1995.
Turkle, S., ed. *Evocative Objects*. Cambridge, MA: MIT Press, 2007.
Turner, M. *The Literary Mind*. Oxford: Oxford University Press, 1996.
Turner, V. W., and E. M. Bruner, eds. *The Anthropology of Experience*. Urbana: University of Illinois Press, 1986.
Tyler, T. R. *Psychology and the Design of Legal Institutions*. Tilburg: Wolf Legal Publishers, 2007.
Verges, J. *Justice et Littérature*. Paris: PUF, 2011.
Vining, J, *From Newton's Sleep*. Princeton: Princeton University Press, 1995.
Vismann, C. *Files: Law and Media Technology*. Translated by G. Winthrop-Young. Palo Alto, CA: Stanford University Press, 2008.

Vismann, C. *Medien der Rechtsprechung.* Frankfurt: S. Fischer Verlag, 2011.
Wall, J. *Moral Creativity: Paul Ricoeur and the Poetics of Possibility.* Oxford: Oxford University Press, 2005.
Ward, I. *Law and Literature: Possibilities and Perspectives.* Cambridge: Cambridge University Press, 1995.
Watt, G. *Dress, Law and Naked Truth: A Cultural Study of Fashion and Form.* London: Bloomsbury Academic, 2013.
Watt, G. *Equity Stirring: The Story of Justice beyond Law.* Oxford: Hart Publishing, 2009.
Weisberg, R. H. *Poethics and Other Strategies of Law and Literature.* New York: Columbia University Press, 1992.
Weisberg, R. H. *The Failure of the Word.* (New Haven, CT: Yale University Press, 1984.
Weizenbaum, J. *Computer Power and Human Reason: From Judgment to Calculation.* New York: W. H. Freeman, 1976.
White, G. E. *The American Judicial Tradition: Profiles of Leading American Judges*, 3rd edition. Oxford: Oxford University Press, 2007.
White, J. B. *The Legal Imagination, Studies in the Nature of Legal Thought and Expression.* Boston: Little, Brown and Company, 1973.
White, J. B. *When Words Lose Their Meaning: Constitutions and Reconstitutions of Language, Character, and Community.* Chicago: University of Chicago Press, 1984.
White, J. B. *Heracles' Bow: Essays on the Rhetoric and Poetics of the Law.* Madison: University of Wisconsin Press, 1985.
White, J. B. *Justice as Translation: An Essay in Cultural and Legal Criticism.* Chicago: University of Chicago Press, 1990.
White, J. B. *Acts of Hope: Creating Authority in Literature, Law, and Politics.* Chicago: University of Chicago Press, 1994.
White, J. B. *"This Book of Starres": Learning to Read George Herbert.* Ann Arbor: University of Michigan Press, 1994.
White, J. B. *From Expectation to Experience: Essays on Law and Legal Education.* Ann Arbor: University of Michigan Press, 1999.
White, J. B. *The Edge of Meaning.* Chicago: University of Chicago Press, 2001.
White, J. B. *Living Speech: Resisting the Empire of Force.* Princeton, NJ: Princeton University Press, 2006.
White, J. B. *When Language Meets the Mind: Three Questions.* Nijmegen: Wolf Legal Publishers, 2007.
White, J. B. *Connecting to the Gospel – Texts, Sermons, and Commentaries.* (Eugene, OR: Wipf & Stock Publishing, 2010.
Witherspoon, G. *Dynamic Symmetry and Holistic Asymmetry in Navajo and Western Art and Cosmology.* New York: Peter Lang, 1995.
Witherspoon, G. *Language and Art in the Navajo Universe.* Ann Arbor: University of Michigan Press, 1977.
Wittgenstein, L. *Philosophical Investigations.* Oxford: Basil Blackwell, 1953.
Wordsworth, W. *The Collected Poems of William Wordsworth.* Ware, Hertfordshire, UK: Wordsworth Editions Limited, 1994.

Contributors

Richard Dawson has held teaching positions in economics, law, and politics and published work on the economic role of government, on colonization, and on literary dimensions of law. He was annual Henry Lang Fellow for 2000, which led in 2001 to the publication of *The Treaty of Waitangi and the Control of Language*, based on his economics doctoral thesis. In 2010, he completed a law doctoral thesis engaging with the work of James Boyd White. A revised version of the thesis, titled *Justice as Attunement*, was published in 2014.

Thomas D. Eisele is a professor of law at the University of Cincinnati, where he has taught for twenty years, having previously taught at the University of Tennessee and before that as a Bigelow Fellow at the University of Chicago Law School (1978–79). These three law schools have been remarkable institutions of learning for him as a teacher, building on what he learned as a student at the University of Wisconsin (BA, 1970), Harvard University (JD, 1973), and the University of Michigan (PhD Philosophy, 1984). His current teaching is in property law, wills & trusts, and jurisprudence. His five years in the practice of law in Chicago are the subject of his essay in this collection.

Julen Etxabe completed his doctoral dissertation with James Boyd White, at the University of Michigan Law School, and currently works as a research fellow at the Helsinki Collegium for Advanced Studies. He is coeditor of the journal *No Foundations: An Interdisciplinary Journal of Law and Justice* and the author of *The Experience of Tragic Judgment* (2013).

Jeanne Gaakeer holds degrees in English literature, Dutch law, and philosophy. She wrote her dissertation (1995) on the history and development of *Law and Literature*, and the works of James Boyd White. She is currently endowed professor of legal theory and associate professor of jurisprudence at Erasmus School of Law, Erasmus University Rotterdam, the Netherlands. The focus of her research is on interdisciplinary movements in legal theory (specifically Law and Literature and Law and the Humanities) and their relevance to legal practice. She is cofounder, with Greta Olson (Giessen University), of the European Network for Law and Literature (www.eurnll.org) and the 2013 recipient of the James Boyd White Award (bestowed by the Association for the Study of Law, Culture and Humanities). She currently serves as a justice in the criminal law section of the Appellate Court of The Hague.

Rebecca Johnson is a professor of law at the Law Faculty, University of Victoria, Vancouver. Professor Johnson clerked at the Supreme Court of Canada for Madame Justice L'Heureux-Dubé from 1993 to 1995, and was a member of the Faculty of Law of the University of New Brunswick from 1995 to 2001. Her book, *Taxing Choices: Taxing Choices: The Intersection of Class, Gender, Parenthood, and the Law (Vancouver: University of British Columbia Press, 2002)*, received the Harold Adams Innis Prize.

François Ost is professor of law and Vice-Rector of the Facultes Universitaires Saint Louis of Brussels, where he also served as a Dean of Law from 1982 to 1993. Professor Ost is codirector of the European Academy of Legal Theory and editor of the *Revue Interdisciplinaire d'Ètudes Juridiques*. Professor Ost has published numerous books and his work has been translated into English, Spanish, Italian, and Portuguese. His latest books include *Shakespeare—La Comédie de la Loi* (2012), *Traduire: Défense et Ilustration du Multilinguisme* (Fayard, 2009), and *Raconter La Loi: Aux Sources de L'Imaginaire Juridique* (Odile Jabob 2004), for which he was awarded a Quinquennial Prize by the Francophone Community of Belgium in 2006.

H. Jefferson Powell is a professor of law at Duke University. He has served as a lawyer in the United States Department of Justice and as special counsel to the Attorney General of North Carolina and is the author or editor of several books. Powell also holds a PhD in Christian theology and is interested in the relationship between religious faith and poetry.

Jack L. Sammons is Griffin B. Bell Professor of Law Emeritus at the Walter F. George School of Law, Mercer University, where, in addition to teaching for thirty-five years, he has also served as Director of Clinical Education, Associate Dean, and Vice President for Finance. A graduate of the universities of Georgia, Duke, and Antioch, he did postgraduate work in professional ethics at the University of Nebraska under the guidance of Professor Robert Audi. Professor Sammons is the author of *Legal*

Professionalism, published by the Carolina Academic Press, and numerous articles, videos, and poems engaging with a wide range of subjects including legal ethics and legal education. He is also the author of a commissioned play.

Joseph Vining is Hutchins Professor of Law Emeritus at the University of Michigan. He received a BA in zoology from Yale University, an MA in history from Cambridge University, and a JD from Harvard University. He is a Fellow of the American Academy of the Arts and Sciences, and has been a Senior Fellow of the National Endowment for the Humanities and a Rockefeller Foundation Bellagio Fellow. His work includes *Legal Identity* (1978), *The Authoritative and the Authoritarian* (1986), *From Newton's Sleep* (1995), and *The Song Sparrow and the Child* (2004).

Gary Watt is a professor in the School of Law at The University of Warwick. He is a National Teaching Fellow and was named national "Law Teacher of the Year" in 2009. His monograph books include *Trusts and Equity* 6th ed. (Oxford: Oxford University Press, 2014), *Dress, Law and Naked Truth: A Cultural Study of Fashion and Form* (London: Bloomsbury Academic, 2013), and *Equity Stirring: The Story of Justice Beyond Law* (Oxford: Hart, 2009). He is coeditor of the collection *Shakespeare and the Law* and is one of the founding coeditors of the journal *Law and Humanities*.

Mark Weisberg is professor of law (Emeritus) at Queen's University in Kingston, Ontario, where he also served as professor of education (cross-appointed) and Educational Development Faculty Associate at the Queen's Centre for Teaching and Learning. For his work with colleagues and students, professor Weisberg has received national, provincial, and university-wide awards. Most recently he is the author, together with Jean Koh Peters, of *A Teacher's Reflection Book: Exercises, Stories, Invitations* (Carolina Academic Press, 2011).

Willem Witteveen is a professor of Jurisprudence and Rhetoric at Tilburg University, where he has also served as the first dean of the Liberal Arts and Sciences Bachelor Program. His publications in English include "Reading Vico for the School of Law" (Chicago/Kent L. Rev. 2008) and the edited collection "Social and Symbolic Effects of Legislation Under the Rule of Law" (Edwin Mellen, 2006). Most recently he has edited, with Maartje de Visser, *The Jurisprudence of Aharon Barak: Views from Europe* (Wolf, 2011).